# SIX
# MINUTES
# IN ETERNITY

Published by Lisa Hagan Books 2023

www.lisahaganbooks.com

Cover photography Jonathan Borba

Cover and interior layout by Simon Hartshorne

# SIX
# MINUTES
# IN ETERNITY

— A Memoir —

PHILIP
HASHEIDER

*To Mary,*
*The love of my life.*

# CONTENTS

# Prologue

---

For six minutes I was dead. I met all the requirements: heart not beating, lungs no longer breathing, skin an ashen-color turning blue. I was lifeless, flat on the floor.

This is my story about the events of an early October morning leading to my sudden cardiac death and what I experienced during that time away from my body. It is my explanation of how I interpret the experience I had here and in another dimension. By no request or fault of my own, I had suddenly, in an instant, become an expert on dying; something I had never really aspired to.

Perhaps more than this, it is also my meditation on how I now perceive life, as I worked to understand what happened to me, and how I now examine death, after what I experienced during the time I was being revived, and the full awareness that life has been opened for me with a new set of eyes.

I didn't experience my death as a result of a car crash or other physical tragedy. I collapsed during an exercise session, and then not even while handling the equipment. I stood where I was, next to a machine in the room, and simply collapsed to the floor.

Those six minutes stretched any physical presence I might retain to the farthermost edge of my existence here. I was within seconds of my life being entirely severed from this world, my inner flame being fully extinguished. Yet, those critical moments became the catalyst to change and transform my life forever.

It's been a rebirth for me. Not only in a physical sense because I have never before experienced a complete separation of myself from this life and then returned that I'm aware of, but also, by being brought back from the edge of death, this gift has given me a second chance to reflect upon and re-examine former attitudes and long-held beliefs which I had used to construct my life around. It has given me a presence that allows me now to examine death itself, unflinching and toe-to-toe, to confront any fears attached to it. My experience has allowed me to examine everything I now encounter from a new perspective and to realize that my fears are only an illusion that I have a choice to embrace or not. Much of what I thought was important before that October morning, no longer has the same relevance or attraction that it did before while other aspects of my life have increased in their significance to me.

What is six minutes? It is the time it takes to brew a cup of coffee or make a sandwich. Take a shower. Fry a burger. Fill your car tank with gas. Empty the dishwasher. Clean out and sort through your purse. Yet within those six minutes, whether I consider them long or short, I witnessed and experienced what eternity is like, and that has put my life here on a new trajectory.

The easy part of my story is to explain how I got to that dimension. Finding the words that I can use to adequately convey the feelings and sensations I experienced while in an alternate dimension is the real challenge.

*How do I find human words to explain something not of this world?* I often thought. How do I translate an extraordinary experience that was, to me, non-verbal and non-linguistic, into a configuration of meaning that others can understand in a different dimension—ours? It is like trying to explain all the different colors of gratitude, or describing in human terms what an octave sounds like if you haven't heard one.

I understand that all words carry a certain vibration with them, or have become encased within a certain history of explanation. Words that are of the same height, length and width used between two people, may have vastly different meanings to each and are especially dependent upon how each relates to that word, or their history with it. The tone of the word I emit whether written or spoken—the temperature or the volume of that word—can have a significant impact on how it is received by someone else.

If we allow the vibrations that encode the words to expand beyond the boundaries of the individual letters we allocate or use for our comprehension, or, if we are willing to crack the shell they have become encased within via their descent through generations of our history, then we can open ourselves to an understanding and alignment with them that exists beyond language.

This is what I intend for you: that these words be read with the hearing of the vibrations and frequency they possess as my transcription of what I witnessed in another dimension that contains no human language. I intend the meaning of my words, as we ascribe definitions to them, to be welded together with the vibrations of the visualizations and wonder I witnessed to express and enhance the full essence of my experience in another dimension.

My intent is not to use my words to dictate how anyone should relate to them, but to explain my encounter with another dimension. I know that once a word has been spoken it has *always* been spoken and echoes through time, to still be heard by ears of a different dimension. In this way, I believe we re-hear words in different oscillations as we remember them later. The phrases, poems, essays, speeches, or other words that have the greatest connection with our own vibrational plateau are the ones that we remember most because they continue to resonate best.

My awareness of what I experienced in a different dimension was then, and is still to this day, crystal clear. Parts of my story relate events that occurred while I was not conscious during the time of my collapse or in the hours that followed when, although I was breathing again, I was not cognizant of what was going on around me. One of the driving forces for me to investigate and understand what happened during that October day was to talk with those involved. Six months later, I began my investigation. It consumed dozens of hours of interviews with the eleven people intimately involved with saving my life. These included the staff of my local hospital's Wellspring fitness center, where my collapse occurred, and whose initial efforts made my survival possible; the Sauk Prairie Emergency Medical Technicians (EMTs), who finally revived me; the local police officers who responded to the scene; and later, upon arrival at the hospital, my wife Mary, our son Marcus, and our daughter and her fiancé, Julia and Victor.

From these interviews I have been able to assemble their accounts to accurately interpret the actions taking place during the time I was unconscious, and for the following eight hours after I regained consciousness and was attended to by the hospital's Emergency Room (ER) doctors and staff. I secured all my medical reports to study the timeline of the events that occurred, to examine the procedures used on me, and to clarify statements made to me that I couldn't understand. Those eight hours were, and still are, missing from my human memory and the only way to reconstruct them was to speak with those who were around me during that time. Each person I interviewed could remember their precise actions during those six minutes. They may not have been aware of what others were doing at the same moment but they were explicit in recalling what actions they performed.

As I conducted these interviews and collected the medical information, I began to better understand the actions that were taken to save my life. Without their expertise, I would not be writing this. My understanding of what they did, while simply saying that it was important, would be a vast understatement. It is not the full story, but it was the incentive—the motivation—for me to look at the whole event and try to make sense of all that occurred that morning and through the next critical days.

I admit that some time passed before I could find words to explain what I had witnessed to my family and close friends. There was some hesitation on my part whether they would want to hear about it. I didn't care if they believed me or not because I knew what my experience was. And that's all that really mattered to me. But I needed to share such an exciting adventure with someone. It was too good to keep to myself. My biggest hesitation was that I wasn't sure I could adequately describe it.

Because of that, I kept putting off writing about my experience for over a year. I made notes from time to time as I sketched out thoughts as a way to help understand my feelings at any particular moment. This changed when I talked with Dean and found he had a parallel experience but had never said anything because he didn't think people would believe him. I then realized there are likely many others who've had a similar experience. Perhaps I could help them give voice to what they encountered. Keeping inside such an extraordinary experience may make a person feel isolated, like they are in a cage without a key to get out. They may have felt that no one wanted to hear about it. I thought that by telling my story it would allow them to realize they were free to express it, too. And perhaps that may give them a release from their self-imposed captivity.

So, a part of my journey back to recovery has been to commit my experience to paper. This is my effort to transpose the feelings and sensations I witnessed in another dimension into words that others may find useful in their own way in this one. This is also a means to publicly acknowledge the unselfish efforts and professional dedication of the many people who helped me at my time of greatest need.

I can accept the fact that what I write about may seem implausible to some. It may appear incredulous to others. And the skeptical may find it fanciful or deluded. All are welcome to their opinions or interpretations. But that will not change my experience or the way I relate to it now. My emergency and medical reports confirm the physical dynamics involved in my rescue. Those who assisted me serve as my witnesses to the events described here.

I don't believe my near-death experience makes me more special than anyone else. I am another human being sharing the experiences of this world just as anyone else. But I have no doubts there were others through time, or even contemporaries of myself now, who have encountered a similar experience. I realize I was given an extraordinary gift during those six minutes of seeing the dimension of Eternity, and it seems selfish not to share it. Maybe others will find something within these pages to be useful in their journey while here.

When I recognize and accept the fact that my human body isn't meant or constructed to last for eternity, much like my fragility at the fitness center, I can reconcile that reality with the reason of why I will physically die some day. But the death I experienced was not the end. It was a portal of energetic transference through which I passed into a higher plane of experience and understanding that I now know is the journey for everyone. Knowing what happens after my physical death is a profound revelation. I was given an unexpected gift by experiencing it and then returning. If I can give you a glimpse of the transition we all will make, or that those before us have already made in their own way, then perhaps the fear will no longer have the power to frighten.

It is because of my experience that I now understand why people most fear death—because it means loss and an uncertainty of the unknown. The most frightening aspect of death for us may be the fear that we will not know or remember who we were when the light of our physical body goes out, or that we will continue to exist. My experience showed me that we won't understand our memory from this dimension in the same way we consider it as part of our cognitive process now.

It is far beyond that.

Fear pretends to be our caretaker, a protector in its masquerade. It becomes a magnet for our expectations. I've learned from my own experience that my fears have no more power over me than what I am willing to give or surrender to them.

So, I invite you to enter my experience of a sudden cardiac death and my recovery with an open-handed willingness. A willingness to consider that possibilities exist, not only to help us to fully delight in our human form and the world each of us inhabit, but also to consider that it is an endless journey that we are on. If but one person can then step beyond their fears, especially their fear of dying and of death, and reach out to embrace life in a new and vibrant way, then the message I present will be in gratitude for the gift I have been given for my return.

My story is for those who are frightened. It is for those who feel lost. It is for those who feel there is no hope beyond this existence. And, it is for those who have a willingness to consider the seemingly impossible possibilities that exist outside of our normal, everyday, human experience.

There is hope. I've seen it. I've felt it. I can now live it. And so can you because it is what presents itself to each of us, if we choose to accept it. Perhaps with these words written within these pages, you also can *hear* the voices of another dimension. This is my hope for you.

I offer this freely to you because it has been a gift given freely to me.

# Chapter One

It began as a normal day on our hundred acre farm where we raise and pasture-graze beef cattle. Soon enough it turned into one that involved an abruptly ended exercise session, a dozen emergency response personnel, an ambulance ride, admittance to an emergency room, and a bed in a cardiac care unit with wires hooked to my chest leading to a beeping monitor.

The wheels were set in motion that morning when I stepped out the back door of our century-old farmhouse and walked towards the large flat pasture to check on our beef cattle. I took those same steps each time I went out there. And each time it was without the slightest thought that it would be any different than my walk was the previous day. Why should that morning diverge from any other? How could I possibly imagine that that particular walk, on that particular morning, would be the one to set me on a path to another dimension?

But it soon would.

Mary was getting ready to leave for her work in Madison. She was on the staff as the director of connecting ministries. The hour drive usually meant that she left by eight, or a bit earlier, trying to time it so that she hit a sweet spot when the traffic going into the downtown area lightened up.

We sat at opposite ends of our oak kitchen table—she all dressed and primed for work, me in work shirt and blue jeans—as we discussed the day's schedule. That morning Mary would take one vehicle and I would take her car to have new tires put on. An appointment was set up the previous week and I was to be there at one that afternoon. No problem. Plenty of time to get there, I had said.

"Are you going for a work out after that?" Mary asked as she got up from her chair. She walked over and set her dishes in the sink and her empty tea cup on the counter. This had become a frequent morning question because I had developed a routine over the previous eight months trying to improve my cardiovascular fitness at our local hospital's Wellspring Center that was located in Prairie du Sac, a village that adjoined its twin, Sauk City, to the north. It was a fifteen minute drive from our farm so it took some effort to go because I couldn't simply walk to it. My every-other-day routine of going for a workout fell on that morning.

"Probably after. I'm not sure yet," was my non-committal response. I hadn't decided if I wanted to spend that time away from the farm. There were things I wanted to get ready for the coming winter while the weather was still pleasant to work in. I needed to empty and pull up the outside cattle water tank. Fix some loose wires around the perimeter of our pasture fences. Little things that weren't pressing but still needed doing before it became too cold to do.

"Maybe I'll just come back here after getting the tires changed," was the best I could offer.

Mary slings the strap of her carry bag bulging with files over her shoulder, then reached for her purse and cell phone, and walked over to me.

"Hug?" she asked.

*Sure.* Even after twenty-eight years of marriage, she is still the one I want to curl up with. It's a long embrace that felt different to me that morning but I left it at that.

After we separated I grabbed my sunglasses before we descended the steps, me trailing behind, and walked out the back door. I reached for my baseball cap hanging on a hook and pulled it on just above my rims, and turned left to head for the pasture while Mary turned right to the garage.

"See you tonight," I said as I back-stepped away from her and then turned around already lost in my thoughts. My right hand held my walking stick as I headed to the field.

Little did I realize how fragile that short walk could have been for me.

It's always a pleasant walk over the pasture's grass, particularly in the fall. The land is always more inviting to walk on rather than riding over it with a pickup truck, a tractor, or even a four-wheeler, if we had one. Walking allowed me to feel the slight undulations of the field's terrain under my feet. The soil beneath my feet was laid down by a deep lake that sat over this little prairie as the last glacier receded north thousands of years ago. The sediment left behind after the lake drained was rich silt loam spreading across the open prairie that now supported the grass that fed our cattle. *It's an amazing cycle*, I thought as I kicked at the grass to jostle the bugs from their cozy nests. If they took to the air I could watch as swallows skimmed the surface of the grass stems, swooping and nabbing their unexpected feast of available insects. The grass fed more than our animals.

Our pastures grow slowly as it reaches October. There's less sunlight in late fall as it arcs lower during the day and dips into the west earlier each night, only to rise a minute later the next morning. This limited light lulls the grass into thinking a long nighttime is coming, so they slow down too.

Things are shifting more noticeably this time of year than they are in the full swing of summer with its abundant sunshine. Pastures have their own rhythm, depending on the season. In the summer the grass expands as it grows like stretching an elastic band. While late in the season, the pasture grass contracts as it gently beds down for the winter that is coming.

As I walked, I noticed there was plenty of grass left for our cattle to graze on and, maybe, if the first snow held off to say, mid- to late-November, they could stay out for quite some time yet before I would need to feed them round bales of dry hay that I had stored in our barn and shed and baled earlier in the summer. Our cattle ate in winter from the same plants they grazed on through the spring, summer and fall.

I walked to within twenty feet of our herd of twenty-eight head. They generally ignored me when I approached. Partly, I was sure, because of familiarity but also because they were more interested in chomping at the grass. They likely thought I could wait for their attention but their breakfast couldn't.

They were slow-motion harvesters as they took one step forward, then paused to grab a mouthful of grass just inches in front of them, then take another step forward, then stop, as they snail-paced themselves across the field. It was like watching a sluggish animal caravan that never quite reached any particular destination point. They keep moving until they were satisfied and then would lie down on the soft grass carpet to rest and chew their cuds.

I began to talk to them as I normally did. Several looked up at me, almost alarmed, with ears pricked forward to listen.

*That's unusual,* I thought. But the more words I spoke, the more alert they became.

*What's going on?* Suddenly, there were twenty-eight burgundy-colored, Red Angus bodies giving me their full attention. The rest had stopped eating at the same moment. I was almost embarrassed that they found me so interesting.

I said a few more words and suddenly two shot off running away at half speed until the rest joined them in a full race across the wide field.

*What's this about?* They acted like they'd seen a ghost.

My jaw must have dropped in disbelief because they'd never done that before.

*What's going on?* I wondered. When they finally stopped, they were three hundred yards away. Then they all turned to stare back at me, ears pricked up again, intently listening for the slightest sound.

*Was I some aberration? A cipher to them?* I wondered.

Anyway, I saw what I needed to see of them. None had a physical problem that required my attention so I turned with my walking stick in hand and headed back to the house.

I was in the middle of the pasture, half way to the gate, when I turned to look back at them but they hadn't moved an inch and were still looking at me as if responding to a high alert siren. Then four minutes later I had crossed the quarter-mile and closed and locked the gate behind me.

The walk changed my mind. I decided that I would go into town that morning instead of waiting for the afternoon appointment. Since I'd be in town sooner than I expected, I'd have time for a short workout. I showered and changed. I grabbed my canvas gym bag stuffed with my workout clothes as I headed out the door to the car.

The fifteen-minute, twelve-mile drive took me past neighboring farms until I reached Sauk City. Now that I had plenty of time on my hands, I turned left up the street leading to the fitness center's parking lot. I parked the car, walked in and took the steps down to the changing room. Then it was back up to the first floor room for my exercise session.

I looked at the wall clock as I said hello to Sarah, who was monitoring the room. It was eleven. After warming up, I stepped to the arm curl machine, sat down on the cushioned bench, placed my elbows on the arm pads in front of me and grabbed the two handles.

As I did, I could never have guessed in a million years that I was only moments away from eternity.

# Chapter Two

Picture my pallid, lifeless body lying outstretched on the thin exercise room carpet, wedged next to the base of a lift machine. The speed camera of the room's activities has instantly dialed down to slow motion as the yells for help begin to bounce off the walls.

I am lying unconscious on the floor, my sweating body cooling with each passing second, turning shades of gray in each unresponsive moment as blood drains from my face. Not speaking. Not thinking. Not breathing. Not even knowing I am slowly dying.

Frenetic activity erupts in the room as the staff members fly into action, their training overriding any hesitation. Diane drops her clipboard and abandons her rehab client to begin chest compressions once she realizes I'm not breathing. Sarah races across the room to call emergency services. Sandy jumps from her desk, abruptly ending her phone call, and grabs the automated external defibrillator (AED) from its glass box, until eleven local EMTs shortly arrive to assist and take over. Josh, who had stopped by for a workout before resuming his role as a school athletic trainer, jumps off his treadmill and runs over to assist Diane.

Time is running out. For me, and for all of them to help. There's no response as Diane and Josh alternate on the chest compressions. Sarah gives information to a 9-1-1 operator who is notifying the local ambulance team at the same moment. Sandy drops to her knees to open and unpack the AED. She pulls out the patches and attaches them to my stone-still body. Their tenacious activity struggles to restart a heart whose inner light is slowly dimming, but they forge on without the awareness of their own adrenalin fatigue.

At this critical moment, nothing is a given. No guarantee the end result will satisfy them or me. No assurance their efforts will revive me.

Yet they continue. They work against the odds they face knowing the first minutes are most critical and can mean the difference between life and death. They step outside of their staff positions, outside of their individual routines, outside of their own lives, to focus their intense actions on my unresponsive form.

This chaotic scene slowly settles into a rhythm of one unified collaboration as the disparate individual parts begin to coalesce. It is like they are sections of an orchestra following different themes until an unseen conductor brings them into synchronized movement. Then, just before the crescendo is reached, the screeching voice from the AED calls everyone to clear away and forces each of them to witness what is about to happen. Time itself stands still, now motionless as it watches impassively from the sidelines to the activity displayed before it, positioned alongside the gasping staff members. In that brief suspended moment, all possibilities exist—life, death, eternity—until one single, simple movement with the push of a button releases an energetic explosion into my body to try to restart my heart.

My body jerks and twitches. They wait for a sign. Any sign. Nothing.

Their pause instantly erupts back into action because the shock doesn't trigger a response. The furious chest compressions restart. More instructions come from the AED as it recharges.

More calls for help. People are moved from the room. Incoming appointments to the rehab area are directed down the hall to stand and wait.

If I were conscious during this time, I would be embarrassed and might have felt guilty for making all these people do so much on my behalf. Or, at least, I might have a sense of wonder at the absurdity of it all. How could the twenty moderate arm curls I had just finished moments before equate to my heart stopping? I could never have imagined, even in my wildest dreams, that when Sarah corrected my posture on the machine only a few moments before, I was only seconds away from experiencing another dimension of time and space. Why hadn't it happened a few hours earlier while I was walking alone in our pasture to check our beef cattle?

In my most vivid imagination, how could I ever think that my forearms would be the last thing I saw in this life? Not my wife. Not my son. Not my daughter. Just my arms as I stood up from the curl machine and looked down at both. I had felt a tingling sensation start to course through every muscle like they had fallen asleep. That would be the last thing I remembered from this life.

I now realize that death doesn't wait for us to come to terms with it beforehand because I didn't get a chance to discuss it. I had sometimes wondered what it might be like to die and had asked myself that question dozens of times. Little did I realize that, at that moment, I was getting my answer.

Through those final minutes as I was being worked on, I had no overhead spectator's vantage point as a disinterested party, and no recording of it to view later. I had no sense of hovering above my body or watching from a room corner what these people were doing to me.

Everything was out of my hands. I had no control over the outcome. Those who were present in the room had accepted the challenge of trying to bring me back to a life they continued to chase.

Besides, I didn't witness any of this activity because my conscious self hadn't bothered to stick around to see what happened next. I was already present in another dimension. I was gone from my body. I was somewhere else.

It was Monday morning, 11:15 a.m., the fifth of October. That was my last moment on earth. I collapsed to the floor and began a journey that has changed my life forever.

# Chapter Three

In less than a blink of an eye, I found myself in an entirely new place.

It was like I decided to take a trip and left in such a hurry that I forget everything—my luggage, my food, my car, my wallet, my passport, even my underwear. There were no goodbyes. No final messages. No forwarding address. I just left.

And then, I arrived. But where?

I didn't wonder *why* I was there, it was just that I *was* there and I hadn't asked to leave.

I didn't yet comprehend that my lifeless body was still back at the fitness center and lying on the floor being frantically worked on. I didn't recognize I had died because I didn't feel dead.

The place *seemed* vaguely familiar, like visiting a place that you sense you had visited before but can't put your finger on it. But I couldn't explain to myself why it felt that way.

Regardless of what had happened, I recognized that I had somehow stripped away the entire weight of my human form. I felt I had dropped a heavy backpack that allowed my inner being – my in-dwelling self – to leave without a second thought. I was now somewhere that didn't hold a physical space that I recognized. I looked around and found myself in the largest outdoor theatre I'd ever seen but there weren't any stars that I could see in the sky.

Then I realized there was no sky!

There were no walls, no ceiling, no basement. It didn't have a dimensional form that I could recognize or distinguish. Yet I could see all that spread out before me.

I then sensed I was floating. I looked around and saw I was sitting in what seemed to be a small "structure" of some sort. I could best describe it as being akin to a raft and I instinctively knew as the only occupant that it was made specifically for me. It's like it had my name engraved on it although I didn't recall making a reservation for it.

*Well*, I thought, *if this is for me then surely there are others here as well.*

Then, I heard the stillness. I listened because it was peaceful. It was warm, welcoming. It was as if a clear fog enveloped and squeezed me with a hug. It pressed in on me. There were no clouds into which I'd ascended. There was no dungeon of chains or fiery pit for me to look down into. It was wonderfully quiet and calm, at first, as if I was re-adjusting from jet lag.

My "hearing" was re-orienting itself to the realization that I didn't have ears when I raised my hands to rub them. I stared at both hands as if remembering I had looked at my forearms only seconds before. But now they held the *outline* of the physical form I knew before—with ten fingers—but these "arms and hands" were not made of bones or muscles anymore. I supposed that I had survived some trauma or whatever pain my body may have experienced. But the only feeling I had was peace, not pain.

What I had perceived in this physical world as the outline of my human body had now transformed into a pattern stitched together with energetic filaments and tonal threads that were synchronized by vibrations whose alignment then compressed and fashioned "the me" into what I recognized as my former human shape. I was seeing myself as a textured hologram that had been woven into an energetic silhouette and I was now present to witness this reconstruction. This new form was a translucent remembrance of what *once was me*, but *now is me*—there, in that dimension in which I'd newly arrived. I was realizing myself as a very different vibration than I had experienced here on this plane.

It took a blink before I realized that this wasn't the fitness center any more. That barely registered as a thought. But it didn't bother me, nor did I consider why I wasn't there anymore. It didn't matter. I wasn't frightened by what was before me because it felt like returning to a former residence I had inhabited before. It was so comfortable that I started to settle in.

I examined the structure I was in. It felt like I had sailed down a river and flowed out into a vibratory ocean where I then found myself. I was floating on waves, gently rising and falling as their ripples spread out into the vastness beyond. I was fascinated because I didn't drift anywhere or towards anything. I stayed floating upon this sea of silken energy vibrations that surrounded and enfolded me like a warm cocoon and bathed me like a gentle rain. I watched those waves approach and then pass through me as they continued on.

I took all this in as I continued to look to my sides, over the edge of my raft, being able to face all four directions at the same time, before I finally focused on what was right in front of me. It had always been there, I supposed, but now I finally noticed it as my "eyes" came into focus of these new surroundings.

I looked up to see a gigantic sphere of light. Then I realized it was more than that. It was infinite. It was immense. It expanded to the outer rim of this borderless space before me yet I felt I could reach out and touch it because I was that close. But I also seemed so far away that I could see the entirety of its rim. It glowed with the energy of millions of suns although I could still look into it. I was seated before it without getting burnt. I wasn't consumed but became the flame as I merged with it. This deep yellow and golden orb pulsed with a consciousness that made all things instantly knowable as those waves that passed through me transmitted a vibration of intelligence to identify every purpose. It was mega-data on an infinite scale. I realized that here were all the answers to all the questions that I could ever ask.

I was looking at the origin of my answers.

*If only I could tell this to someone,* I thought.

I was a witness to what was right in front of me as I was being melded with waves emanating from this Source. It drew me in like a magnet. It seemed so natural, so easy, so effortless to say, yes. There was nothing complicated about any of this.

In that moment of experiencing a sensation of Forever, I *knew* I had arrived back to where I originally came from. I was being invited to unite with this Source as it sent waves to enfold me. I didn't even have to question it because I then instantly knew that I had shed the physical consciousness of my life on earth as well, and now was in the presence of what I could only explain as the Source of All Creation.

I was unchained from everything I had known myself to be, all that held me to my life on earth, and I was being soothed like gentle hands that smooth out the creases of the life I had lived here.

In that moment of awareness, in that dimension that transcends our concepts of Time and Space, I was being permeated with vibrations that were in full union with the Source before me. As these silken waves of light washed over and through me, I was bathed with a pure energy of warmth and acceptance. Like liquid love, these waves cleansed and washed away any residue from my physical life that may have secretly tagged along with me. I was breathing in the illuminative breath of the Eternal Source of Love.

Yet, *in that same moment* the staff and EMTs were still furiously working to revive me. The EMTs arrived and flooded into the exercise room, and took over for the exhausted Wellspring staff. In the next few minutes a device was inserted into the back of my throat for breathing should that ever start up again. An access point was drilled into my left tibia below the knee for an intravenous needle. The room had been quickly emptied of all others. All that occurred while the chest compressions continued between the applications of two electrical shocks that didn't create any response. The local police arrived to take command of the street for the ambulance and the rescue scene. And my wife Mary was called and informed of my collapse.

*If they only knew where I was at that moment.*

Imagine that you're standing in a warm shower after having come in from the bitter cold, say the dead of winter. You stand naked and feel the water cascade onto your body as it begins to warm you from head to toe. Now imagine this as a pulsing, glowing energy that washes over you. It enters at the top of your head and you feel it descend in a slow wave as it ripples inside your body until it reaches your feet and leaves through your toes. It flows, wave upon wave, top to bottom, inside and out, as it completely bathes your entire essence. It is like being energetically marinated. It is not the deep, soothing warmth emanating from an ambient temperature but from the enfoldment of a peace and calmness that will not release me now.

*This is where I was and what I was feeling.*

There were no expectations for me there other than *to be as I was*. I did not have to justify myself to *anyone*. Being in the presence of the Source was a welcome of generosity with no questions asked. I was accepted simply because *I was now there*. And nothing from my life on this planet could touch me. None of it existed there and all that I was before did not matter to me anymore.

I sensed there were other spirit energies around but I had not yet *seen* them. Perhaps they knew I wouldn't be staying and the only way I could comprehend them in their form would be to join with them in their spirit consciousness and be completely cleaved from my human experience here. Perhaps I would see them fully only if I stayed. But *something* was there because I felt unseen *hands* that surrounded and lifted me as if I'd been assigned to them in my passage.

As I sat where I was, floating on the waves, I became so enthralled at the immensity of the infinite energy before me that I almost neglected to look around. It was like going on a trip and forgetting to look down the side roads. I noticed flickering sparkles of light all over. Millions upon millions of them wherever I looked. They were like little twinkling stars, or maybe like fireflies all glowing around me. Each separate and each floating in their own place like I was. Then some darted off and others appeared. It was like watching the arrivals and departures at an international airport.

*Was I leaving soon too?* I wondered.

I turned away from them and then I saw what I can only describe as Infinity. It was beyond anything I could imagine here. It stretched out before me in all directions. In human terms, it spread forward, backward, down, sideways and at all angles. But it was limitless and its vastness held me outside of Time and Space as we understand it here.

It would be inaccurate to say there was no color because we would interpret that as being solid black. But there was no need for color as we discern it with our eyes. There was no black. No white. No red. The spectrum through which we perceive the light of illumination on this planet was a minute fraction of the immeasurable translucent collection of embroidered alignments presented before me – a mosaic cohesion holding everything together.

The amplification of that pigmental display melded with the octaves of aural vibration to compose a crystalline, transparent diffusion through which everything beyond it could be distinctly seen. It was as if my vision through this glass-like ethereal suspension had channeled a magnification of the farthest reaches of Infinity into absolute clarity and drew it back for my examination.

It was a kaleidoscope of vibrations and complexion that constantly changed as each intensely aligned with the waves passing through me and beyond. Forms and shapes of the vibration waves shifted as if encountering other arrivals.

I then realized, because of the sensation of already being there forever, that I was *existing* in Eternity. Now I was *seeing* it.

Imagine that you drive across an endless highway on earth. As it leads to the horizon, the land before you bends and joins it until both become indistinguishable with the sky. However, there was no bend of my sight into Infinity. I was looking straight into it and it simply kept going in all directions. Incredibly, the farther and deeper I looked, the clearer it became because of that vibrational magnification.

I was seeing through a different lens those things I could never see with the low wattage of my human eyes. It was like getting new glasses that refocused the expression of light and energy and allowed me to see a clearer and wider vision of that which lies beyond our human sight. A door had been opened for me in a completely different dimension and somehow I had stepped through it.

*So is this what eternity is like?* I thought. And an answer came back before I had even finished my question.

*Yes. For you.*

It was in an octave of tone fashioned from a consciousness that was being expressed through the articulation of familiar words so that I could understand the intention of a new dimensional language I had just encountered.

Within that space before me, multitudes of dimensions appeared. To describe what I saw I have to use the *entire* universe in which we presently reside—all that we can see and all that is beyond our telescopes to the farthest "edges" of this dimension's existence.

I can explain it best by taking all this vastness and compressing it into a single, thin sheet of paper that is suspended in space. Then imagine another entire universe, perhaps the size of ours, as a thin sheet positioned a micro-millimeter right beside it, and then another beside that one, and then another, and another, and another on into as far as you can imagine—forever. All these universes being separate from each other in a row that continues in both directions.

On top of this row is another row of universes, each separate from the others stretching in both directions like the one just below. Then, another row on top of that, and another on top of that, and another in an upwards direction going in an infinite a distance as you can imagine.

Now, back to the first row we started with (of which we are a part), there are rows below it that go "downwards" in an infinite direction. Then each of these rows have other universes going laterally in both directions—all suspended in the vastness of eternal space. Then think of each possessing different physics, geometry, light, matter, life forms, non-life forms – whatever you can imagine.

That is what I saw.

The threads which suspend these universes within the vastness all connected them together with spider web-like energy filaments that were themselves part of a larger web-like structure to which they are attached. I saw all these threads leading back to the incandescent energy of the Source that was and is pulsing life into every one of the sheet-like dimensions.

Yet, in all this cosmic spaciousness, I had no sense of falling into emptiness, or a pit, or pulled in any direction. The energetic waves that passed through me continued to ripple onward into the far distance of Eternity.

This was certainly not a confined space. It was not a special room or house into which I was parked forever. I was not tied to our planet or even our universe anymore. I was free from all the constraints, all the boundaries, and all the limitations I encountered in human form. I suppose some may call it heaven if they wish. But it was not someplace *up in the clouds* because there were no clouds. It is an eternal dimension that exists beyond human logic or the concepts we use to understand our world.

Along with the release of all constrictions, I was freed from all expectations, all judgments and all guilt that may be ascribed by religious edicts or by others. Any inadequacies or disappointments I may have felt during my life on earth no longer mattered. There was no residue of my past actions for which I had to atone. No shame as to what I had been or had done. There was no material wealth I had accumulated. There was no emotional or physical pain I still had to embrace. All of that was gone. Perhaps the greatest freedom I felt was my release from fear because there was nothing to be afraid of there. Fear did not exist here and it wasn't even acknowledged as a concept.

I felt safe, safer than I've ever been in this life. And that, to me, meant that all who were there beside me were safe as well. I realized I was beyond the reach of any human influence and I accepted that I would remain beyond anyone's reach. No one could harm me because I was entwined within the braided threads of love woven into the fabric of infinite time. And I understood that it was for all who I had now joined or those who encountered me here in my truest energetic expression.

Whatever emotional and physical tethers may have held me had been cut away as the vastness of Time and Space spread out before me, and I understood that the physical destiny of each of us is a reunion with the Source of All Creation.

Then I turned back around again. I saw the Source energy waves spreading out in all directions as we comprehend linear dimensions emanating from a central sphere. It was a ceaseless stream of vibrating, radio-like waves that flowed and never reversed, and I didn't move or drift away with them because I was anchored to an eternal Presence.

I saw millions of singular bursts jetting out every instant from this divine Source and racing into Infinity like bright energetic slivers of light. I instantly understand each of these to be the creation of a new form seeking a dimension enabled by Source. Not necessarily in our planet system or universe, but somewhere into the infinite matrix that spread out before me.

Those bursts streaked in all directions like shooting stars, each a clarion announcement as an aspect formed into an energetic entity with its own likeness and variation of Source. Some were human forms, some were animal, some were trees, some were water, some were flowers, some were forms I probably couldn't understand while I was on earth, but all came from within the depths of Source as waves of brilliance that glowed with the light of beauty and the vibration of truth and love.

I understood that this was the *Nest of the Source of All Creation*, where everything is formed and molded in the Creator's likeness. Here, birth was given to all that is, all that ever was, and all that will ever be, in all the forms, in all essences, in all the infinite possibilities that the Source can contemplate and then create. All was infused with the same energy of the Divine.

Everything I saw before me was at the cusp of Creation. I instantly knew that this was where my own spirit consciousness was formed—in the sparkles of laughter, in the joy and from the love of Source. Each sparkle was coalesced and fused, and then forged into a single spirit entity which I knew became my *internal self*—my soul—that I was in presence with. My physical configuration that I had inhabited here on this earth was the visual expression of the same spiritual essences I saw being fashioned before me, and what I understood to be for everyone else too.

When I first arrived I thought it was incredibly quiet and spectacularly peaceful. Then slowly I became aware of a sound in the background. It was like a deep, steady harmonic bass violin's tone that rose and descended through an infinite range of octaves. Its vibration seemed to be speaking a language I had yet to decipher. But as I listened it echoed across the matrix of dimensions spread before me.

I felt no urge to leave. I had no feelings of longing or absence from where I had left my body behind. I had no particular desire to return to this life on earth. I could say I was surprised to find myself here in the first place. But I did recognize that for some reason unknown to me then, I had effortlessly slipped from a physical embodiment and dimension to one of a completely different expression, and one in which I could comfortably and contentedly stay forever.

But I didn't.

Back at the fitness center I was still just a motionless, unresponsive human form. Frantic minutes had been ticking away for the EMTs. I couldn't call to them and tell them I wasn't there anymore. That I was somewhere else. I couldn't tell them that they shouldn't bother to keep working on me because everything was fine where I was in another dimension—all while people I had never met were desperately working to pull me back from it and return me to the body I had known before.

Finally, there was a blip. Kevin saw a signal. Then a scratch on a printout.

Again a beep. And then another. My heart had started beating. I was coming alive again.

In less than a split second, I was drawn back from the sanctuary I had inhabited. Back into the body I had left behind. Back from the longest trip I had ever taken in six minutes. Back from an experience that would take a long time to understand and still longer to explain.

# Chapter Four

Kevin had been scrutinizing the paper trail spitting out of the defibrillator from the moment he had arrived and set up their machine. As the EMS Director, he was in the office when my call came in. The fitness center was located just across the street, half a block away, so he and Chris raced over on foot instead of waiting for the ambulance to pull out and drive over.

With both a screen monitor and a printout, Kevin focused his attention to the lines and squiggles on the paper, holding it close to his eyes so he didn't miss anything while looking for any tell-tale tick on the read-out that would indicate abnormalities to my rhythm.

Behind Kevin's smile and quick laugh, that made him a pleasing boss to volunteers serving under his direction, is a tenacious perfectionist who had worked in emergency situations for over twelve years, and had seen the full spectrum of human trauma.

When he arrived in the room, Kevin had unloaded the backpack he shouldered across the lawn that included the portable defib machine. He quickly switched the lead wires from the fitness center's AED machine to his so he could immediately use his printout. He satisfied himself that the patches were properly positioned and went to work.

Chris took over for the exhausted fitness staff once he arrived and was applying the intense chest compressions when more

EMTs flooded into the room. Kevin glanced at the monitor screen, comparing it with the squiggles that began appearing on the paper. Nothing changed.

As he powered up his machine, he was told that one shock had already been given by Sandy. He was looking for any signal that might explain why that didn't work when everything on his printout suggested it should have. He could read there were signs in my heart and that it still had electrical activity. There was hope yet, but still no response.

Chris kept vigorously pumping on my chest until Dean took over to relieve him. Dean had been handling role-management as their training director but was kneeling beside me. His medium height and thin features suggested a marathon runner who had gotten side-tracked and ended up working on an ambulance call. He took his turn. Dean was then relieved by Keifpher, who had just arrived from his short ride to join Chris and Kevin, the police officers and others, to find one shock had already been administered.

As crew chief, Chris was responsible for coordinating his team through their response procedures and assigned tasks as more EMTs filtered into the room. They had trained for this type of event so he no longer needed to scrutinize their every move as he concentrated on my body lying below him.

Rikky raced into the room to find most tasks already being handled, but not the Intraosseous (IO). She immediately sliced my sweatpants leg to my thigh, then grabbed the medical drill from Chris's bag and pulled it from its pouch. She attached a large-bore, fifteen gauge needle one-inch long and pressed it against the skin just below my left knee and pushed to drill the needle into the marrow of my tibia. Then she detached the drill from the needle and left it behind still stuck in my leg. She unpackaged an IV tube, attached it to the needle, and began forcing bagged saline fluid into my leg.

When my heart stopped, so did everything else. Fluids no longer moved through my body. My blood vessels had collapsed and provided no access points for needles because there was no pressure from pulsing blood to keep them expanded and available. No fluids could spread through my body except via the bone marrow which functioned almost on its own. The default option was to drill to gain access to it.

Dean knelt beside me readying himself with a device to insert into my throat that would allow him to pump oxygen into my lungs. Until then I had gone without breathing on my own for almost five minutes. He forced air into me by squeezing a bag after Chris had taken over again with the chest compressions.

Kevin began to sweat. Time was ticking away too fast without a result. Chris was already drenched in his own perspiration when Keifpher took over for him.

Finally. Kevin recognized something in a squiggle.

A signal appeared that showed ventricular defibrillation. That was a rhythm he could work with. My heart still wasn't beating but there were enough active electrical impulses inside it yet that he would try to reorient them with an electrical shock. It was maybe a last chance.

He told the EMTs to stop what they were doing and clear away from my unmoving body.

At the machine's command Kevin pushed the button that sent another charge exploding into my chest. I flinched again. He immediately returned to read the printout, looking for any sign of a change in heart activity. The EMTs quickly moved back in and the chest compressions aggressively restarted.

Kevin was hoping against hope as he read the printout. He knew that *a lot* of time had passed by then but later said that he tried to push it out of his thoughts.

He looked at the screen, almost willing it to show him something to believe in what he saw. Then, a slight blip and he checked the paper. Same thing there.

Then another. It was stronger.

Then another. Everyone exhaled.

It got stronger. My blood pressure began to return and slowly elevate.

It had been over six minutes since my last heart beat.

They saw me slightly lift a finger of my right hand.

Dean was ready to remove the King Airway from my throat. He had set a suction tube beside himself to be available once the tube was out. They knew from experience that heart attack victims often vomit once consciousness was regained. The suction tube would be used to remove particles that got expelled from the stomach to prevent them from being inhaled into the lungs.

But he waited.

Kevin said out loud that my heart beat was getting stronger. Then I jerked my hand up to grab at the thing stuck in my throat. That was a welcome sign because it was a natural response for anyone regaining consciousness to grab at it to get it out of their throat.

While EMTs held my arms down, Dean carefully eased the banana-shaped tube out of my throat. An oxygen tip was positioned under my nose and its strap wrapped around my ears to hold it in place.

Rikky held my left leg with an iron grip, making it immobile, as I tried to lift it and reach down for it. A tall, willowy woman with glasses and shoulder-length hair, she had the strength in her long lean arms to arm-wrestle any man to submission, and crush his hands in the process.

Fifteen minutes had passed since I collapsed.

The previously silent EMT voices exploded as excitement and satisfaction rippled between members of the group now that they had a positive response. They forgot about fatigue and continued their tasks. None of them knew what shape I was in but they'd take any positive signal they could get.

Chris hovered over my face like a mother hen looking for the slightest sign I might re-arrest in the first few moments after I start breathing. His fixation on me distorted the personal satisfaction he felt from witnessing *any* movement coming from my once lifeless body. He'd responded to over four hundred emergency calls in his eight years as a first responder and could cite only two other successful recoveries after a heart stoppage.

I'd be his third. But that wasn't guaranteed yet. He'd seen that too many times before. The patient looking good one moment and then gone again the next.

So he hovered. And kept a determined vigil.

In his late thirty's, Chris is a large man with boyish features but with big fists and the weight he used as he applied each chest compression would make any pro wrestler proud. Yet beneath the short dark beard was a gentle person with a large heart of kindness and concern for others.

Dean had begun making preparations for my removal regardless of the outcome while Chris was still pushing on my chest. He'd confirmed that the hospital had been called to be ready for my arrival, alive or not.

During that time Lieut. Travis of the local police department had arrived soon after the call came in. He was the second officer on the scene and surveyed the room to make sure everything was being attended to. He moved outside to control the street for the ambulance and made sure the exit path was clear. He asked if Mary had been called and learned that the reception desk had not been able to contact her yet.

Travis called and Mary answered. He identified himself and Mary recognized Travis' name but had no idea why he was calling. He was standing in the middle of the street, getting transport information from the dispatcher and the hospital, while explaining to Mary what happened.

He said I had a sudden cardiac death. The Wellspring staff and EMTs had done CPR. They had shocked me at least twice. I was awake. I was alive. I was now talking. No news about my condition except I was breathing. He hadn't found out yet which hospital I would be sent to.

Diane and Josh stood off to one side after the EMTs arrived and watched. The emotional adrenalin release after their work finished had forced them to sit down after they were replaced. They could only observe the activity with hopeful anticipation as the EMTs took over. They could do no more. It was completely out of their hands. For Diane that was the most emotionally charged experience she'd had in her twenty-six years of health care work.

Drivers were standing near the ambulance parked outside waiting for a body to transport.

There had been a pause in activity as the EMTs waited and watched. They needed to allow time for me to regain consciousness before I was moved. Dean directed that a cot be set up next to me.

Ever so slowly my eyes began to open and look up at them. They were like two round pieces of glass set into deathly gray-colored goblets.

No one was in a hurry and their movements became less frantic as my breathing got stronger. My movements became more deliberate. The five people kneeling over me firmly held me against the floor so that I didn't try to get up or reach for my leg.

I wouldn't be moved until they were certain I was stable enough to be lifted off the floor on their long board. It was only a two-foot lift onto their cot but they waited until the critical first minutes passed without further incident, all while Chris continued his vigil over my face.

The assessment of residual damage to my body was postponed since I wasn't bleeding externally. Now that I was awake, their job was to get me safely out the door and transported so they could pass me off to the hospital emergency room staff.

As an oxygen tube was readjusted below my nose, Dean and Keifpher rolled me over onto my right side and held me tight so that I was perpendicular with the floor. Dean grabbed the suction tube and watched because I began coughing. He was ready for any vomit that might be ejected, but none appeared.

When he was satisfied I'd passed that point, he asked for the long board to be slipped behind me. Dean and Keifpher eased me back flat onto the hard wood surface. Then five EMTs grabbed the board and lifted me, gently setting me back down onto their cot. Chris was hovering again and closely watched my breathing. Rikky was holding both my legs tight so they couldn't move as I was repositioned on the cot. Someone checked my pulse even though it showed on Kevin's monitor. Only then did Kevin and Chris give the ok to roll me out through the fitness room door.

Lieutenant Travis apologized to Mary for making her wait on the phone but he asked her to hold while he rechecked that everything was going alright with my exit. He was then back on.

Mary was caught off guard because she didn't know I had changed my plans to go for a workout. She thought I was still at home.

"No. No," Travis said. "He was here in Prairie. At the fitness center."

He paused as he listened to his monitor. He was getting conflicting directives from the ambulance and the hospital. Finally he said they were taking me to the local hospital. He told Mary that I was in excellent hands. Then he asked if she could hold again because he heard new instructions coming in.

While Kevin walked alongside the rolling cot, he listened to the monitor now packed inside his shoulder case for any signal that might alert him that my heart had stopped again during that short move.

Six EMTs shepherded me down five steps that led to sliding doors and out to the middle of the street where the ambulance was parked. They reached the open doors at the rear of the ambulance and together lifted the cot and rolled the wheels into the floor track where the locks were set to hold me in place.

Chris climbed into the back with Keifpher and Kelli and began hovering above my face again while they talked to me. He was asking questions, trying to engage with me, even if I didn't make any sense.

Kevin switched the wires from his shoulder unit to the monitor inside the ambulance. He checked that everything was working and then left. He had just handed me off for my next stop.

Lieut. Travis received updated information as the driver turned on the red flashing lights. The rear doors were closed and secured. The siren started. The ambulance began to move and headed to the local hospital.

But there was a sudden change of plan.

Travis told Mary that I would to be taken to Madison and the University hospital instead. The local hospital had directed the ambulance to go there because it's a Level One Trauma Unit and they had a cardiac catheter unit that I needed.

When the ambulance was a mile up the street heading in the direction of the local hospital, they were informed of the change and received the directive to proceed to Madison. They turned around in the downtown and sped in the opposite direction for the twenty-five mile trip.

After my removal the Wellspring staff convened to construct their assessment of the incident. Sarah spoke with Sandy and told her that I had appeared normal when we had our brief conversation at the arm curl machine. Then ten seconds later I was on the floor. Diane and Josh added comments because their report needed to be filed quickly so the medical staff at University Hospital had access to it and up-to-the-minute information about what happened, what my condition was, and anything else that would help their emergency personnel with their assessment once I arrived.

The exercise room needed to be put back in order after I was out. EMTs helped reposition the heavy machines that were moved to work on me. They picked up all their equipment before they left.

The ambulance screamed back through the twin villages after it turned around. At the stoplights Kelli got out to make room for the paramedics that would join the ambulance along the highway. I couldn't see a thing because Chris was still hovering over me and if he moved away for a second all I would see was the interior ceiling of the vehicle. During the ride to Madison Keifpher tried to give me aspirin as a protocol to avert another heart attack.

I refused to take it until he explained why I should take it.

Keifpher insisted again.

"Not until you tell me," he recalled me saying.

He said, "You were dead and you need to take the aspirin!"

That, apparently, was all it took.

One more stop was made along the way.

The EMTs requested assistance from their colleagues at the Middleton station. They asked for paramedic support in case I needed any drugs during a possible re-arrest, which the local EMTs weren't licensed to carry.

The two vehicles met on the side of the heavily-traveled state highway with cars speeding past. Two Middleton paramedics jumped out of their vehicle and ran to the back of the open door of my ambulance. It got awfully crowded with four standing people, a cot with me on it, and all the medical tote bags lying on the floor.

Seventeen minutes later, we pulled into the emergency bay of the University of Wisconsin Hospital.

Chris finally stopped hovering as he and Keifpher helped the ER staff unload me.

Then he went to look for Mary.

# Chapter Five

———————

I opened my eyes. Or thought I had. And even if they were open, I couldn't see or recognize anyone. If it was the case that my eyes could see people, then my mind didn't register their presence.

People may have spoken to me and I may have spoken back, but I didn't hear their words or mine. I was in a vacuum where no sights or sounds engaged my senses even if I was surrounded by them. That went on for a long time and even though I was later told I had interacted with people surrounding me in the ER, eight hours passed before any awareness registered in my mind that my senses were still working.

It felt like I had been sluggishly peeling off layers of veneer that coated my eyes with a clear film that had obscured my surroundings in the fitness center, the ambulance, the ER, and the hospital room. Then slowly over the period of hours, each layer that was removed took me one tiny step closer to becoming conscious of myself and those around me. The shadows sharpened. The forms developed with slow, but increasing clarity. The words became less garbled until finally, as the last layer was removed, my mind finally could comprehend fully what was in front of me—my family.

When the last layer was gone I could once again—in my own mind even though others thought I had already been doing that—recognize myself at some level of mental consciousness that I had known before I left. Only now with those layers removed,

I recognized it as the body I had previously lived in, the people I had previously known, and air I had been breathing.

When I awakened fully to this life again, when that last layer was removed, it was 8:30 Monday evening, and I had been reattached to the construct of time we use here.

Sometime later, after I finally reconciled my presence to these new surroundings, I asked myself a question.

*Why is everyone here?*

I glanced at anything I could try to focus on. I stopped to feel myself breathe. Boy, that really hurt! There was tightness in my chest. I gulped for my next breath and someone stirred next to me. I glanced around but my eye muscles ached. Slowly, very slowly I realized I wasn't in the exercise room.

*Something's not right. This is weird.* I thought.

Another question came to me, but I must have said it out loud.

*What am I doing here?*

There were people standing above me. One. Two. Three. I lost count. My head was pounding. Each person stared back with grave concern. Had I said something wrong?

Someone was standing to my left. It looked like Marcus. But that wasn't possible because he lived in Minneapolis.

*Where the heck am I?* I must have said it loud enough because he chuckled.

"You don't remember?" he asked. He said he was Marcus as he looked down on my body flattened against the sheets.

"What are you doing here?" I asked. He just smiled and slightly shook his head.

My inside voice wouldn't stop asking questions, even if I couldn't say them out loud. I wasn't getting answers from anyone, or even myself.

*Boy it's loud in here*, I thought. Now my ears were throbbing from the noise just like my head.

I looked down at my feet and saw a white sheet had been pulled over me.

*When did I change? Where are my shoes?*

I lifted my left arm to bring my wrist close to my face as if I was reading a watch with incredibly tiny numbers. I had a plastic bracelet on my wrist. *What's this?* I didn't recognize the letters or the name on it.

I noticed needles were stuck into my right arm, and when I raised it someone quickly eased it back down beside me.

*Why does my left leg hurt so much?* It felt like I had broken it. *Man that hurts.* More questions kept coming from above me just as I was beginning to have more questions for myself.

The bright lights glared so that I had to squint. I lifted my hand to shade my eyes but someone again eased my arm back down. I didn't have the strength to offer resistance. The noise seemed so loud I wanted to tell everyone to shut up. It was like swimming underneath water with everyone talking to me from above it. The voices bubbled and gargled as the sounds sloshed around in my ears, like shaking a half filled bottle of water.

I could tell there were people in the room although I couldn't see them very clearly yet. They were like silhouettes that moved in and then out of a picture frame. I gave up and tried to focus on only one person. It looked like Mary standing at my feet and she seemed to be rubbing them with her hands.

*What's she doing here?*

I stared for a long time trying to comprehend what was happening. I had a fleeting thought when I looked at the white sheet draped over my body. Maybe I was dead and she's performing some sort of funeral preparation by washing my body and had just reached my feet. But I couldn't feel them or her hands.

I looked back at Marcus.

"Why are you here?" I asked as I tried to bring him into a clearer fix in my sight.

He shook his head. "You just asked me that, dad."

*When did I ask that?* I thought.

"Well?"

"You had a heart attack this morning while exercising," he said without alarm. He shifted himself from leaning against the wall to move closer.

"We talked about this before."

"When?" I asked.

"About an hour ago. Don't you remember?"

"No."

I didn't pursue it. *This is some strange dream I'm having. That's all*, I said to myself. *It can get over now.*

A doctor and nurse came by. One held my wrist and the other listened to my chest.

*What are they doing to me?*

I glanced around to try to see where I was while they fiddled with me. It was a large room. There were beeping sounds. Shuffling feet. My eyes settled on something I finally recognized—a wall clock. It read eight o'clock.

*That can't be right.* I thought. I just went to exercise at eleven and clocks don't run backwards.

AT LEAST NOT HERE!

I must have shouted that out loud because eyebrows arched in surprise from those around me. Someone leaned over and checked my eyes with a small flashlight. Another put a stethoscope and listened to the pulsing in my neck that even I could feel. The furtive glances between the medical staff made me wonder if I had said something wrong.

"It's eight *at night*," one finally said, seeming half amused and half alarmed.

"That doesn't make any sense," I said.

But I decided to retreat and regroup within myself.

*That can't be right* was the only thought I could grab hold of. *It just can't be.*

I had no way of understanding that hours had passed me by. *How can I lose eight hours? If I did, where have I been?*

It was confusing. So awfully confusing.

The questions kept circling. If I was at exercise like Marcus said I was, then why was I in a hospital? He said a heart attack. But I'm breathing, I could tell that much. I had pain all over, like I had just been beaten up. But what especially hurt was my left leg as I reached down to touch it.

"Please don't move like that!" Although said gently, it came across like a command from a drill sergeant who was standing next to me. The young man with a clipboard and pen seemed intent on noting every twitch I made. My first instinct was to lift my right leg to see if I got a reaction.

"Please don't," he repeated but more firmly.

*Well, ok then.* I'm thought. Piss me off by telling me I can't do something and I'm likely to try it.

I shifted as if I was about to raise my left leg but his look suggested I had better not.

Being flat on my back didn't provide me with much range to look around. I barely saw the tips of my toes that Mary was still rubbing. Now I could feel her hands as she gently stroked first one and then the other. It was like different parts of me were waking up from a deep hibernation at different moments, totally unsynchronized from each other. First my arms, then my legs, and finally my feet.

*What is she doing here?* The last I saw her she went off to work.

Then I finally recognized Julia and Victor.

*They're in Ripon. Why are they here?*

I then made the simplest connection. Everyone's here!

I felt like I was in some homemade video taken at a family gathering that had surfaced after being lost for years. Maybe I was dying and they were here to see me off. Like a last visit before final departure. I didn't have the faintest idea why all this was happening to me.

Was all this a dream I was having? Although I could finally recognize them no one seemed to hear the thoughts I had that I couldn't get out. When I tried to ask a question, no one answered. Maybe it was all inside my head and the questions simply weren't getting out. When I stumbled trying to say anything, I tripped over whatever words I could find. I made muffled sounds like I had a mouth full of cotton until I realized I was groaning from my pain. I noticed their eyes glance back and forth between each other. It seemed like no one was talking except me.

The sounds in the room got louder the more I became reactivated to myself and my surroundings. The ringing in my ears was piercing. Every movement anyone made seemed to be ploddingly deliberate as if time had intentionally dialed itself down to a snail's pace like some slow motion movie.

I felt *soooooo* tired. I couldn't remember ever being that exhausted. I just wanted to sleep. I kept drifting off but then more questions came for me to answer and woke me up.

*Leave me alone!* I screamed inside.

I withdrew into myself and ignored the talk around the room and the questions because I recognized these were not the sights and sounds I had just witnessed. And I suddenly felt a rush of incredible sadness because I realized I wasn't floating on waves of any kind anymore.

I couldn't see past my feet. The lights above me were not golden. I had people grabbing my wrists. Others were listening to my chest, my neck, my throat. This room was alien to me. It wasn't comfortable. It wasn't welcoming. I felt like I shouldn't be there or here or anywhere. I felt absolutely lost without having any idea why.

When I tried to lift my head it felt like a boat anchor that slammed back onto the thin pillow after I gave up.

I had been admitted to the hospital at 12:51 p.m., Monday afternoon. A chest X-ray and metabolic panel were ordered within the first two minutes after my arrival. Within seven minutes, the X-rays had been taken and blood was drawn from my arm for a panel profile. Things had moved quickly. At least light speed faster than I could think because I seemed to be two sentences behind everything being said.

Someone explained that no pulmonary embolism showed on the X-ray. I supposed that was good news but it didn't mean anything to me.

As if I could possibly comprehend it, I was told my main pulmonary artery and the thoracic aorta were of normal caliber, and my heart was a normal size. That didn't make any difference because I simply didn't care at that moment.

I didn't have any identification when I arrived so I was listed on their manifest as Patient Puerto Rico XXX. That unexplained name was given to me as an unidentified person entering their facility. I was simply an unknown quantity to them, dropped into their laps. I didn't arrive with a slip of paper pinned to my chest with my name on it.

Sometime later after I'd been admitted, my identification surfaced. It was a bit like waiting in a morgue for a positive ID of the victim to arrive.

By evening I was repeatedly told that all my vital signs were normal. Perhaps they didn't think I could comprehend it because they repeated it over and over. My blood pressure and pulse had quickly stabilized, much to their surprise. There was confusion about why my heart stopped because I appeared normal to anyone who saw me that afternoon. I may have looked normal to them but I don't feel it myself. I felt like I was in two different places and that I was performing an imitation of myself for them in that room, when I was really somewhere else at the same time.

It was between 8:30 and 9:00 o'clock before I fully comprehended that I was in a different place than an exercise room. To that point, nothing made any sense. I may have been awake to others but my mind wasn't fully present for me. When the awareness of my surroundings and the people in the room began to slowly converge together in my mind, it was like I was adjusting a set of binoculars that brought all the blurriness into clear focus. The kaleidoscope of my vision, hearing, and feeling began to merge all at once.

I was just beginning *to see* the people around me for the first time. Those wavy, out-of-focus forms began to transpose into solid human beings. They had many colors. Many sizes. Different sexes. Different hair. Some had glasses, some didn't. Some smiled, some seemed serious. Some asked questions, some gave commands.

That's when my *real* confusion began.

If I had been *there*, then why am I *here*?

My head was still throbbing. It felt about to explode from some information overload. But other than the new pains I had before I walked into my exercise session, I couldn't say that I felt any differently.

I stopped at that thought. Maybe something happened to me there. But I couldn't possibly guess what that might be.

My breathing seemed normal although I had an oxygen tip attached to the bottom of my nose. My vision seemed a little better, and when I said I had my contacts in, Julia asked a nurse to help take them out. Then things went blurry again because I didn't have my glasses or any idea where they were.

Two doctors and a nurse talked off to the side between themselves and I heard an agreement that I needed to be closely monitored during the night. Apparently I wouldn't be going home.

Somehow I had lost eight hours of my life. That much was slowly starting to sink in. It wasn't a fog through which I struggled to navigate. It was a loss of my equilibrium. I suddenly felt completely off balance like I was teetering on the edge of a cliff on one foot with my mind listing to one side. I kept grabbing the sides of my bed to steady myself as I pressed my head back into my pillow trying to make the dizziness stop. When it eased, I looked around carefully before it started again. I didn't need another command from someone with a clipboard.

I couldn't reconstruct what happened because I couldn't remember anything happening to me. I could remember being in another dimension immersed in a great light and bathed in powerful waves. But my mind couldn't reach back any farther than that to retrieve anything. Besides, I was too tired.

I now found myself boxed in a white room with four walls, stainless steel equipment, people poking me, and my family standing at the outer edges. It was like they were watching me as I stood in a boat on some distant shore, and I was waving as I slowly floated away from them and they're helpless to do anything about it.

Or, were they watching me drift back to the shore where they were standing and waiting in anticipation for me to arrive again? I had no way of knowing if either was right.

Everything around me seemed unreal. Surreal. Like it was happening but really wasn't. Any answers would have to wait until morning because I was too tired to think. I was numb. My whole body felt anaesthetized.

Maybe there would be time for talk later. Maybe not. I drifted off to sleep not caring one way or the other. Perhaps there would be time to learn more. Perhaps there would be more still to come.

But it would be nothing compared to what I learned really happened.

# Chapter Six

The next time I opened my eyes, it was quiet. Deathly quiet. Not a sound. But, thankfully, no one held a clipboard beside me. No one was asking me questions either. But there was no Mary. No Marcus. No Julia and Victor.

*Where did everyone go?* For a blip, I thought I might have dreamt it all. But as the reality set in, I was flat on my back in a hospital bed, without knowing why.

During the night they must have brought me up to that room from the ER but it was all lost on me. I didn't remember the ride as they settled me into an Intensive Care Unit (ICU) room. I knew that much because the sign on the desk at the other side of the room, as I peeked over the tops of my linen-covered feet and squinted at it, said so in dark letters.

The curtain was pulled halfway around my bed. If I had a heart attack as Marcus said I did, where was the incessant beeping of the heart monitor? I half-expected to hear it because that's what happened on high-drama TV shows, right? Loud beeping to alert you that something dramatic is about to happen, or might not.

Nothing.

The silence wafted around the room riding its own currents, ready to shatter at the slightest disturbance. The rattling of a cart echoed somewhere in the next room. I turned to look at the open door to my right.

*Why am I in here?*

I had a nagging sense that I had been woken constantly during the night. Over and over and over. Waking up, then falling back to sleep, then up again, then drifting off. It seemed like everyone wanted something from me while I slept.

I felt like I was drifting in and out of a foggy ride to nowhere. It reminded me of the time I had a two-week, farm-related business trip during which Mary had rearranged our bedroom while I was gone. I was exhausted from driving the eighteen hundred mile trip when I got home in the early evening. I ate and went straight to bed.

I got up in total darkness during the middle of the night and opened what I thought was the door to the hallway that led to the bathroom. Instead, it was the door to Mary's closet and I found myself wrapped up amongst her hanging dresses, skirts and coats. I began floundering, flinging my arms to push them out of the way, only to bump into a wall.

"Where the hell am I?" I muttered in frustration. In the dark, I couldn't find the door I had just come through. Mary turned on the bed light to see what the ruckus was all about. She began laughing hysterically as she rolled from side to side thinking this was the best entertainment she'd had since I left fourteen days before.

So in that hospital room, I felt I had stumbled back into a foggy closet from which I couldn't find my way out. The only thing missing was the light and Mary's laughing that I could use to find an exit.

There were people in white uniforms I didn't know, who kept asking me the same questions. Over and over and over. Did I feel ok? Does my chest hurt? Can I breathe ok?

I must have said yes each time because after they finished checking everything they left. Only to have another round of the same questions after what seemed like only ten minutes later.

One time I woke up and tried to lift my leg but with little result. It wouldn't move. But it was enough to trigger some monitor alarm because two people rushed in and placed their hands on my shoulders to ease me back onto my pillow, and to block any dismount from the bed I might have been considering.

"You need to lie still," one said as she pulled the sheet cover back up to my chin and leaned over to check the monitor leads on my chest so they weren't tangled.

The other checked the plastic line making sure the flow from the hanging IV wasn't interrupted. Then he said, "We prefer that you don't get out of bed, ok?" He lightly patted my shoulder as if to nail that point to me. His seemingly polite question, with its soft tone, had the sharp edge of a directive.

I nodded. "Ok."

Everything seemed straightened out. After they were satisfied I wouldn't chuck myself onto the floor, they quietly left. But not before the male nurse raised the side bar to my bed and locked it in place. The curled corner of his smile implied that I couldn't be naughty anymore.

At least they didn't strap me to the bed or put an ankle monitor on me . . . hmm, well, I was pretty sure they didn't. But I didn't move my leg to confirm that because I didn't want them rushing in again.

I was awake again so I looked at the clock high on the wall that said it was six.

*Is that morning or night?* I wondered. I couldn't tell because there were no windows to let either the light or dark into the room.

The pain in my head had settled from excruciating to throbbing except for when I moved it quickly on the pillow. Then the drums started pounding again. So I laid there looking straight ahead at nothing but the wall and ceiling. It was all really boring at that moment and I wasn't given a remote. I looked around and saw there wasn't any TV monitor to look at either, so it didn't make any difference.

No nurse or doctor appeared ready to come in just then so I began to explore and make mental notes for later use.

I lifted my left arm and saw an IV needle attached to the back of my hand with what seemed like half a roll of tape holding it in place. That looked familiar. Ok, check that off my list.

I felt the monitor patches attached to my chest. Check.

*No, wait.*

I rub. Someone had shaved my chest! *I don't remember that.*

I slid my right hand under my gown since it didn't have any back to it and it more or less just laid on top of me. I walked my fingers up to my throat exploring my skin as I moved it from side to side.

*They'd shaved my whole chest and stomach!*

I had a moment of feeling violated because I wasn't asked if they could do that. I let that thought recede and figured that at least from now on they wouldn't be ripping the hair off in clumps if they replaced the patches with new ones.

*What else?*

I tried to rub my painful left knee but that meant crossing my right arm over my stomach and hips. My chest screamed in pain when I made my first attempt. So I quit. I took a deep breath as I relaxed back onto my pillow. I coughed and that sent shockwaves through the muscles across my chest. They felt like they'd been pummeled from a boxing match in which I'd been beaten to a pulp.

Besides my leg, my inner chest felt tender and really hurt. For a second I thought *I am* having a heart attack because it hurt so much. I glanced at the numbers on the monitor but nothing changed.

I stopped and assessed it for a moment. No. The muscles on the outside hurt but not anything inside. Ok, then, check.

Then I had a guy-thought.

Just to make sure, I gently inched my hand down my stomach, over my hips, and down in between my legs. I count.

*One. Two.* Ok, they're still there. I continue. *Thank goodness, it's still there.* Retracted a bit but still there. Check. Check. Check. Whew! That was close.

*Wait. Something's not right.*

I felt around some more.

*I'm shaved down there too! How'd that happen?*

Another question for Mary later. So I guess, check.

My thin pillow puffed out on the ends as I slapped my head back down. I think in between heavy breaths.

*Ok, my chest hasn't been cut open like many heart attack patients. I'm not cut anywhere else. So on the whole, that's not bad. Right?*

My eyelids got heavy as I started to relax. I gave up my check-list exploration and began to drift off. Then I had a flashback. It surprised me because I hadn't been able to remember anything from yesterday. So why should I suddenly recall my grandfather's heart attack from fifty-three years ago? In that particular moment? Was there some message for me? Or was it simply short memory loss that couldn't remember the current and had to resort to the far past in order to tell itself it was still viable?

I hadn't thought about it in decades. Maybe now, because I was having my own chance to understand what he must have gone through, there was a message for me. Maybe I should listen.

It had happened during the night of October 28, 1962. I was woken by the shouting in our upstairs farmhouse. My grandmother was calling down the steps to Dad who came bounding up two at a time. She and Grandpa slept in the room across the hall from my two brothers and me.

A sliver of light filtered into our room as I kept the door cracked slightly open to look out to see what the hollering was about. Grandma glanced over her shoulder to see me but didn't say anything as she held Grandpa's hand, lightly stroking it as his unsteady breathing came in short gasps, followed by low groans. *He must be hurt* was the thought my ten-year-old mind had.

There wasn't any clock in our room to tell me the time. Maybe eleven, maybe four. I couldn't recall how many minutes passed between when I heard my dad make a phone call and when a car finally came to a sliding stop on the gravel county road that passed by our farm. It found the driveway and turned into our yard.

There were muffled voices downstairs, followed by a rush of two men up the stairs. My dad raced first, followed by the newly arrived doctor from the Ukraine who had taken up practice in a small village eight miles away. Even in the soft hallway light I noticed a slightly-built young man with a great shock of dark hair, alert eyes, and a determined, can-do attitude.

He quickly examined Grandpa and then instructed Dad to help carry him down to his car. He said there was no time to wait for the ambulance, such as it was in those days. Usually the local undertaker's station wagon served as the ambulance and would have taken at least a half hour to get to our farm.

They leaned him forward on the bed and together slipped their right and left arms under Grandpa's legs and then locked their free arms together behind his back. They lifted and cradled him like a hammock, and moved quickly out of the room, along the short hallway and down the steps with Grandma close behind.

I ran to the upstairs window that overlooked our farmyard and watched them settle Grandpa into the back seat, where Dad sat beside him. The young doctor scrambled around to the driver's seat and away they went, spraying loose gravel against the wheel wells as they sped off. The quiet returned to the house like it had to the hospital room I found myself.

When I finally got to visit my grandfather in the hospital, I walked into his room and saw him lying underneath clear plastic sheeting which I was told was an oxygen tent. I wasn't underneath a tent but I had an oxygen nasal tip attached to my nose.

I shook my head as if to loosen the rest of this memory from its shelf. But nothing more came and it dissolved almost as quickly as it arrived. There was more to it but I couldn't touch it then. It was gone for the time being. Maybe I'd remember the rest later.

I was staying at University Hospital only through the morning because of our insurance coverage. I would be transferred to St. Mary's Hospital but only if they felt I was stable enough to handle the ride and movement. A final evaluation was to be made before I would be discharged. Or not. In that case, I'd be there another day and probably another night.

Outside my ICU room, I heard what I assumed were several doctors and nurses talking. As I was the only one in this particular unit, I assumed they probably were talking about me.

I heard one say, "Look at what this guy answered." Which was immediately followed by a short burst of stifled group laughter. There was a pause before one doctor came in bearing a slight smile. I had no idea what I'd done that was so funny. Maybe it was my hair, since it hadn't been washed for awhile and probably reeked of sweat.

The doctor explained that they felt it was safe for me to be transferred. After they had finished the paperwork, I would be moved as soon as the ambulance came for me.

Two men from a private ambulance service arrived later and after they entered my room, I was shifted from the bed to their rolling cot. A nurse checked my IV bag as it needed to be unplugged from my hand. Another ICU nurse switched the wires that attached me to their monitoring machine to the ambulance's portable unit. Then I was whisked away through the doorway, past other patients who I didn't know were right outside my door, and out into the corridor.

We rode down an elevator and then I was rolled outside where they lifted me into the back of their ambulance. I was hooked to another IV bag and heart monitoring unit. The gurney was locked into place and we left at 8:15 on Tuesday morning.

One EMT drove while the other remained in back with me, constantly writing on papers held by his clipboard, and checking numbers on the monitors. I must not have seemed a serious case with so little overt supervision being applied. Or perhaps they were just really good at their jobs.

Once in the parking bay at St. Mary's, they lifted me out and rolled me directly to an elevator. There was no check-in as I was expected. We rode up to the fourth floor Cardiac Care Unit, and then they wheeled me into a room directly across from the nurse's station.

As they helped me to sit up on the gurney, they asked if I could stand to move onto the bed. I was steadied as they slowly swung my legs over the side, and helped to step down onto the floor. Six people now surrounded me.

I was in the most intensive observation area and all the staff members watched to make sure nothing happened while I was moved to their bed. They were ready for anything and, as I glanced out the corner of my eye, I saw they had positioned a crash cart at the doorway that wasn't there when I entered the room.

I shifted to the bed and was eased onto my back. The covers were pulled up to my stomach. I was breathing fast. That was exhausting work. A station nurse moved in quickly and listened to my heart while another checked my blood pressure. Someone held my hand steady and afterwards I found I had been banded with a new wrist tag. The transfer was complete and I was their responsibility.

All day I was to be monitored. One nurse explained that tests were scheduled for later that morning but said she didn't know anymore than that. I wouldn't be allowed to eat anything until the doctor came for a consultation.

Dr. Alan walked in shortly and introduced himself as the cardiologist who would be working with me.

He was about six-foot, with short hair speckled dark and white, and glasses that were still in his breast pocket. He held himself with an air of confidence and said he should be able to help. That is, if he could find out what was wrong. But first there needed to be tests. He'd reviewed all the information he had about my collapse. He'd read the EMT report, the Wellsprings staff report, the ER report from UW Hospital, and from the ICU.

"You've had quite a ride," he said.

He admitted that after reviewing all my reports, he was surprised that I looked so normal and my readings appeared as they would in a healthy person.

"That's very unusual for the kind of event you've just gone through."

He said that a normal response after a heart stops was elevated blood pressure and pulse rates. There were usually signs of proteins in the blood that showed if the heart had been affected. He said if it was a heart attack, there would be specific blood proteins indicating some degree of damage to it they would be looking for. The panel profile taken from my samples during the night didn't show *any* elevated protein levels to indicate that.

"But something caused your collapse. We *need* to find out what that was," he added in his even, mild tone. But a sense of urgency was evident in how he said it. If he couldn't wait, probably I shouldn't want to either.

I would be prepped shortly for an echocardiogram (ECG/EKG) which would give him a better picture of what was going on with my heart. It needed to be done that day because he couldn't risk leaving me overnight even though I didn't *appear* to be in any imminent danger. He didn't want to take any chances.

I sat there silently. I didn't have any feelings about this one way or the other. I still wasn't sure what happened but I seemed to be stuck where I was at the moment without any other options. Aside from my left knee that hurt and my chest muscles that were really sore, and the headaches I had, the dizziness, and the desire to sleep all the time because I felt exhausted, I didn't think anything was wrong with me.

Dr. Alan briefly explained that the ECG/EKG would record my heart's electrical activity by using sound waves while showing live, moving images of it. The ultrasound would spot any damage or problems in my heart and surrounding vessels that might not show up on a typical X-ray. I thought that would be something to see. I'd never seen the inside of my body before let alone what my heart looked like.

Two hours later I was helped onto another gurney and wheeled down the hall. I went through several doors and into a side room. A technician explained the procedure and I entered a room where I was confronted with a large circular machine that almost touched the ceiling. For a fleeting second, I felt I was about to become an extraterrestrial experiment.

I pointed to it.

"It's a non-invasive procedure. Nothing to be frightened of." I was told by the technician.

*I'm not frightened for Pete's sake. I'm wondering what it is.* I said under my breath. That surprised me because I'm not the kind of person who snaps at someone who is trying to help me. Or at least I wasn't that person before. Did something change me? I wondered.

I was shifted from the gurney to a flat table and positioned adjacent to the machine. The technician instructed me to lie still as I passed through. "This will take a few minutes."

He promised I wouldn't feel a thing.

Feet first, I slowly moved into the machine's central entry point until my chest was directly under the large rotating donut-like machine. I felt like the jelly filling being pushed into the center hole.

"Ready," the man at the keyboard said. I wasn't sure if it was a statement about his readiness or if it was a rhetorical question directed to me. I guessed I was ready because within seconds the donut started moving. First slowly, and then picking up speed until it was spinning like a top. It whirled around and around so silently I opened my eyes to watch it and just as quickly closed them because it made me dizzy.

Blue lights blinked. And with the sound of the machine whirring away, I thought we just might have lift off.

The process was completed after several minutes. When all the pictures were taken, it was powered down and the spinning became slower with each revolution until it settled to a complete stop. He touched a button and the table retracted and pulled me back out until my feet cleared the machine. I was helped off and into a waiting wheel chair, and taken back to my room. I was told I could order something to eat but only soft food, like yogurt. I couldn't cheat because I was told the kitchen had my room number and my name that was on a restricted diet list.

I chuckled. I hadn't been on anyone's restricted list since I was a kid.

Their plan for me wouldn't be made until the pictures were read. It was past one in the afternoon by the time I was back in my room. At least I had some idea of what part of the day it was. While I worked my way down to the bottom of the yogurt cup, Mary stepped back into the room.

She looked at me and then around the rest of the room.

"This is nice," she said.

"Um, yeah, I guess," I replied. I hadn't really given it much thought. I was more interested in eating. She seemed to imply that I'd checked into a four-star hotel. Without available food.

She walked over to my bed, leaned down and gave me a kiss. Then a hug.

"Want to climb in?" I asked.

"No," she said. "But thanks anyway."

I explained where I had been and she told me she wanted to talk about what she'd just been through. It wasn't meant as a competition so I said she should go first since she was the guest in my room.

She said that after she left the hospital to go back home, she and Marcus stopped to get something to eat. Victor and Julia drove back to Ripon. Marcus had the longest day because he had driven to Minneapolis and then turned around within an hour and drove back to Madison. Four hours each way.

I couldn't top that, so all I said was that I didn't have any clothes, just the thin hospital gown I was wearing.

"I brought some with me," Mary said. But she didn't think I'd be going anywhere soon.

She said she and Marcus went into town to get the car from the parking lot, and to pick up my clothes at the Wellspring Center because they were still hanging in my locker. They dropped the car off to have the tires changed. While they were there, they ran into one of the owners whom we've done farm business with. Marcus talked with him while Mary explained why I'd missed the appointment.

Marcus needed directions to get to my locker once he got to the fitness center so he stopped at the front desk. The staff members asked how I was doing and he explained to them what I looked like.

It was Tuesday morning and Mary hadn't gone to work yet. But she said she wanted to get there later to retrieve her laptop. She was helping a family plan for a funeral reception.

She said she was sorry if she didn't seem concerned last night. She was still getting over the phone call from Travis about my collapse. Then having to call Marcus and Julia, and my mom. That was a lot of balls to juggle at one time. Plus, she had to deal with the insurance issues.

I didn't say anything while she continued with her list.

She said she rubbed my feet to at least do something helpful instead of just standing there.

"It was the not knowing how you might be afterwards," she said with tears welling in her eyes.

She explained that I had been repeating myself while I was in the ER. Over and over, asking the same questions. Like I had lost all short term memory. Maybe my whole memory. No one knew. And that worried her.

"You do seem better this morning though. Although you haven't said much."

I explained the donut machine I'd been in and she gave me a look like I was pulling her leg. I explained that a Dr. Alan had been in and then I was sent to a room to take pictures of my heart.

"The machine looks like a donut, honestly," I said pleading my case.

I told her how I was slipped into it before it began to spin around.

"But I haven't heard anything from them yet," I added. I was now finished with what I could remember.

"Oh, there was one more thing," I said to Mary.

Before I was about to be sent over from the UW hospital, they did some final evaluations before they would let me go. I was in bed and there was some laughing outside my door. I didn't know what that was about.

She grinned and said, "You don't remember?"

"No."

"Well, at one point in the ICU, you were answering questions for the pharmacist. He was going over any medications that you were taking while I stood beside you. I said you weren't taking any."

"Then he asked if you were allergic to anything. And without skipping a beat you made some political comment. It came out so fast you couldn't have had time to think about his question."

"The poor guy almost broke out laughing because he didn't expect that. Especially from a patient in your condition. He tried to stifle it but he couldn't help chuckling. He tried to think of something to say and finally said, 'Well, we'll try to keep them away from you.'"

"Marcus, just rolled his eyes and said, 'Why couldn't he have just said something else, like peanuts?'"

I looked at her with disbelief. "So that was what the doctors and nurses outside my room had been laughing at?"

"Probably," Mary said.

Since we now had time to talk, or at least while I was still awake, I asked Mary to explain what happened yesterday because I had no idea.

Mary replayed the scene to me.

She served as director of connecting ministries at First Church in downtown Madison, and was on her lunch break with two other staff members when she got a call that registered a Baraboo number she didn't recognize. She said she didn't normally keep her phone with her while eating but for some reason yesterday she did. She said she answered it and got up to walk into an empty conference room to talk.

"Lieutenant Travis identified himself. He said you had collapsed in the fitness room. That you were in the ambulance. You were on your way to the local hospital. But that changed quickly and they were then taking you to a Madison hospital. But you were awake and breathing. You were still alive."

He was still getting information about my transport. After some back and forth conversation in the background, he told Mary it would be the UW Hospital.

"I went back to the lunch room and said I was leaving for the hospital and took off."

Mary said she grabbed her purse and coat, and headed out from her second floor office. She was told they were taking me to the UW hospital because it's a Trauma One Center.

"That's all I knew. I couldn't believe it at first because I had just seen you that morning and you looked fine. It seemed surreal."

She said she drove down University Avenue in what should have been a ten minute trip to the hospital but it took longer. Her first thought was to call Marcus and Julia.

"I called Marcus as soon as I could while waiting at a stop light. But I couldn't get him. So I tried Julia and got her right away and explained what happened." Julia called her fiancé Victor and she left work immediately.

Her second call to Marcus worked. He had just driven back to Minneapolis when he answered and was dropping off a rental car after being in Madison on a business trip the past few days. Mary turned off University Avenue and pulled into what she thought was the emergency parking lot.

"I couldn't find it," she continued. "I'd been in it enough times to know where to go but I came in from a direction I had never used and I pulled into the wrong lot. I was flustered. I was upset. I could have cried. I finally found someone at a pay booth who told me I needed to go around to the other side."

She said if she hadn't done that she would have beaten me to the emergency room.

"That would have been interesting because I would have been asking for you and for an ambulance that still hadn't arrived."

Mary slid into a parking spot that opened near the emergency entrance and speed-walked through the sliding doors and into the reception area. Chris met her in the hallway and explained what happened. That the trip went well. That I missed out on a med-flight because of the weather so they brought me by ambulance. That I had finally responded after several shocks. That I talked to him during the ride. As far as he could tell I was doing as well as could be expected. There weren't any guarantees but my chances looked good to him.

"Most of what he said was lost on me. I was in a fog. I didn't know what to expect. Then I saw you and you're in bed talking with everyone. You looked great. You looked like nothing had happened. You were wide awake. I didn't know what to think."

She said they asked me all kinds of questions from "Do you know what day it is?" to "Who is the President?" to "What did you last eat?"

She mentioned that she didn't say much because I had all their questions to answer.

"I was numb anyway. That feeling probably was related to flashbacks I had of my parents and the number of times I went to the emergency room with them. This was too close to that."

Mary said I made jokes and funny comments to those around me. She wasn't sure that they were interested in what I said but they wanted to keep me awake and that seemed one reason for the questions. So that I would engage with them.

She said that I was continually monitored as they watched for any change in my condition. All my vital signs had gone back to normal which seemed to surprise them every time they checked.

"You *didn't look* like you just had a heart attack," she said.

Mary was there when Julia and Victor arrived from Ripon, and when Marcus arrived much later. It must have seemed like an impromptu family reunion.

Mary said it was getting late when they finally brought the paperwork. They told her I'd be kept in the critical care unit that night so I could be closely monitored.

Before they moved me from the ER, they wanted Mary to sign a form saying she would be responsible for payment.

"I said I needed time to check that our insurance would cover treatment at UW Hospital. So, while you were still in the ER, I was pulled away from my husband and had to spend a half hour on the phone checking insurance coverage."

She said someone in the hospital's admissions office finally got involved and decided I would be staying overnight. Thanks to Mary, I wouldn't be pitched out into the street and they would work with her to handle the insurance issues in the morning.

"So, yes, I had the pleasure of sitting for a half hour dealing with insurance issues. Plus, I still was working on making arrangements to handle a funeral reception at church. I certainly didn't want to be involved with two of them."

There was more.

"I can't say I was mad at you for what happened. But it was like reliving the past. I had gone through this with my parents. Mom called me from the hospital when she was taken to ER. Then later, when my dad fell at the Assisted Living place. Getting that call and then having to run to the hospital. So I had a lot of practice with emergency calls and then just having to deal with it."

She said that later I was taken up to a second floor room in the Critical Care Unit and they all followed me up.

Mary stopped. Even though it was somewhere around noon, she suddenly looked exhausted. She sat down in the chair next to my bed. I thought for a second that she might fall asleep.

We both sat in silence for a minute.

I said I felt bad for causing all this trouble.

"I didn't mean for it to happen," I said as I looked over to her. She just gave a nod and a little smile, and as she looked down at her hands she seemed slightly relieved. I never wanted to put her through something like this. Or Marcus, or Julia, or Victor. Not willingly.

We kept to our own thoughts until the silence was broken when Dr. Alan stepped into the room. He was clutching a bunch of papers and pictures in his hands. He looked first at me and then at Mary.

"We've found the problem," he said before he paused. "Well, problems."

That didn't sound good.

# Chapter Seven

―――――――――

"You have two blockages."

I shrugged because the words from Dr. Alan didn't have any meaning for me. Well, he should know, I supposed, because he had a bunch of official-looking papers in his hands. He stopped for a moment, standing five feet away from my bed, to let his findings sink in with me. But it really didn't.

"Oh?" was all I could muster. *You don't say,* was what I was thinking. I couldn't conjure up any other emotions because I didn't feel any pain inside me. Outside, yes. But nothing inside to coincide with what he just described.

I looked over at Mary but couldn't tell if she was reacting or not. She sat motionless. Her hands still rested on her lap. Her eyes were only half open. She seemed not to notice him at first. Then she raised her head to look over at the cardiologist she'd never met. Her face registered nothing.

Dr. Alan broke into our silence as he stepped over to Mary to introduce himself and his position. He was warm and seemed to be genuinely interested in how both of us were taking that news. He said he realized this had been a strain but that I was in better shape after seeing me in person than what he would expect if he just saw me on my medical report. I wasn't sure if he expected more of a reaction or if ours was a typical patient-spouse response—stunned silence as the implications sank in. I hadn't had any experience with that subject before. There didn't seem to be any how-to-react manual available to guide us.

He pressed on with his explanation.

"There's one blockage in the circumflex coronary artery. The other is in the first diagonal branch and its' left anterior descending artery," he said looking down at his papers. I was sure he knew all those terms by heart but, for a second, I imagined him as a newscaster reading off a script or the latest breaking news that came across his desk.

I sat motionless staring blankly at him. I didn't have the *faintest idea* what he was talking about. But it didn't sound good by the way he said it.

He might as well be giving me a lesson in Greek because neither description made any dent in my recognition of the parts of the heart I had to learn in high school science class. We studied diagrams with different colors identifying the aorta, the four chambers, arteries, ventricles, and all the other bits. I might have paid closer attention if I'd known I'd ever need some idea of what he was describing. Still, the technical terms did sound awfully impressive.

That was what I really thought when he paused. I looked at my feet that pushed the sheets up in little tee-pees at the end of my bed. I gravely nodded as if I'd grasped the meaning of what he'd just said. The question I really had for him was *when can I go home?* I didn't get to ask it because he continued.

"The first one is ninety-five percent blocked. And the second one ninety percent."

*Ok,* I thought, *which part was that first one again?* He had just started and already I was two laps behind.

He explained these problems without alarm but he was insistent that they be corrected as soon as they could schedule it, which meant later that afternoon. He said they couldn't afford to take the chance of waiting until tomorrow morning. That implied that I couldn't take the chance either. He didn't say it in such a way but he seemed to be shouldering the responsibility of caring for a patient's best interests, and then one who wasn't in any position to comprehend the seriousness of what he'd said.

It seemed ironic in a certain way that I had gone sixty-three years without anyone paying the slightest attention to my heart. Yes, I'd had two or three complete physicals during those seven decades, with the usual stethoscope listen-in each time. I had played sports in high school—football, basketball and baseball—all which required a cursory, generic physical that involved a local physician listening to our hearts for anything abnormal such as a rhythm problem, and checking all the boys for any sign of a hernia, which would disqualify them from sports until it was remedied. I was glad Dr. Alan didn't seem interested in assessing that now.

In my defense, I had been a runner at one decade-long stage of my life after college. I had run my share of 5K and 10K races but drew the line at competing in a marathon. I was physically active every day after college as I farmed with my father and brother. I milked cows twice a day, pulled calves at difficult births, threw hay bales off a wagon onto an elevator, pitched manure from calf pens or silage out of a silo. I thought I had gotten plenty of exercise.

Now Dr. Alan likened those two vessels in my heart to clogged drain pipes.

"You're fortunate," he said gently, but explained as he drove home the point that it was only because neither vessel was completely closed that I most likely didn't have a full-blown heart attack. Some blood could still pass through those constricted vessels. He said it obviously still could yesterday because I was still alive. But maybe not tomorrow. Or maybe not even tonight. He added that was also the likely reason they could revive me because the blood flow wasn't completely shut off.

He had reviewed my most recent blood test taken that morning. It identified a slight presence of proteins which generally indicated some heart damage. The higher those protein levels were, the more heart damage they typically found. But, my levels were so minute that he'd concluded that what registered was probably caused by the electro-shocks or the chest compressions, and not from anything else.

"It's remarkable," he said. "I can't remember seeing anything similar."

He pursed his lips and raised his eyebrows as if he didn't have anything else to say. It was a look mixed with disbelief and relief all rolled together. I had the feeling he didn't like seeing major problems either. He's likely seen damaged hearts, fully corroded vessels, collapsed veins and arteries, hearts with the consistency of putty, whether the result of genetics, disease or lack of tone from little or no exercise, or even from a patient's diet that would kill an elephant.

For once I didn't mind being the exception.

"So, why did Phil collapse if he didn't have a heart attack?" Mary asked.

Dr. Alan thought for a moment as if trying to find the best way to explain what happened in a normal functioning heart and one that stops. I finally got the high school lesson I missed years ago.

He explained that electrical pulses sent out to the heart's fibers originate in its upper sinoatrial node. These pulses cause the heart fibers to contract—to beat. When a person exercises, there's an increased need in the exchange of calcium and sodium ions inside this node. As one exercises more vigorously, these ion requirements become greater and speed up as required which allows the heart to beat faster and faster. When a heart beats normally or has a normal unimpeded blood flow, things work well.

When something causes this exchange to become altered, say through a lack of normal blood flow due to an arterial blockage or a partial blockage, as in my case, then the four phases of the normal electrical sequence can be shifted to an irregular pattern causing changes in the beats. He said to think of a car wheel hitting a bump so that its balance shifts slightly and then begins to wobble and thump. The heart begins to quiver because its natural rhythm is lost. When that happens, the beating ceases and a heart stoppage occurs.

*Wow!* I'm thought. I never heard that in high school.

"So that's what happened to me?" I asked.

"In general terms, yes," he replied.

"So, how did they bring him back?" Mary asked, now intrigued by his explanation.

"That was due to the AED," Dr. Alan said. "The chest compressions kept the blood moving even if you weren't breathing. That was extremely important because although the heart can exist in a quivering state for a short time, it can't indefinitely. The AED is what got your heart going again."

Then he paused to consider another line of thought.

"An electrical intervention is needed to reset the heart's rhythm," he said. "The heart won't reset itself at that point and the shock from the AED does not automatically restart the heart. It clears all the electrical waves that have created the unnatural rhythm, like wiping a blackboard clean to start over. Once that is done then it's up to the heart to remember, along with the brain waves, that it is supposed to start beating again. At that point it can restart itself."

He explained that to think of it in an odd way, the electrical shock had to completely stop my heart and its electrical impulses—in essence killing me—in order for them to start up again in a normal, organized pattern to begin beating again.

"I was told he was shocked at least twice. Why didn't it work the first time?" Mary asked.

"Sometimes the electrical node doesn't respond to intervention," he replied. "It may take more than one shock to work. And sometimes nothing can be done because of the damage to the heart that's already occurred before anyone arrived to help."

He explained that was why CPR was essential to keep the blood moving through my brain, because it carried oxygen to feed it. Then my brain could continue to function and for it to remember it needed to remind my heart to restart." Later in an interview, EMT Keifpher had said that "they had three to six minutes to intervene before it's a done deal."

Dr. Alan looked through his papers until he found what he wanted, and then stopped a moment to read it.

"Your timeline is interesting," he finally said. "I see they applied two shocks for sure, maybe three, I can't really tell right now, but I can check on that."

*Wow!* I thought.

"But I never felt a thing," I said.

"You wouldn't because you weren't here," he replied. "Well, not physically in the sense that you knew what was happening to you. And that's probably a good thing not to feel what a shock does."

He looked down to study his papers again. Then he frowned and raised his eyebrows. He cleared his throat and began again.

"It looks like, if I'm reading this correctly, that it took about six minutes to get your heart going again."

He shook his head slightly from side to side.

"That's amazing," he said quietly, almost to himself. Then he looked up.

"You're very fortunate," he said. "That's about the outer edge for any heart to restart after being inactive for that long. But everyone is different. Some may not survive three minutes while others may go as long as you did, obviously. After that amount of time, the node will typically cease to fire electrical impulses. When that happens there is no way to reestablish those impulses or bring the person back. It's all over."

The three of us let that statement hang in the air for a moment before he quickly started again.

"But, you're still with us now and we can fix it."

He quickly went through the schedule they'd developed for me for the rest of the day. I would be prepped for surgery. The procedure involved inserting stents in each spot to open the blockages. There would be some recovery time depending on whether they go through my wrist, which meant a short stay, or if they have to go up to my heart from my groin, which usually called for a longer recovery period in the hospital. Unless there was some complication.

"There are no guarantees," he said flatly. "But we'll know what we face before you enter the operating room."

"So, no chest opening?" I asked.

"No. You got lucky. Again." he said smiling. He seemed pleased that it wasn't worse.

He said I would probably be back in my room soon after the procedure. That sounded a bit like hedging. They had already notified the doctor who would do the surgery, and he'd be ready when I got up to the operating theatre.

"Any questions?" he asked. I had a dozen and tried to rifle through them quickly to find one that topped the list.

"Good, then. This will be pretty straight forward, so not to worry. I'll see you later." Then he turned around and walked out the door.

The 'but, I have a question,' got stuck in my throat before he left so I didn't get to ask it. I turned to Mary who was looking back at me with her own puzzled look?

"You wanted to ask him something?" She said.

"Yeah, I did," I replied. "I wanted to know if I can go home after that?"

Mary got up from her chair, straightened her clothes, looked straight at me and asked if I was crazy.

"No. I don't think so," was all I could sheepishly come up with.

She shook her head in disbelief. "Do you *understand* what's happened to you?' she said in exasperation as if she'd given up on explaining it to me again. She rolled her eyes and slapped her arms against her sides as if to say, "I'm done with this."

I tried a different approach.

"Did you understand any of what he explained?" I asked.

"Not the technical stuff, no. But enough to know you'll probably be in here for a couple of days. At least."

I considered that for a moment but then, as if I never heard what she said, I asked about the wedding on Saturday.

"It's Tuesday," she said. "Don't get your hopes up. Let's get through today and this procedure first. Then we'll see."

At least that wasn't a "no".

She said she'd call our friends whose son was getting married to explain what happened to me and that we probably wouldn't make the wedding. She was sure they'd understand.

Now I felt helpless.

It was like I'd fallen onto some conveyor belt that had passed me along through a series of stations over which I have absolutely no control. It started when I collapsed. I didn't have any say in who saved me. Then to an ambulance not of my choosing, the ER, the doctors and nurses, the spinning donut machine, and now surgery. No one had asked me. It was just assumed that all that would be ok with me.

Maybe I need to stop and quit whining, and just be grateful for everything. But after what I had experienced in a different dimension, it all seemed so trivial. How could I explain this to anyone, let alone Mary, and without them thinking I was some sort of Nagging Nellie?

After I calmed down, I realized I probably would be incredibly stupid not to go along with them. But not having a say or being asked if it was alright welled up from inside me and I took it out on Mary. I was used to making my own decisions.

"Yeah, we'll see," I said in my loud, outside voice, laced with the petulance of a child who was determined to get his way if he held his breath long enough.

Mary seemed stunned by the way I said it. She momentarily stopped in her tracks as she walked towards the door to make her call. She didn't turn back to look at me before she left so I didn't see the tears forming or hear her thoughts that I was being incredibly ungrateful. Maybe I could almost read her mind: *Can't you just be thankful you're alive?*

I wanted to say that this was so not like what I'd ever experienced in my life. I was a rookie at being dead, and then being alive again. Couldn't anyone give *me* a break? But I didn't know where to start, or how to form it into words, so I dropped it.

After she left I was alone in the room. I suddenly realized, as if it were some grand new thought, that it wasn't fair of me to use her as a lightning rod for my own frustration. Not with what she had obviously been through the past twenty-four hours.

I supposed that if I had taken the time or had the mental stability at that moment to try to see her side of it, I might have reacted differently. She was running on the vapors of little rest and I was running on—well, I don't know what at that point. Her nerves were frayed from the events, and uncertain about our futures, particularly mine and how it might impact hers.

Would I be able to work again after that procedure? Would I regain my memory or was I about to become a burden to her for the rest of my life, our lives? In some semi-vegetative, no recall state? If that was the case, then I wondered why I would bother going through of all that was being scheduled for me? What happened if something went wrong during that procedure? Maybe it would be better for her if I had died. She could take the insurance and create a different, perhaps better life for herself without me as a millstone.

"See you later?" I said to Mary. But she was gone. Besides, it was a question more than a statement because I really hoped she came back. I wanted her in my life. I wanted to be in her life regardless of how short or long that might be. But not if it meant that I couldn't function normally. I wasn't reconciled yet to wanting to be a millstone. Although I was just in the first few hours of a new life, I wanted her to have a big part in it. If for no other reason than to allow me to keep thanking her for staying beside me.

I realized I needed her to be in my life. Not so she could

take care of me or be a nurse maid if things went south over the next few hours. I could take care of myself. For the last fifty-odd years—I had not depended on anyone else for my well-being. Maybe that was the problem. Maybe I hadn't opened up enough to allow someone else room to come in.

Maybe I'd excluded her too much from things and she felt I'd often pushed her away with my sense of self-sufficiency, which seemed only natural to me. Ever so slightly I began to see it a bit more clearly than just a day earlier. Something had changed and awakened within me since Sunday. I don't *need* her in my life, I *want* her in it.

I was seeing with a new set of glasses on this plane as well. The thought occurred to me that I now had acquired two pair: one for here, one for "there."

My walk down that lane of thought was interrupted by the nurse who came in to prep me for my trip upstairs.

The nurse cleared all liquids away from within my reach. She said I couldn't have anything until after I returned from surgery. She held my hand as she pulled it up close to check the IV needle taped to its back. She glanced at the monitor to register my heart rate and blood pressure, and then attached a small clamp with a cord to the end of my middle finger.

"I'm checking your oxygen levels," she said, and then waited for numbers to light up on the screen.

"Ninety-five percent. You'll do well up there," she said with encouragement. I had no idea what she meant but let it go since she used the word *well*, and, besides, I had become used to not knowing what was happening.

The clock read 4:30. I knew it was late afternoon. Minutes later, when Mary finally walked back into the room she said she went to get something to eat in the cafeteria. And, no, she didn't bring anything for me.

"That's ok," I said. "They'd take it away from me anyway." What I was really thinking was that I was glad she's back. It seemed the time-out for both of us had helped diffuse the tension we both felt before.

The nurse had stepped out just before Mary re-entered the room and then came back in and said everything was ready and that two orderlies would be coming shortly to take me upstairs.

I said that it's late. "I hope the doctors don't knock off at five."

She laughed as if it was the funniest thing she'd heard all day. Or the most preposterous.

"That *won't* be the case I can assure you," she said with emphasis. "You need to be done today. Besides these things go smoothly." She finished everything on her checklist and then just stood next to Mary, both of them patiently waiting in the silence that suddenly engulfed the room.

Two young men soon walked in rolling a cot and pushed it alongside my bed. They helped ease me out of mine and over onto it, lifting my legs first. I was settled into my transport while the nurse checked my pulse and I said goodbye to Mary, who grabbed my hand and squeezed it, and then bent down to give me a kiss.

I looked up and said, "I love you."

If things didn't go well she would at least have heard me say it as my final testament to her. She repeated it back to me as she released my hand.

They pushed me quickly out the door and Mary was left behind because she couldn't come up the elevator.

After entering the elevator and the door closed, we were lifted upwards. I watched the numbers on the console and it seemed the higher I went in the hospital, the more drastic the situation, or serious the problem. First floor, admissions. Second floor, the restaurant. Fourth floor, cardiac care. Fifth floor, surgery. We reached the top floor and the doors opened.

I was rolled into a big room with a profusion of overhead lights shining like lasers as I passed under. What I could see was largely restricted to the ceiling because I was flat on my back on a hard surface with no pillow to prop up my head, and only a thin cloth pad underneath me. I could look from side to side and that was only because the staff members were moving around each other. The size of this room made me feel like I was in the center of a small sports arena but without the bleachers or screaming fans.

One doctor was already present and greeted me as if we were old friends. He even got my name right, which was a comfort to hear because it meant I was in the right place with the right doctor.

He introduced himself as Dr. Joseph and asked if I knew why I was there. I wasn't sure why he asked this unless simply to engage me in conversation while I was still awake. I said that Dr. Alan explained to me earlier what would happen but I didn't understand any of it.

"Basically I just came along for the ride," I said, trying to make a joke of the whole situation.

I couldn't judge any reaction behind the white mask that covered his nose and most of his face. The white cap he wore covered his forehead, down over his eyebrows, so all I could see was a narrow slit through which two eyes stared back at me from behind large glasses. He explained what he was going to do although he didn't mention the serious spots in my heart they had found.

I said I didn't feel uncomfortable so it couldn't be that bad.

Little did I know.

Silence followed his short explanation as he continued his preparations. I heard soft music playing in the background so I asked if he took requests.

"What would you like to hear?"

I said I'd like to hear some jazz if he could manage it, but I was thinking, *If that happened to be the last music I ever heard then that's what I'd like to go out on.*

He said sure, he could find some.

He got off the stool he sat on and I watched him touch some knobs on a machine off to the side beyond my right foot. Dave Brubeck came over the speaker and I thought that would be a good way to leave.

He returned to my table and said that before they put me under he wanted to explain what he would be doing. He was now standing over me and looked down on my prone body. He was tall enough for me to see him from hips up so I figured he had to be at least six-two or more. He had rubber gloves on both hands that he held together in front of his stomach as he talked. He had a gentle manner and a patience as if I'm the only person in the world that mattered to him at the moment. At least I hoped he felt that way. His voice was muffled through the mask and I struggled to understand what he was saying.

"It's called a cardiac catherization," he said. I felt like I was back in school.

"I'll inject a dye into your IV. It then spreads through each artery. That makes your vessels easier for me to see during the procedure."

That seemed reasonable to me, the novice in all this.

"No need to worry. You'll be constantly monitored and then we can take a good look at your problems."

That was fine with me too.

"I'll be doing whatever repair is needed. Everything is going to be fine. Relax."

*Yeah, right, relax, he says.*

The last time any doctor told me to relax in a hospital setting was when I had my colonoscopy, and then it was said right after having been lubricated and just seconds before the steel instrument touched my skin and was inserted.

They had injected the anesthesia into my IV while he explained the procedure and he'd hardly finished his sentence before I passed out. I was completely gone. Maybe he was a distraction or running interference. I didn't hear any more jazz either.

My operation was stopped dead in its tracks while he was in the middle of performing it. Murphy's Law had raised its ugly head shortly after he started. Whatever can go wrong, will go wrong.

The procedure that I was assured would make me whole again began a little after 5:30 p.m. By this point I'd been fully prepped. The IVs had been inserted and the dye was flowing into my veins. The oxygen tip had been fitted under my nose and the medication given according to the directions of the pre-procedure checklist at 5:47.

The entire procedure was halted at 5:52, when Doctor Joseph was called away for another emergency. He returned four minutes later to begin the prep-work again which ended at 6:04, after a twelve minute delay. It took him six minutes to insert the first wire and perform the left coronary angiography. Thirty minutes later the first stent was put in place and deployed for twenty-nine seconds before the stent deployment system was removed.

Work then began on the second blockage and eight minutes later that stent was in place and deployed for twenty-six seconds. All the medical hardware used inside me was then retracted.

At 6:54 the implants were finished. One hour and twenty-four minutes after the start, Dr. Joseph was finally finished with me. The rest would be in other's hands. After I stabilized in the operating room, I was transferred back to my cardiac care room at 7:10. I had been gone for over two hours. I didn't wake up until 7:38, when I was checked for signs of mobility, motion and alertness.

For the second time in two days, I was once more among the living after having been totally unconscious. It took a long time for me to come to any sense of awareness after having been heavily sedated. When my mind was clear enough to understand my surroundings, I realized I was back in my hospital room. I looked around and saw Mary was there. Then I noticed she was smiling. The nurse who was standing next to her was chuckling too.

"Give me a minute," I slurred.

Mary waited for what seemed a long time before she felt I could understand her.

*I can't even talk straight,* I thought. *I must have been out a long time.*

It felt like having work done at the dentist after they freeze your mouth. Only it felt like my whole body had been frozen because I was numb all over.

The nurse stepped out of the room to give Mary and me a moment together.

Mary said she was going to leave now that I was back in the room and awake. She didn't want to leave without knowing that I had come out of the anesthesia alright. And she didn't want to have to return to the hospital if things went wrong. She would see me sometime in the morning but said she was going to sleep in late. Marcus made her promise that she wouldn't drive home

Tuesday night, so she'd booked herself into her favorite Madison B & B and would be staying a short distance from the hospital.

Mary squeezed my hands with both of hers and gave me a kiss and said goodnight.

"Oh," she said as she stopped before the door. "I have something to tell you tomorrow. You'll probably find it funny. Just think Murphy's Law."

# Chapter Eight

I lie flat on my back. It's early Wednesday morning.

I was pretty sure I wanted to open my eyes but the rest of my body was dead set against moving at all. I was mentally scanning each body part, trying to find some spot on me that didn't hurt. My leg still felt broken. My chest ached like a dead weight had been dropped on it. Pain shot through my chest muscles as I drew in a deep breath. My left hand was tightly taped to an IV drip needle. My eyes hurt but I thought they worked until I realized I couldn't open them.

*What's next?*

I thought that maybe I'd gone blind during the night because I couldn't see anything. My eyelids felt like lead. The reasons why I would want to open them eluded me. I'm not sure what I'd see, if anything. Besides, each of the last few times I had, it was nothing but strange. A strange room. Strange people around. Strange body sensations. Strange questions.

Blindly listening around, I didn't hear anyone rustling around my room. I began my own checklist again to inventory my body as I ran my hands over my chest and pelvis. All my bits still seemed to be there and in the right spots. The bed cover was pulled half-way up to my shoulders. It appeared that I didn't move an inch during the night. I felt molded to the mattress.

I reached for my eyelids that were stuck together. As I jerked my fingers up to rub them, I felt the IV tube flip away from resting on the bed cover as it fell beside my bed. I used my forefingers and rubbed, and rubbed before I could finally see some light filter through the crust.

I finally saw I was in the same room as the night before. Once my lids opened, I looked at the flakes of residue on my fingers and wiped them on the sheet. *At least I'm not blind*, I thought and took a breath in relief.

I lifted my arm and turned my head to take a sniff.

*Wow! That's ripe.*

I hadn't showered since Monday morning before I went to town. I didn't look like death warmed over. I smelled like it.

Yesterday had seemed a v-e-r-y long day even if all I did was lie in bed napping. I still felt like I had been hit by something really big. I was roused several times during the night as they took more blood samples. I wondered if I'd have anything left by the time I went home. I'd get that answer if they set up an IV with red liquid rather than the clear stuff my veins had been drinking.

I looked around since my eyes were mostly open. I knew it was Wednesday morning because that's what was written at the top of the wall white board across from me. My name headed the list, just above the doctor's name, then the nurse on duty which appeared to have been rubbed off and then rewritten with another name because two different color markers have been used and, at the bottom, the room attendant whose name was different from the last one I saw.

My stomach growled and it occurred to me that I hadn't eaten in two days. A nurse burst into the room to check my IV and said good morning. I thought she might stop to chat so I could ask about some food, but she recorded the monitor numbers, tapped the drip of my IV, lifted the tube back onto my bed and checked to make sure it was straight and still intact in the back of my hand, and then hustled back out the door.

"Do you . . . .?" My question trailed off and fell like a rock onto the floor because she was gone before I could get it fully framed in my mind. My eyes itched so I rubbed them some more and removed more dried goop from my lashes.

The next two hours were a constant stream of nurses and attendants making their morning rounds to check patients as they came on duty. It seemed each one who came into my room checked all the same numbers as the person before. Except for the room attendant who came in to sweep and mop the floor. But I did notice her glance over once at the monitor's flashing numbers. I fanaticized that maybe she was a secret hospital agent on an undercover assignment to watch me.

I was left alone most of the morning except for the periodic explosions of staff members coming in. Several knocked first as if they were entering forbidden territory. One time a nurse did stop to chat and said that they would try to get me up to take a shower later. She must have noticed the aromatic fragrance that radiated from my bed but didn't mention it.

During the quiet moments between their visits, I realized my head wasn't throbbing like before. Maybe the drugs I'd been given had eased it or just maybe my circulation got better in only a few short hours. I stared up at the blank TV screen suspended from the far wall to the right of the white assignment board when Mary walked in. I wasn't expecting her for a while and my surprise must have shown because she smiled as if she'd played a trick on me.

"Surprised to see me?" she asked. There was more bounce in her voice that morning. She looked refreshed.

"Yes I am," I replied. I was pleased to see her after the stress of yesterday.

When I mentioned that she looked better this morning, she said she got the best night's sleep she'd had in days. And also because the surgery went well even if there was a glitch in the process.

I listened, meekly, realizing that she probably had it worse than I did. I was either out of it entirely while wide awake or totally unconscious. I had missed it all either way. But she experienced all the uncertainty and horror that any caring spouse, partner, friend or family member must feel after being thrown unexpectedly into an emotional cauldron. One that stirred up a mixture that combined feelings of hopelessness, anger, dread, and perhaps a dozen more emotions, and ladles it all onto your plate without you asking for it in the first place. The body may take in all that it sees but the senses are hammered so suddenly, so unexpectedly, that they often recoil, or slip into denial. It takes time to mentally process what happened, especially if all by oneself, before the realization of the consequences fully registered.

I had been fully absent from all that.

Mary has a kind heart. Kinder than me, I suspect. She feels things to a depth I admired but didn't often acknowledge to her.

*That will change.* I silently vowed as I looked up at her.

When I finally got a chance to ask one nurse, she explained that I wouldn't be allowed to eat until the doctor said it was ok.

"Why?" I asked after she told me that.

"Just in case," she said. It sounded like she was hedging about something.

"In case of what?" I pressed.

"The doctor will be in soon." She maybe didn't ignore my question but she didn't answer it either, and then she left.

I looked at Mary. She'd taken the chair and moved it so she faced me with her back to the window. She had just enough of a little smile that I knew she was about to say something.

"Do you remember what you said to the nurse before they took you upstairs?" she asked.

"Um. Sort of. Something about work?" I struggled to remember.

"You joked that you hoped the doctors didn't quit at five."

"So?"

"Well, the nurse came back after you went up and was really embarrassed. She said this had never happened before but they would need to delay the surgery on you because an emergency case came in that they had to deal with first. She kept apologizing and saying that this had never happened before."

"So it happened because I made a joke?"

"Maybe. Who knows? Thought you'd find that interesting," her smile broke into a big grin.

I asked about the car and tires. Mary proceeded through a litany of what happened the previous morning and how she and Marcus handled it all. Marcus collected my stuff from my locker at the fitness center. They both went to get the tires changed and decided that since I looked out of danger Marcus would go back to Minneapolis so he wouldn't miss any more work.

Mary had just finished her explanation when a tall man, with glasses propped up on his head, stepped into the room. He wore a white lab coat and stood about eight feet away from my bed and filled the whole doorway. I didn't have the faintest idea who he was but the tone of his voice, when he said good morning, reminded me vaguely of someone I'd recently met.

"Remember me?" he asked. He was smiling and his question suggested we were already on friendly terms. He stepped over to my bed and reached across it for my right wrist. He slowly turned it over and examined both sides and then ran his hand the length of my arm up to my shoulder looking at my veins from the outside.

After he finished, he said it all looked good.

I was still stuck back at his question and it must have seemed to him that I was in slow motion when I finally said, "Not really."

"It's the mask, right? Confuses everyone later," he grinned.

His hair was parted on one side. His face was clean shaven. No mustache like mine. No short sideburns like I have. But he had a smile that lit up the room.

"Ok …" I stumbled and then stopped trying to remember.

Finally I said, "Jazz?" It was just a wild guess.

"Right." His quick reply suggested I'd just won a quiz contest. "I'm Doctor Joseph. I did your surgery yesterday. Well, last night."

"Thanks," I said and mentioned that I didn't really feel any different than before. Except for being a bit groggy from the anesthesia.

He said I probably wouldn't notice anything right away but as I recovered and got stronger I likely would feel overall better general health.

"What did you do?" I asked.

"I implanted two stents to fix your blockages. I opened them up. It all went well."

*Oh, really? It all went well?* I thought to myself as I remembered what Mary had just told me.

He explained that I was a high risk patient because the blockage problems were there waiting to happen. My risk of any problems now had dropped significantly. He knew that I didn't have any warning and simply collapsed.

"Blockages typically have two outcomes. Neither of which is good for the patient."

He said he didn't need to sugarcoat his explanation to either Mary or me because we'd been through the most difficult period of not knowing how the surgery would turn out. That part was over. Now that he's seen me, he was optimistic that I likely would fully recover since there was no damage done to my heart. The initial X-rays showed nothing and he didn't see anything while he worked on me that would suggest otherwise.

"But," he said. "Sometimes the spouse or partner doesn't want to hear a full explanation and relive it again."

He turned to Mary as he talked but she just shrugged her shoulders to say it didn't bother her.

He explained that one outcome from an uncorrected blockage was that it could lead to a massive heart attack with no hope for recovery. The other was heart damage that could range from minor to debilitating.

"Dr. Alan said he explained your blood tests. The microscopic damage we saw is *atypical* of a case such as yours. That's good for you because you'll likely have a good recovery now that we've opened your vessels in time."

He said that what they could tell from the blood tests, my consistent vital signs, and the high oxygen numbers at this early point after surgery was that my blood flow had improved.

I pointed to my right wrist.

"Oh, that," he said. "That's where I went in." He said it like it was the most natural thing in the world for him to do. Which, it probably was, being his line of business. He reached for my wrist again and turned it one way and then the other as if admiring his handiwork.

I waited for him to finish looking at it.

He checked by lifting the edge of the tape on my wrist to make sure there was no bleeding. Satisfied, he turned his attention back to me and explained what he did.

He tapped the tape with his index finger and said he cut open an entry point in my right wrist artery. Then he inserted a catheter through which he could pass a special balloon. This was then threaded up the large vein in my arm, across the inside of my chest and to the site of the worst blockage. He inflated the balloon to open up the artery and then inserted the stent. This was left behind after he retracted the wire and balloon.

"Going through your wrist has the advantage for you of needing less recovery time," he added. He said I'd be in the hospital longer if he found my wrist artery too small and had to use the alternate entry site in my groin.

He said that if it had been a complete blockage he likely wouldn't have even met me. We wouldn't be having this discussion because I wouldn't have made it to the hospital alive.

Because there was a miniscule opening within that blockage the blood could still get through. He passed the balloon-tipped catheter through the constricted part of the artery to put the stent in place. He then inflated the balloon to press the stent up against the inside artery wall. As it expanded it created a large opening for the blood to flow through. Then he deflated the balloon to remove it. He said the stent stays behind and I'll just have to live with that. Literally.

He smiled after he said that. That must be an inside hospital or surgery joke.

He said that each stent would release medication over time to keep scar tissue from developing as the artery heals. That helps prevent a new blockage from reforming in the same spot. Nothing was guaranteed, he cautioned, and it's possible that I could develop another one in a different location.

"But," he said smiling. "That's probably so far down the road that you're more likely to die of old age than another blockage."

Good for now. Bad for later. It was almost like kicking a problem down the road. The upside was that if I hadn't survived this round of blockages in the first place, I wouldn't even have a chance to develop another one in the future.

*So, I'll take it,* I thought.

"After I finished the most significant blockage, I moved on to the second," he continued.

When he finished the second implant, they observed me until they were sure my blood pressure readings were at levels they knew were holding steady. Only then was I sent back to my room.

He got up to leave.

"Let me know if you start to feel differently than you do now. Immediately."

I nodded as he extended his hand. He turned, said goodbye to Mary, and walked out leaving us alone again. There was a quiet between us until she said she already knew that I was going to ask her about the wedding.

*Was I so transparent that she could read my mind?* I thought.

"I called Jim and Kathy and told them we likely wouldn't be coming." Mary was going to get ahead of me and said it more as a final statement than with any room for negotiation. So I let it drop. For the moment.

She got up saying she was going for a walk. She had been sitting listening to the discussion about the procedures and wanted to leave the room and get some fresh air. But she stopped when another doctor arrived at the door.

The first round of the day's doctor visits had started. They must have passed each other in the hallway because right after Dr. Joseph left, Dr. Alan stepped in.

It was encouraging to see the pleased look on his face as he smiled at Mary and said hello. Then he turned to ask how I felt.

I said my headache was gone. My knee still hurt and so did the muscles of my chest a little. I tried hard not to give myself away too much, that both hurt more than I would admit, because I didn't want it to affect my chances of getting out of there.

He walked over to my bed while pulling the stethoscope out from his coat pocket. He positioned it on my chest and shifted it from side to side as he listened intently. He asked me to lean forward and for several seconds settled at one spot on my back and then another.

"Your lungs sound fine," he finally said as he replaced the stethoscope back into the pocket of his white coat. "So does your heart."

He had a look on his face as if he might be expecting to find something else. With his extensive experience with heart patients it was difficult to know what he expected to find in me.

"I wish I could explain it," he said.

He said that cardiac doctors rarely saw such low numbers for blood pressure, a heart rate, or the protein counts after a collapse like I'd had.

"We know they gave you CPR," he continued. "We know you had several shocks. I wish I had an explanation for why you look so good and why you've returned to normal so quickly. But I don't."

He had crossed his arms in front of his chest and looked down at the floor momentarily. It seemed to me that he might have been looking for an answer in other places and maybe he thought it was written in the tiles.

I didn't blame him for not having an answer.

He said that the reason why it happened at that precise moment in the fitness center or the fact that it could have happened somewhere else was simply a matter of luck or good fortune to him.

But even in my muddled thinking at that moment, I began to sense that something else was in play behind all of it. I couldn't put my finger on it yet but there was too much that happened in the sequence of it that was unexplained. The timing of when it happened—not at night but in broad daylight. The place where it happened at that precise time—in the fitness room and not at our farm. The ready and quick assistance was available at both that time and place—the number of trained staff that were on hand and available to help. And the closeness of the EMTs and ambulance—just across the street.

It was obvious it wasn't explainable to them except, perhaps, by luck. I just couldn't buy that but at that moment I didn't have a better explanation myself.

He said the stents were now mine permanently but I won't ever notice they're in there. He was leaving instructions for the nurses that they would get me out of bed later to walk. Not a lot but to get me moving again and up on my feet. He wanted to see how I reacted to the exertion of moving while I was still in the hospital.

There was a pause and he seemed ready to leave. *Better ask it now or never*, I thought.

"By the way," I said. "We'd made plans some time ago to attend a wedding up north. Is that still possible?"

Mary shot me a look of disbelief that I would even consider it let alone ask about it.

He looked straight at me without flinching. I saw his eyes move a little from side to side as if he was searching for an answer that was accurate while not flat-out rejecting it because he wasn't sure.

"Well . . . " he said slowly. He used that pause to give himself another moment or two.

"Let me check on you tomorrow morning and if everything looks good I might be able to at least let you *go home*. Or maybe Friday. But I'll wait until tomorrow before making my decision."

That was fair enough I said, self-satisfied that I asked it. Then he turned and left.

I could see Mary wasn't sure that was a good idea. I told her I'd like to go if we could. I'd gotten a new lease on life and I didn't want to waste it. She said she thought I might be wanting to spend my lease too soon.

Thus endeth that conversation. For the moment.

The urge to do *something, anything* had swirled around inside me. Maybe it was because the blood was flowing again. Maybe it was because I was tired of lying around in hospital beds. Maybe it was because I felt the lethargy towards life draining from me and being replaced with a new additive. I sensed a little bud was starting to grow inside and I needed to nurture it to sprout.

A nurse came in with a laminated double-fold card and handed it to me. It was a menu from the cafeteria.

*Finally. Finally. Finally.* I was able to order some real food. Not the IV drinks that had been my steady diet for three days. I struggled to add up the numbers but I calculated that it was something like thirty-six hours since I last had anything of consequence to eat. At that moment anything looked good.

I asked what I was allowed. She said that no restrictions had been put on me so I could order anything.

"Really?" I asked, thinking she might be pulling my leg. No one had allowed me to do anything for myself so far.

"Yes," she said.

So I did. It was a restricted menu nonetheless but I picked fruit, vegetables, meat, and a lettuce salad. And for good measure, an ice cream cup. That was for starters anyway. I called the number printed at the top of the card and someone answered. I ticked off my list as I deliberately ran my finger down the choices. When I finished the voice said it would be up shortly and asked for my room number. I said I wasn't sure but the voice said to look at the numbers at the top of the white board and repeat them. That did the trick.

I waited on my bed for what seemed like hours listening to my growling stomach before a person in a crisp white uniform walked in holding a tray. It was loaded with a plate covered by a metal shell, a milk carton, some dinner ware wrapped in a napkin and a hot tea in a paper cup topped with a plastic lid. I had already pulled the rolling table over myself in anticipation of a meal. I tucked up my bed sheet to make it feel like I was stuffing a dinner napkin under my chin before I dug into the food.

I ate slowly and tried to taste each bite.

After I finished my lunch, I was full. I was content. I was stuffed. But it felt good.

Then I was ready for a nap. Eating was hard work too. I nodded off quickly.

When I woke up, I looked around to find no one in the room, so I took another snooze. I napped every chance I got on Wednesday. I couldn't believe how tired I was from the past few days.

In between several of those naps a nurse would come in and ask me to urinate into a plastic jug. Sometimes two arrived with that request. They said they needed it to test for proteins and other indicators to determine how my heart, liver and kidney functions were responding to the stent procedure and if there was any noticeable change. Each time a new container was held out for me to use.

I needed help out of bed each time and one nurse always joined me in the bathroom to make sure I didn't collapse. After several of these sessions I became accustomed to the assisted requests and didn't care anymore who saw the complete me. By now I'd been naked in front of so many nurses that the thought occurred to me, after I got back into bed and after they had left, that maybe I could qualify for a spot in the Chippendales revue. Perhaps a career move at this stage would do me good. *Sure, I could do the senior circuit,* I thought.

It all really intrigued me because I couldn't remember another time in my life when so many different people were fixated on how much I peed!

And they were adamant. I needed to perform for them each and every time they arrived with their little plastic jug and deliver something to them, regardless of the quantity. How much could I possibly have? I wasn't sure that they had considered the fact that I had little of any kind of liquids since I'd been there, except for what I got from an IV. After a couple of these communal bathroom sessions it was like trying to get a trickle from a dry radiator.

Plus, each time I was helped off the bed, the pain in my left knee got stronger and it had increased in size because of some belated swelling. It was like my knee realized it was supposed to be swollen and then finally got in gear and did something about it. I still had not been told why it hurt but I reasoned that I probably slammed it onto the floor knee-first when I collapsed.

It was late in the afternoon when I was helped out of bed to take a short walk in the hallway. At least she wasn't carrying a plastic jug for me. That would to be the first extensive walk I had in three days.

The white cotton socks I had worn to exercise at the fitness center had been lost for days. They had been replaced with thin, aqua-colored little booties with gripper spots dotted across the bottom that were supposed to keep me from slipping on a floor.

I was asked to get up and off the bed. The two nurses helped slide my feet to the side so I could sit on the edge. They stood on either side as I raised my arms to offer them as a surrender. As they held firmly, I pulled myself to my feet and stood, slightly swaying. Each held one arm and helped steady me until they were sure I wouldn't collapse. I imagined that, to them, it must have felt like they were handling a delicate glass sculpture, concerned that if they let loose I might fall and shatter.

My head began to spin from the sudden movement and I felt dizzy. But their firm grips were a subtle signal they didn't want me to sit back down. So I stood there breathing deeply as I looked at the doorway, surprised that it now seemed almost out of reach from my standing position. Everything had seemed so easy lying in bed.

I shuffled at first, one tentative step in front of another as if I was testing the strength of the floor. I reached the doorway after what seemed like an hour, and looked across to the nurse's station directly opposite from my room. They also were keeping a close eye even though I had attendants. One nurse left my side and though I was alone with a single nurse, I had a nearby audience.

I shuffled to the left once outside the room as the nurse gently directed me to the hand railing fixed along the wall. I looked down the corridor at the thirty feet she wanted to shepherd me. Through my eyes it looked the length of a football field. She released her hold of my left arm and I used it to grip the wood rail. I took a deep breath and gingerly stepped forward with one foot and put pressure on it before I brought the other forward. Then another step. And another. I stopped to catch my breath.

Onward again. One step. Two. Three. Four. Stop.

It seemed like a half hour went by before we finally reached the end of the railing. I paused again and gripped the rail with both hands while I faced and stared straight at the wall only inches from my face. I leaned my forehead against it for a moment before I slowly shifted myself around to face the direction from where I had just come. One nurse still stood back at my room door. She'd been watching the whole time while the second nurse acted as my chauffeur. I took another deep breath and began my limping return. I never would have thought that it could be that difficult to regain my balance. I hadn't had that much trouble walking probably since taking my first steps as a baby. It felt like I was learning to walk again.

I began my marathon trip back and finally made the doorway to my room. One trip was enough they said. I didn't argue. I was exhausted.

They helped ease me back into bed. I was breathing hard. My chest rose and fell like an accordion as one nurse checked my pulse. I was sweating buckets just from that little walk.

*This isn't good*, I thought. *I'm never going to leave.*

It took a good minute for my breathing to slow down. I was gasping. When I finally caught my breath the nurse decided that was enough for today. I wouldn't be making the second trip that had been scheduled for me that afternoon. I tried to object and said that I was willing to try again but what I really dreaded was what she was going to write in her report. I was almost certain it would be passed to Dr. Alan and that would probably influence his decision about whether I could leave the hospital or even go north that weekend.

Now I really felt sick. Maybe I'd just blown my chance to prove that I was ok. After the nurse left the room I thought about how my reaction from this short walk was really stupid. If I'd done a better job of acting that everything was alright then maybe she'd write something different.

*I blew it!* I said to myself. I relaxed on my pillow and fell asleep.

I was kept in bed most of Wednesday except for the persistent peeing requests that didn't stop even though I didn't feel I had a drop left to contribute to the collection plate. The lights on the monitor were silently, incessantly blinking as if waiting for someone to notice. The room smelled fresh. It must have been mopped sometime earlier but I hadn't noticed. Maybe it happened during my nap.

The TV was off. I thought maybe I should turn it on to see if the world still revolved. My world had been confined to this square room with the window facing towards... *hmmmm*, where exactly? I still didn't know because the view out the window was of another wing of the hospital that never allowed me to figure out the sun's direction. I'd have to ask Mary if I remembered to.

Later that day, Mary worked from my room with her laptop computer. She occasionally stepped out and into the hallway to answer her phone or make a call. She was a welcome presence although there wasn't anything for her to do with my care. She stayed through supper time and then decided to return to the B & B early since I seemed better. After she left, I drifted off for the night.

109

The fourth morning arrived with such a stillness in my room that it was disorienting. I was alone, dressed in a backless night-gown tied only at my neck. In a way it reminded me of a BBC TV show, *Red Dwarf*. It was set on a gigantic space ship with only a few crew members. The control room was always quiet except for the low humming of the air conditioner. It simulated an atmosphere that was noiseless as their ship drifted through the quiet of space. That's what my room felt like to me then. I felt I was drifting in the quiet of space with few people on board.

My left knee grew to the size of a large grapefruit. It had swelled during the previous two days and had finally gotten stiff because of my lack of movement.

On early Thursday morning, I was gotten up, I peed for them, and then I was taken out to the paddock for another short walk. Now I felt like a racehorse being led out to exercise, primed for a potential run. Only I wouldn't be running for a long time. I wasn't sure I would leaving by Friday like I hoped. Or maybe ever.

I was miserable because I was frustrated. I was frustrated because I was tired. I was tired because, well . . . I was tired. *None* of this was in my plans for that week. And there didn't seem to be anything that would change that and magically transform it back to what I had planned. There was absolutely nothing I could do about any of it. So, yes, I was frustrated to the hilt. I felt I could scream from my helplessness. But I didn't want any of that to show. It might lessen my chances of leaving in time to go to the wedding.

If I had stopped to think about it clearly, I might have realized that my desire to go was so out of proportion from the reality of my condition that it would have seemed unfathomable to any-one else that I'd want to make such a journey. Why not just stay home and rest? I doubt I could have fully explained the drive I felt within myself to go. Go anywhere. Go somewhere besides a hospital. Go find something alive.

Or did I simply want to go because I was running away from something? Was I subtly afraid it might catch up with me if I stopped?

I settled down and figured that instead of fuming I'd order breakfast. Scrambled eggs sounded nice. And toast. Some milk. Tea. A fruit cup. *Wow.* The idea of food almost made me giddy with the choices available. I was like a kid left loose in a candy shop. Maybe I'd order one of everything just to get even with the phantom causes of my situation.

I had just finished eating when Dr. Alan walked in for his morning check with me. He didn't say anything about my leaving but mentioned he would review all my tests later that morning.

So I took another nap. Mary called to say she'd be in soon.

"Great. See you then," I said as she rang off.

*Try to sound upbeat, like everything's ok*, I told myself. *That's better than moping around.*

During that time I was helped up again and taken out for my two-way walk in the hallway. That time I tried to act like it was going better and I often bit my tongue so as not to let the pain in my knee get the best of me. I moved faster than before but not too fast so that I tripped over my feet. The last thing I wanted was to be picked up off the floor. That might cause tremors through the nurse's station.

But as things went better during that walk, I hoped that maybe the nurse would observe my "improvement" and note it for the doctor.

An hour had passed from when Dr. Alan finished his first morning stop at my room. Now Dr. Alan stood next to my bed with charts in his hands. He moved each page from one hand to the other as he slowly shuffled through them like a deck of cards until he reached the one he obviously was looking for. He stopped and studied it again and then raised his head to look at me.

"Everything looks really good. I don't think there's much more we can do for you now. You seem able to handle being out on your feet. I'll authorize your release for later this afternoon."

It took a moment for me to realize what he had just said. I almost didn't believe what I had just heard. It was good that he paused while looking at the papers so his words could sink in.

*That's great!* I told myself. But then I realized I needed to get his official clearance for this weekend so that I could tell Mary and convince her.

I asked him about going to the wedding that weekend. He said that shouldn't be a problem. Then he smiled and said I might want to take it easy and not over-do the dancing.

With his go-ahead now secured, I felt I didn't have to hide anything. I told him that the way my leg still hurt there probably wouldn't be much dancing. It was the four or five hour ride that might be harder.

"You should be fine," he said. But we would need to stop more often than usual so I could get out and stretch.

"I'll set up an appointment for you to see your doctor in two weeks. I'll want to see you in two months. Good luck." He reached out his hand to shake mine and then left.

Deep down I was ecstatic. Just like that, I was getting out of here. Then, for a split second, I had the strangest feeling that this was all a hoax, or a bad dream, and he'd come back in and say he was just kidding. He was pulling my leg, right?

I waited. I watched the doorway, but he didn't come back in.

I waited some more until I was pretty sure he wouldn't return. *I'm home free*, I thought.

I called Mary at work to confirm my scheduled release. She didn't seem convinced.

When she arrived, I couldn't tell if she was reluctant to pick me up or not. If she had mixed feelings about my release, she didn't say anything. She had brought a fresh change of clothes for me yesterday so I had something to wear other than the flimsy gown.

I was to have a counseling session before I could be discharged. A female medical assistant came in with her clipboard and a pile of papers she needed to go over with me. There were medications being prescribed that I needed to understand. But it was Mary who listened closely to the instructions. She wrote down on her note pad the dosages and units to be taken each day as they were explained. It was a confusing list to me. The assistant said the hospital pharmacy was located on the way to the exit and they would have my medications ready when I left.

After she left the room, I could finally change from my gown to my street clothes. It felt different this time. It was like I put on a whole new wardrobe even if they were the same clothes I had often worn before. I buttoned my shirt. I stepped into my blue jeans while seated in the room chair and then cinched up my belt. *I've lost weight!* I thought because it tightened a notch closer to my stomach. That was one heck of a weight loss program.

I almost felt ready and dressed for the ball but I had to wait for the final release order to leave. I realized I still had time to order lunch, so I did. A last meal of sorts. I could eat while sitting in the room chair and already it felt different. Eating while sitting up in a chair seemed a novel activity. I didn't feel like a patient anymore as I sat and ate, just a visitor who had ordered something from the kitchen.

I was informed that my discharge was set for Thursday afternoon at 3:30. Minutes before that time arrived—they certainly cut it short—an attendant came into my room with a wheel chair and said he would be taking me down to the lobby and front door because I wouldn't be walking. Although he asked, I didn't need help getting into it.

He unlocked the wheels and as he pushed me out into the hallway, I was able to wave to the nurses at their stations when they turned to watch me leave and wished me luck.

Mary had gone on ahead of us by several minutes to bring the car around and park at the entrance by the time we rolled out of the hospital. For the first time in four days I was outside of a hospital or ambulance. I drew in my first breath of fresh air only to find it was laced with exhaust fumes from other waiting cars with idling motors and I started coughing. And that hurt because my chest muscles were still awfully sore.

I was thankful that Mary brought a light jacket for me. I had put it on before I left my room. The outside October chill had settled in even though it was mid-afternoon on a sunny day. The breeze that came off the Madison lakes swept through the corridor between the hospital proper and its parking ramp across the narrow street. It acted like a wind tunnel outside the front entrance. I shook myself from the crispness as I slid into the passenger seat and buckled in.

I was told I wasn't allowed to drive for at least three days. *Fine*, I thought. The way my leg hurt it would be difficult and awkward even if I did.

The normally heavy downtown traffic hadn't changed but at

least it was moving. On the drive out of Madison I noticed the colors had turned brighter from Monday when I last saw them. Tall corn in the farm fields that glided past my car window was drying to the brown of harvest time.

Less than an hour later I was back in our house. I was tired but at least I was home!

Once inside, I sat down. Mary wouldn't let me lift my bag or do anything else. She'd been mostly quiet on the drive and my comments about what I saw in the fields mostly got an *uh, huh.*

Her silence made me think that maybe now she's not sure she wanted me home yet. Maybe it would have been better if I had stayed a couple more days and just forgot about the wedding. But how much would that have helped?

Mary asked if I wanted anything to eat or drink. I said I wanted to sit for a bit and then go outside to look at the cattle. Twenty minutes later I got up to head outside. Mary insisted she would walk with me. It took a few minutes to get to a spot on our lawn that overlooked the pasture north of our farm buildings where I can locate them in the field. They were as far away at the other end as they could possibly get. So much for a welcome home, guys and gals.

"That's a half mile," I said. "Even I know I can't make it that distance. Or even a fraction of it."

With that realization, I settled for looking at them across the distance between us.

"Another day," I said to Mary. She seemed relieved that I didn't make an issue of it and walked beside me with her arm wrapped around mine as we made our way back to the house. We were both quiet, lost in our own thoughts. Mine were of tomorrow. I'm not sure what hers were yet.

I stopped and told her thanks for everything. She simply squeezed my hand as we stepped to the back door.

Once inside again, I plopped myself down on the kitchen chair and distractingly flipped through all the mail that had piled up. Life went on even while I was in the hospital. It would have gone on even if I had died. The proof of that was lying before me in that stack.

I got bored with all of it because it seemed pointless. I called my mother to tell her I was home and that we were still planning to head north to the wedding sometime the next morning. Mary looked over and slightly shook her head because she still wasn't for it.

Mom said she would come over in the morning to see me and we could talk then after I got some rest. Later on Mary started to pack for both of us, finally reconciled to the fact that I wanted to go no matter what.

I went to bed early.

Tomorrow would come. I was pretty sure of it.

# Chapter Nine

The crisp fall air greeted me on Friday morning. I felt like crap but I certainly wouldn't admit that to anyone. I might end right back in Madison. It felt a lot like my whole body was anesthetized while still awake. I was numb inside.

It was after eight o'clock before I found the strength to pull myself out of bed. I stood up from the edge of our bed and looked out the north window where I could see our green-roofed, white-sided barn three hundred feet away. Between the east side of the barn and the trees on our lawn I could scan the distance and see the cattle out in the pasture. It had cooled down over night but hadn't frosted the grass.

I pulled up on our bedroom window to open it and take in a deep breath of cool air. And just as quickly I coughed it out. *Boy that hurts*, I said to no one in the room.

I turned and shuffled to the bedroom door, then shuffled down the short hallway and to the steps. *I'll try not to pitch myself down*, I thought as I stared down to the landing. It seemed quiet downstairs so I had no idea where Mary was at that moment. I didn't call out for her because I would have to yell and that would, well, hurt a lot. I felt I could walk down on my own even if she had instructed me to let her know when I was going to use the stairs. I figured I would have to do it by myself sometime anyway. Why not start now?

I thought I finally understood what it must feel like to be hit by a truck, but without actually being thrown under it. Almost every part of me hurt. My chest. My legs. My hands from the IV needles. My back from lying in hospital beds for so long. My head was throbbing again. I felt I was a composite of all the aches and pains I'd ever had, all rolled into one.

*But at least I was home,* I conceded.

I hardly ever used the round hand rail along the inside staircase that Mary's father had installed years ago when Marcus and Julia were young. Now I grabbed it and said a belated thank you to him for it. My right hand steadied me as I began my descent. Each step down seemed a long stride to the next one. I never thought to notice that before. First my right foot. Then I dragged my swollen left knee behind. It was more like sliding it down to the step because I couldn't bend or put much pressure on it without the pain shooting through it.

It took excruciating effort just to get down the first seven steps to the landing and the three bay windows that looked out onto our south lawn and across to a neighboring field of ripened corn on the opposite side of our farm's property fence line.

I stood for a moment to admire the window casings that I had fixed earlier that summer in a sudden fit of unexplainable handyman resourcefulness. I had removed the framework from each casing to get at the window weights and replaced the deteriorated cords that once held the windows up. Half were broken and we had resorted to using sticks to prop them open in the summer. I got fed up with that and dove into a home improvement project that took on a life of its own until it was finished.

After I caught my breath and coughed again, I turned to confront the final nine steps down to the first floor hallway. *That's a long way down*, I thought as I stared at the incline for a long time, weighing my options and calculating the result of any misstep. Not once in all the years after these handrails were installed had our kids fallen down any of these steps. I didn't relish the idea of being labeled the first.

Mary was adamant that the stairs to the basement, and the basement itself, was strictly off-limits. It had ten steps and she didn't want to find me flat out on the floor and having to extricate me from there. Where I could safely go and what I could do was framed by the joint considerations of how anyone would get to me if I collapsed again, and then how they would get me out to an ambulance. That became my overriding rule for any activity I might do. Could they get to me if I collapsed here? Or there? I needed to assess all my movements before I even took them. For how long, I had no idea.

I started down the remaining steps and made landfall on our first floor, just outside the kitchen door. I plopped myself onto the chair at one end of the table. From there I could look out the two north windows framed with the same style woodwork the bay windows had.

After finishing my break, I still had no idea where Mary was. I stood and moved to the right to navigate the four steps from the kitchen down to the back door before I could get myself outside. It was all downhill so I reasoned that if I tumbled I'd be going in the right direction until I slammed into the base of the white metal storm door that opened to the outside.

I gingerly reached the bottom and stepped through the doorway while I held the door knob in my right hand and steadied myself against the door frame with my left as I stepped outside and onto the small cement walkway. The storm door slammed shut behind me. *That'll alert her*, I thought. I had stepped from one dimension of our house out into another in the open, and that sensation felt vaguely familiar.

I wore only my flannel pajamas. My cotton socks had replaced the booties from the hospital. I stood for a minute not moving. Just looking around. For an instant I realized I probably was lucky to see this backyard again. I had imagined that one day I wouldn't but I hadn't anticipated that my last view of it would be at age sixty-three.

The sun had risen hours before so I didn't witness it peeking over the horizon as I faced it rising above the tall trees that dotted our lawn. The light sprinkled through the colored leaves on the three black walnut trees that stood fifteen feet away from our two-vehicle garage on my right. Their ripened nuts would soon begin to fall, like someone pulling a ripcord and letting them loose all at once as they simulate an aerial bombardment and pummel the ground below after releasing their hold on the branches.

Mary came outside to join me but didn't say anything about my descent down the steps alone or not letting her know I was up. She had been on the phone making final arrangements for our weekend and hadn't heard me come downstairs. She had been organizing for our departure later that morning.

"Your mom called last night," she said.

I had already gone to bed when she phoned. Now Mom wanted to come over to see me before we left for up north.

Shirley's a survivor. Since hospitals were on my mind, I recalled her bout with cancer in the early 1970s that would have devastated many others. The drugs she was given to attack her lymphoma were still experimental. But they worked.

I now saw a healthy, sprightly ninety-year-old who still drove herself to a twice-weekly exercise class in town. She stayed busy with her church. She still made meals and washed clothes. She wrote notes to family and friends almost daily. She gardened. She had kept a daily diary for over fifty years. She had no intention of stopping any of it. She's a survivor.

My mother was a transplant of sorts. She lived on her parent's farm in the next township when she began dating my father in high school. The roads in the early 1940s were largely unpaved and I can imagine my father pushing hard against the gas pedal of his 1940 Ford as he sped across the eighteen miles of gravel roads, leaving trails of dust, to see his girlfriend. She was too good to wait for. Not unlike my attitude when I first started dating Mary. They later married and she moved across townships to a new life. Six children followed as they farmed together with my dad's parents, who lived in an upstairs room in the farmhouse Grandpa had built in the early 1920s. Three generations were gathered and living under one roof.

Howard, my father, was a good six-foot, and stout man. He was a thickly-muscled farmer with a sensibility of knowing exactly who he was, and he was a terrific livestock man. His sense of humor could be infectious and he only raised his voice when it became absolutely necessary. And when that happened, we kids knew there would be a reckoning. But he never once laid a finger on any of us in anger.

With five brothers and sisters, how I perceived him likely was different from the others. If he did get upset with us I always had the fallback position of being the middle child and could sometimes just blend into the background because I neither was in the point position like my oldest sister, nor was I the most vulnerable as my youngest sister was. I could get lost easily amongst the confusion and sorting out the details of any infraction. That was how I remembered him almost forty years after his death from colon cancer.

It was a cruel twist in my parent's lives. Mom was the first to develop cancer and was eventually subjected to experimental drugs because no other standard treatment seemed to work, but it did. They had no idea if those would either. Dad developed colon cancer half a decade later and received the standard treatment protocol that had largely proven effective in many patients, but didn't in his.

Sometimes Dad drove Mom to her chemo treatments. Sometimes one of Mom's friends if he couldn't. She always drove my father to his treatments in Madison. By that time she was in complete remission and became a support and encouragement for Dad until the realization settled in that his treatment wasn't going to be successful. His end here finally came in March 1979.

My mother survived the funeral, the probate, the aftermath of anguish in questioning why it was Dad and not her, and the readjustment of our farm operation with my brother. She survived the subsequent feckless inquiries of older single or widowed men who thought she was ripe for the picking and certainly must be ready to go out on a date. And she has survived the four decades without the man she loved.

Mom likely didn't realize it at the time but all these survival traits had not gone unnoticed by her grown children. We learned from them even if we didn't say so.

In the years that followed, Mom encouraged her friends and many acquaintances she met at the yearly Relays for Life local cancer survivor events. She became their cheerleader just like she had been in high school. She was coming over that morning to be mine.

I turned and stepped back into the house. Mary watched as I gingerly made my way up the back door steps and into the kitchen.

"You ok?' she asked once I sat down. Her concern was still at a razor's edge.

I said I was but that my knee hurt and was really stiff. She'd heard that probably a dozen times already but had the patience not to comment on my complaints, or from her view my foolishness.

"She's coming over now," Mary said. Mom had called while I stood outside.

A car soon arrived and parked along the south side of our house. It didn't take long for Mom to drive the mile from her house that I could see across the open fields. She still lived on the farm where I grew up along the county highway. For the past twenty-five years, Mary and I lived on a dead end township road that led into our farm, which was my dad's second farm and we bought it from my mother in 1994. Marcus and Julia were raised here. The beauty of where we lived was that our farm sat in the middle of a relatively flat prairie with small hills a mile to the west but a fully open view to the east that leads to the Wisconsin River Valley. The only traffic we got was from those who specifically wanted to see us, those we had invited to come, or those who mistook the dead-end town road for the next one which was a mile and a half away and led to somewhere else. I was constantly amazed that people thought the Dead End sign clearly posted at the entrance to our narrow town road meant it was a through way.

Mom is a short, gray-haired woman with a full nine decade's worth of living behind her. She got out of the car and walked over to the back door. One would not suspect that the five-foot frame that shut the car door would have such a life story of survival to tell. With all that she had been through, she still wanted more out of life. That was inspirational and infectious.

"How are you feeling?" she asked as I bent down to accept her strong embrace.

"Numb mostly," I said. Then I rattled off a list of complaints before I caught myself and stopped. We both laughed. She didn't come over to hear about that. She'd been through a lot worse so she knew the score without me reciting it play by play.

"I'm happy to still be here." That's what I really wanted to say as it came out.

I said that yesterday seemed better than the day before. And that morning seemed better than yesterday.

"Good!" she said with emphasis.

There was a pause that hung in the air. We both realized things could have ended much differently. She could have been coming over to console Mary before my funeral instead. Her face showed concern as she examined mine and mentioned that my color looked good. I apologized for not remembering that I talked with her in the ER because Mary said I had.

"You sounded normal," she said. From listening to my voice over the phone she wouldn't have thought anything had happened to me if Mary hadn't explained it first.

She was glad Mary had called my niece Heidi. Mary thought that Mom should be told what happened to me but didn't want her to be alone when she heard about it. Mary had called my niece because Heidi seemed to be the closest available family member, being ten miles away. Mary asked if she could go to Grandma's and explain to her what happened to me. Heidi said she could take her two young girls along without alarming them because they would think it was just another visit to Grandma's house.

124

We all moved into the kitchen as Mary took the lead while I slowly made my way up the steps, and sat down. We faced each other from opposite sides of the table.

"Well, I guess your time wasn't ready," Mom said. She was tapping the table with her index finger as if to put an exclamation point on it. It was her not-so-subtle way of saying, *You're lucky. Now make the most of it.* She was still the cheerleader.

After a short conversation, she said she would go and let us finish packing. Mom said she just wanted to see me again. We were to have a good trip but to take it easy.

"We'll talk again when you get back," she said without a hint of doubt.

"Now don't do too much dancing on your knee, but do some!" she admonished me with a quick laugh. Those were her instructions for the day and I wasn't offended by a mother's advice. She gave me a big hug and a kiss on the cheek as she slid her hands down both of my arms. I wondered if what she was really thinking was that she might be touching me for the last time.

I didn't go outside with her but I watched from my office window as she backed out our driveway and then headed home to her house.

Mary and I had packed our two cases on Thursday night. Neither of us wanted to wait until the morning to do it before we left.

I hadn't had a chance to really discuss the week with Mary with all that happened every day. I thought we could do it on the five hour drive. There wouldn't be any way to side-step talking about it. Everything that had happened since Monday was a constant, uninvited presence in our lives. I didn't have all the pieces put together and hadn't the faintest idea when I would.

I faced a Hobson's Choice. That is, of accepting one of two or more equal alternatives regarding any discussion I made about what happened to me.

I could choose to ask about what happened and not get an answer, which would still leave everything unresolved. Or, I could choose to ask and take the risk that my questions might trigger some feelings Mary had experienced during the week that she didn't want to revisit or talk about. Either path I chose she was likely to be affected. So if she was going to be affected either way, would it make any difference to even talk about it? It was the elephant in the room.

It was ten o'clock. We were packed and ready to head out. The silence inside our car was broken when I inserted a jazz CD before I adjusted the passenger seat where Mary usually sat, to fit my leg or back profile from hers.

Little was said between us as we took two county roads and one state highway to arrive at the north-south interstate that splits Wisconsin in half. If you could fold the east edge of the state over to the banks of the Mississippi River, the crease in the center would be I-39.

We passed Portage on our way towards Wisconsin's Central Plains, the remains of the last glacier's scrapings. Westfield, Plainfield, Stevens Point, and Wausau all glided past my view as co-pilot. We stopped twice so I could get out to stretch my legs and use the restroom. I was now drinking lots of fluids as instructed at my hospital release and with the new medications kicking in, a new experience that I needed to pee more often than the week before had presented itself in full blast. But, thankfully, not into a jug held out for me each time.

The jazz softly filled the empty space between us and became the background for any discussions. I thought maybe some soft music would ease us into talking. What short discussions we did have didn't take a straight, linear path. Instead they wandered from one random topic to another as something popped into my head. Then another random question. Another answer. More music. More silence.

Mary was focused on the road and finally she revealed what she was really thinking. She was constantly on high alert the whole drive but didn't want to let on.

"I've kept checking the exits for hospital signs in case I needed to use one of them, if you want to know," she admitted.

To her way of thinking, I was still acutely vulnerable even if I was too stubborn to admit it or didn't realize it myself. She had been afraid that she might lose me at the beginning of the week. She needed her own connection with me—any connection. And she didn't want to lose me at the end of the week because of my foolish desire to go on a long trip the day after getting out of the cardiac care unit.

"The only thing I could do for you in the ER was to rub your feet because you kept saying your leg hurt," she said. "At least I could do that much."

She said it felt good to touch some part of me and know I was still alive. It sounded like she was trying to ground me to this world with her hands so I wouldn't leave.

I knew she wasn't in favor of making the trip and had put up a small protest every time I mentioned it.

"But you wanted to go so much, so I thought, ok."

I told her I wanted to feel alive. I needed to feel alive. I wanted to be a participant in some human activity other than just limp down a hospital corridor and then end up sitting at home. I wasn't sure she agreed with any of my logic.

I said I had realized I wouldn't get a chance to do something like this for a long time. Maybe ever. Julia and Victor's wedding wasn't until next summer.

*I might not make it to then,* I secretly thought to myself as I turned from watching the white lines zipping beside our car in the middle of the highway to look at the passing fields beyond the interstate fence line.

We reached Merrill where the four-lane interstate highway downgraded to a two-lane state road. We made a pit stop because the distances between towns from there on would stretch out as if you're pulling a rubber band from place to place.

We had a two-hour drive yet. We'd made good time and didn't need to rush anymore as we'd be there before the sun set. We could enjoy the scenic drive as long as I held out. It would be awful to have to turn back now and go back home because I got sick or needed to find that hospital she was worried about.

The trees still held their fall colors. The sumac along the roadside was ablaze in orange and reds. Freezing temperatures usually settled in earlier up North, often beginning two weeks before we got them at our farm in the south central part of the state. The season seemed to have slowed down the farther north we went.

Frosted leaves go through a metamorphosis as they turn color. I couldn't help but think about the metaphor it presented as the miles slid by on this lightly-traveled road. As the green chlorophyll drains from the leaves they change to a color specific to their species. Maples, red. Oak, brown. Beech, yellow. After the color dries, the leaves die and fall off. No one to pick up them up.

When Mary asked about the distance, I grabbed the map to see how far we still had to go.

"Not far," I said and shortly we passed the lodge's roadside sign emblazoned with colored lettering that said it was just ahead. That's a relative term regarding distance when talking with any Midwesterner. It could mean fifty miles or it could mean two. It all depends.

It was five.

We made a right turn onto a road that led towards the town named for the lake, or maybe the lake was named for the town. I wasn't sure. The lodge where we had made our reservations at the suggestion of the bride and groom surprised us when it unexpectedly appeared after we made the turn. It wasn't noticeable from the main road because it was nestled among the pines and shielded from the highway.

Mary turned into the parking lot and chose a spot close to the front entrance. We stepped out of the car and the air that hit our faces was fresh and crystal clear. The pine scent wafted in layers as the gentle breeze teased our hair. It was a welcome shock because at the last stop we made far down the road, the air was infused with industrial-strength diesel emissions from all the idling semi-trucks.

It was shortly after four and we could check in, unpack, and I could lie down before we went to the evening party being held at the bride's parent's summer house.

Mary said she was tired from the drive. We checked in, found our room, unpacked our luggage and tested the mattress. We both laid down side-by-side on the covers of the bed. Still in our street clothes, I reached over and took hold of her loose hand and drifted off soon after my head hit the pillow.

When I woke up I turned to look at the digital clock on the small table beside the bed. Six o'clock. Another two hours gone.

Man, if that keeps up at this rate, Mary would have to file a missing person's report for all the time I'd lost that week.

Groggy didn't begin to explain how I felt after waking up. *Displaced*, possibly. *Numb*, certainly. *Confused*, definitely. And just for a second, I had no idea where I was. It was another dark closet.

I didn't move my head quicker than I needed to. If I did it seemed like marbles were rolling around the inside edges of a spinning bowl. Dizziness was my new companion and when it said hello, I had to grab hold of a stable piece of furniture or sit down, which I did because I had just gotten off the bed. I could lie back down but that would make it worse.

Mary was still asleep as I shuffled to the bathroom to wash my face and tried to wake up. She finally rustled on the bed so I guessed she was awake. I asked a question. But no answer.

"What?" she finally said with some sharpness at being woken from her nap.

"I know I haven't talked with you much this week. It's mostly because I was tired. But it's also more than that," I said. I explained that I was still trying to understand all that happened. In my own way and in my own terms. I told her that I only had bits and pieces to go on that something major happened to me. I had *huge* gaps in remembering what happened. I didn't have the whole picture in a way that she may have seen it.

I said that maybe I *thought* that before or said I did. But now it was more real because I hurt, I was tired, I couldn't think straight, I was dizzy and my head spun around a lot.

"And you wanted to come all this way with all that's going on with your body?" she asked.

I shuffled back into the room and around to her side of the bed, and sat down on the covers. She looked up at me as I took her hand and held it against my cheek. I hoped the magic was still there or it was going to be a long ride from here on for both of us. *We'll have to wait and see how it works out*, I thought.

But in that moment, looking into her sparkling eyes, even if somewhat clouded by fatigue, I remembered why I was so pleased that she agreed to marry me. I really couldn't care less if the world ended right now for me. If she was the last person I saw on this earth, I could die an extremely happy man. That would be enough for me.

Of course I didn't say that out loud.

While it was intended as a compliment, I wasn't sure it would be taken that way because of another allusion to my death. I kept it to myself and simply continued to rub her hand against my cheek until she thought it was time to go.

We dressed and drove to the party. We slowly navigated our way around the small side roads that were supposed to lead to the house. We weren't sure where we were most of the time. It was dark and there were no street lights to help read the small signs with the road names at intersections. The only things we could read were the little signs with fire numbers that reflected back to us as they seemed to jump into the beams of our headlights. We keep counting down out loud as we passed each one until we were sure it was right around the corner.

Nope. Not that one. Well, maybe the next corner.

The tall pines above us blocked out what little light was left from the evening's sunset. We could see remnants of the fading light above the tree tops but it was of no help at ground level.

"There's the number," we both shout in unison. It appeared so quickly that Mary slammed on the brakes as if she was avoiding a deer in the road. She turned and we drove into a narrow lane that wound its way to the house. She found a place to park among the scattered trees, positioning it so we wouldn't get blocked in before we wanted to leave.

Our plan was to make an appearance, maybe get a bite to eat, greet the bride and groom, meet her parents, see our friends, and then leave. That was a long list to complete in an hour but we accomplished it all.

We headed back to the lodge and I had my first memory challenge in a week trying to remember all the different roads we took to get to the house. If I was honest and not just being polite, I knew that even in the best of times Mary had trouble with retracing steps. Julia learned the same gift from her mother. They were two peas in a pod when it came to being directionally challenged.

Now I found *I* was the one having problems with direction, especially in the dark. We made turns that took us farther into the forest. We emerged only to find more crossroads to choose from. Like Hansel and Gretel, we needed bread crumbs to find our way out. The zig-zagging we did on the back roads finally, mercifully, ended when we stumbled upon the state highway that led us back to our bed.

We arrived in the parking lot and stepped out into the crisp air. We met at the back of the car and walked hand-in-hand across the parking lot to our room door. Even though there was a chill in the air, I deliberately slowed my steps so that I got a few more moments with her outside.

It seemed like an appropriate moment as we stood outside our door. It almost felt as if we were on our honeymoon. I gave her a long kiss as we meshed together in the cool air. For once I wasn't chilled in the cool air as the warmth generated from that kiss and embrace swept through me. I told Mary how much I loved her and how grateful I was that she was my wife.

She smiled that smile that first caught my attention decades ago and said she was glad too, even if that week wasn't the most fun she'd ever had on a date with me.

I fell asleep like a baby, content that no matter what tomorrow brought, I was alive tonight.

# Chapter Ten

I was reminded the next morning that I was still alive when I woke up with a sharp, burning pain that shot up and down the length of my left leg. It felt like it was on fire. I reached down to make sure there weren't any flames.

*Man that hurts.*

I tried to shift myself from lying flat to sitting on the edge of our bed but found that only my right knee would bend. I looked around half expecting to see nurses come rushing in to tell me to lie back down. But no alarms went off except ones in my head.

The nightstand clock read seven. I threw the covers off in disgust and swung my right leg over the edge but I couldn't bend my left knee. It was locked in a straight position. That wasn't good.

*Maybe Mary was right. Maybe it would have been better if we hadn't come,* I thought. *I'll end up in some hospital again.*

She woke up because of my loud groaning and thought something horrible had just happened to me.

I explained what it was. She got up and came around to my side. She pulled on both of my outstretched hands and helped me up off the bed so that I could stand up. My tentative first step was more like a hop on one leg that made me feel like Chester on *Gun Smoke*. But that seemed to loosen it a bit so I took another hopping step.

I leaned against the door frame when I finally made it over to the bathroom. The more I stretched my knee the easier it became to bend it. Getting into the shower wasn't going to be easy because it was a combination shower and bath tub, and lifting my stiff leg over the upper edge without slipping would be a challenge.

Small things I had taken for granted before became logistical and tactical challenges. I was sure other people had worse situations to cope with after hospital stays but that was bad enough for me.

*Why do I have to deal with this?* I could whine but through it all that morning, Mary didn't comment.

Oddly, my question seemed the start to an evolving realization of what was really important. Yes, I could complain, but I was still here to be able to complain. My mother's directive when she tapped our kitchen table rang in my ears.

*You're lucky. Now make the most of it.*

An hour later we left the room to go find a light breakfast in the commons area of the lodge. There was fresh fruit, dry cereal, granola bars, yogurt, rolls, and assorted berries. Just what the doctor ordered, literally.

My appetite hadn't fully returned so I really wasn't interested in a big breakfast. I assumed the medications were suppressing any hunger pangs I had. But I hadn't done any physical work to warrant being hungry either.

Mary wanted to sit outside to eat if it wasn't too cool for me. There wasn't any competition for the two wood deck chairs that we settled into. We faced the lawn of the back lot that stretched out to the tall pines thirty feet away. The enclosed green space had enough room for a softball game.

Mary opened her fruit cup and scooped with her spoon. I opened my granola bar wrapper and took a bite. I waited another minute before I pulled the tea bag from the mug of hot water sitting on the small round table between us. The steam rose off the top and curled up before it quickly disappeared and dissolved in the chilly morning air.

Mary looked over at me and asked. "Is this spot ok? We can go back in if you want."

"This is fine," I said. Actually it was a bit chilly but I'd tough it out since this was where she wanted to sit. I could make *some* concessions and not have to be the one who got his preferences catered to exclusively.

Mary knew I didn't tolerate cold any better than she could tolerate heat. While I would most likely follow her anywhere, I drew the line at traipsing behind her to the North Pole. She would have to send me a post card. You could ask why I lived in the cold Wisconsin winters? I asked myself that question every year, especially during minus thirty degree days. As of that morning, I had spent all of my life's sixty-three years in the upper Midwest and I still didn't have an answer to the question of why. I was better when I think sun, wind, beaches, sand, Hawaiian, Mediterranean, even South Pacific. That was my inner nirvana.

Mary pointed to the late fall flowers on our left that rose above the brown grass that framed and surrounded them. They still showed signs of life late in the season. The quiet was broken only by the birds calling in the trees. Those that typically migrated had left weeks ago. I was willing to bet it was to some place warm. Maybe I need to get a pair of wings.

We sat in silence and soaked up the morning air lathered with the scent of heavy pine as if someone had gone around with a can of freshener before we sat down. It drifted toward us in waves from the base of the trees.

I reached over to grab Mary's hand and hold it. There was no resistance. I hoped it was out of mutual desire and not from being exhausted. She seemed to relax now that she had put some distance between the hospital stay and that moment.

"What would you like to do?" I asked because I didn't have any plans. What plans I did have were now accomplished. I had made it that far and from there on I didn't care what we did.

The wedding wasn't for several hours yet so we could drive around, we could sit here all morning, or find something else.

"I'd like to go for a drive," she finally answered after considering it for several moments.

Neither of us had ever been to this area and one thing we did share in common was to go explore a new place. So off we went. To have ourselves an adventure together.

After driving through the area most of the morning, we stopped at a coffee and tea shop before noon for a break. It was quiet that time of year as the major tourist season was long over. The shop served as a magnet for local residents, and the occasional out-of-town visitors like us. Only a few customers milled about the double room.

We placed our order at the counter and I went to sit down. A man sat by himself at a rectangular table with several empty chairs. I didn't feel any particular need to sit solely with Mary so I asked if I could join him.

He moved his cup away from his lips as he stopped sipping his coffee and looked up.

He eyed me with curiosity, "That would be fine. I'd like the company."

I pulled out a chair and sat directly across from him. His baseball cap sat on the wood top to his right, suggesting he was probably right-handed. His short-cropped hair fit well with his wire rim glasses. He had a deep tan that seemed to etch out the folds on his thin face. I looked at the left sleeve of the light jacket he wore and noticed an EMT patch sewn onto it near his shoulder.

I asked if he lived in the area.

"About eight miles north. I like to stop in here when I can."

Mary joined us and was surprised I'd chosen to sit with someone I'd never met. We introduced ourselves and offered that we were up for a wedding that afternoon.

He nodded in acknowledgement.

I said I had noticed his EMT patch. "Are you a volunteer?" I asked.

"For about a decade now."

"Then I'm in good company," I added.

He stared at me a little bewildered at what I'd said.

"How's that?"

"Well, I met our local EMTs only a few days ago. I just got out of the hospital yesterday."

He studied me for a moment. I wasn't sure if he thought he could believe me or if I was just crazy for being out.

"What happened? If I may ask."

I explained the week's events while he listened. I didn't have any intention of discussing my week with anyone up there but since he asked I feel obliged to talk about it.

"You were very fortunate."

I nodded in agreement. Mary sat quietly not knowing why this conversation she came in on late ever started or that she wanted it to continue now because it hit too close to home for her.

He looked at me closely without leaning over. I could feel his eyes examine my face and then looked at my hands. The bandage patch on the back of my left hand stuck out like a sore thumb for an EMT. He set his cup down and folded his fingers together with each hand and held them in front of his lips while his elbows rested on the table.

"I've had enough experience to know it doesn't always work out that way."

He asked if I had just started exercising when it happened.

"No, since February. Three times a week."

"That's probably what saved you. And the EMTs. Not everyone is in good enough shape to do the things they do when they come up here. I've seen a lot of that."

He paused as he reached down for his cup and slowly took a sip. He paused again before saying anything more. He didn't seem sure if it was best for him to pursue his line of thought.

Another sip.

Then he continued, perhaps trying to find some common ground with me, considering that I had just put him in that position.

"We had to respond once to a visitor."

He stopped as if trying to find the right words that might not offend or scare us away.

"While their group was up here, they decided to rent bicycles and go for a twenty mile bike ride. Twenty miles. At one go."

He shook his head slightly as if he still couldn't believe they thought it was a good idea.

"Thing is, one man in this group collapsed along the way. We later learned that he hadn't been on *any* kind of exercise program. Certainly not one to warrant the sort of activity they had planned. That was the first mistake."

He stopped again as if reconsidering an alternate line of thought.

"You said you've seen some of our area. It's not the most

populated is it? Things are more remote. The towns are a bit far apart and we certainly don't have an abundance of medical facilities that they have in other places. Don't get me wrong. What we have is *good*."

Silence settled in again before he continued.

"Well, by the time they called for help and that help finally arrived, it was too late. He was out on the bike trail, away from the village. There was nothing we could do when we got there."

He seemed like he was apologizing, almost like it was his fault for their carelessness.

"Too much time had passed. People need to think things through when they're up here. Or anywhere."

His staring down at his coffee cup suggested someone whose thoughts still relived that scene on the trail.

Then he looked up again, smiling.

"This is a very beautiful area and that's why my wife and I live up here. In fact we moved up here to stay because we like it so much. Partly because of the remoteness and that's also an attraction for people to come visit this area."

The same remoteness that's so attractive to people also makes it more difficult to get medical assistance if it's quickly needed.

"Not that we don't respond but it takes longer to get there."

I noticed Mary shift uneasily in her high-backed chair. I supposed that was the last thing she wanted to hear this morning.

I took a different tack and shifted the topic. But not by much.

"If I hadn't been at the exercise room I probably wouldn't be talking with you now," I said.

"Like I said, you're fortunate. I hope you have a good time while you are up here. But be smart." He began to get up from his chair, having drained the last of his coffee. But I couldn't leave it at that.

"Perhaps we'll meet again someday," I said. *Only not in your capacity as an EMT. I don't need that again.* I thought to myself.

"Maybe so." With that he pushed his chair back in and walked his tall, lanky figure out the door.

Mary's continued fidgeting signaled to me she'd had enough of this death-talk and wanted to leave. I suggested we get something to eat because I was finally hungry.

We stopped at a local diner that was just around the bend of the road as we left the tea shop. It served a North Woods specialty of fish and chips. The noontime sun shone down as we sat on the outdoor balcony. Only one other couple sat outside at a table across the way. They were probably from the area as the waitress greeted them by their first names. The thermometer on the building corner read a pleasant seventy degrees. It was as brilliant an October day as anyone could hope for. My walleye dinner tasted as fresh as if I had just landed it myself and threw it on a pan.

We sat enjoying the atmosphere. But eating made me drowsy and I began to drop fast. I mentioned this to Mary and she thought we could leave as she was finished too. We drove back to the lodge and I slept for an hour.

After getting up, taking a shower and getting dressed, we set out for the lodge and the outdoor wedding.

Dressing became another adventure. In my loss of many things to remember, I had forgotten how to tie a straight tie with matching ends. I did the steps backwards and couldn't remember the correct way. That was never a problem before. Mary didn't know how so there I was standing in front of the mirror holding the two ends out in front of me as if they would reshape themselves by asking. I turned one end over the top of the other. Then I reversed it. Mary started to laugh while watching me because it looked like I was twisting them both together like two pieces of rope.

"Should I make a noose instead?" I asked her. While intended as a joke that might have been the wrong question because I didn't get an answer. Maybe the silence was her answer.

It was frustrating because I'd tied a tie hundreds of times before. Those little things that didn't require much second-thought before had become major challenges. I suggested not wearing a tie at all but Mary didn't agree.

"Keep trying," She said. "It'll come back to you sooner or later."

"What if later is tomorrow?" I asked.

She said if it took that long, she would go to the wedding by herself.

"Besides, we'd be home by then," she added in jest.

The wedding was held at a lodge on the lake shore with a backdrop of blazing fall colors in the woods across the water. After we were seated, Mary looked around at the view and said it was a stunning place for a wedding.

*Or even a funeral if needed,* I said under my breath.

The brilliant reds and yellows of the birch and poplar trees were interspersed with the greens of the pine and spruce. It was a stunning mosaic across from us that looked as if they'd been painted with a broad brush. For so late that time of year, especially that far north, they dazzled in the radiant afternoon sunshine that stretched all around the lake's edge. It seemed like they were on stage just waiting patiently for an audience to notice.

After the service everyone headed into the lodge for the dinner and dance. We collected our table number and seats from the guest board as we entered the hall. We were seated at a table with our friend Jim's family. During the dinner a jazz band based in the

Chicago-Milwaukee area played in the background. I closed my eyes for a moment and recalled my own request for jazz on the overhead speakers in the hospital's operating theatre. *I'm alive*, I kept saying to myself.

The dinner finished and the dance started after the tables had been cleared. I finally got to meet up with the groom's father. I had only spoken briefly with him the night before. He was aware of what happened because of Mary's call on Wednesday. When she explained that we probably wouldn't be coming up. Now, I was reaching out to shake his hand.

Instead I got a bear hug.

"I didn't think you'd make it," he said as he released me.

All I could get out was a choked up "Thanks."

We'd known each other for over forty-eight years. Almost a lifetime in itself. We first met during the summer of 1968 at the Wisconsin State Fair as competing 4-H exhibitors from different counties. We later spent several years in the same living unit on the University of Wisconsin campus. We had worked together on the kitchen crew that served meals. Mary and I had a long history with Jim and Kathy.

We had been to their wedding but that was long before Mary and I were married, and we came to it from two different directions and times in our lives. I was at their wedding and reception by myself but I ended up at Jim's parent's farm house after their wedding dance. I had driven Jim's younger brother home as it was on my way. Although the party at their wedding reception had finished, it continued at Joe and Esther's until it was almost milking time and I had to leave to go home and do ours. From that night on I was made a *de facto* member of their family and his father never missed a chance to urge me to stop in if I was in his area.

"I can't tell you how good it is to see you, my friend," Jim said, standing there beaming. I appreciated his friendship even more that night because I was alive to be able to.

We headed for the open bar to talk. Although he was father of the groom, he wasn't in great demand at that moment so we could get in some time together before he was called away.

The hospital doctors and staff said that I was allowed three ounces of an alcoholic drink once a day. I thought I'd take advantage of that at the open bar. I rationalized that I could justify it on medical grounds. I told Jim that I intended to make full use of my new directive.

We stood together looking up at the available selections behind the bar.

*So much to choose from, so little time*, I thought.

Finally, I spied a bottle of top-shelf whiskey, literally up on the top shelf. The young lady bartender approached us as I leaned against the counter with my left elbow to steady myself and take the pressure off my knee. Either I was giddy at the prospect of having something almost forbidden or I was just getting shaky from the meds. She asked what I'd like. I pointed up to the top shelf.

"I'd like the Glenfiddich, please."

That must have been her first time pouring something like it because she didn't know what it was—an expensive Speyside single malt Scotch whiskey. She turned and looked up trying to identify the bottle I pointed to. She finally saw where it was and then asked one of the taller bartenders to get it down for her.

"I'm only allowed three ounces," I said as she loosened the cap.

She mis-heard me because once she started, she kept pouring until three inches rested in my cup.

I was beaming. I thought I had just hit the jackpot.

Then she looked up at me.

"Is this about right?"

I couldn't contain myself.

"Just a bit more and that'll be good."

She topped it up and then stopped.

"That looks *juuust* fine!" I said with a broad smile.

Jim was laughing.

"I won't tell Mary," he said as my partner in crime.

Neither would I.

I raised my glass to him. I raised it to life.

*Slainte!*

And then I took a long sip.

I savored that moment as I swished it around in my mouth.

"I think I've found the angel's portion," I announced to Jim.

*In more ways than one*, I thought to myself.

We took our drinks and went off to the side so Mary couldn't find me. I felt like a kid sneaking off to have his first smoke. I told Jim if I was going to drop dead right there, then the last thing I would taste was a great Scotch whiskey and hearing a jazz band.

*There are worse ways to go.*

Nothing happened by the time I reached the bottom of my glass. Then suddenly Mary and Kathy came over to check on me.

Mary took one look at my empty plastic cup and then up at my smiling face.

"Having fun?" she asked with a knowing smile.

"My insurance is paid up. I think. So not to worry."

She shrugged her shoulders as if to say she had done all she could for her mischievous child. I couldn't tell if she was upset, or whether her look signified some mixture of disbelief at what I had just done, or resignation that she couldn't prevent it. Maybe it was simply her reaction to the unexpected absurdity of what she saw before her: some fool who didn't know he died earlier this week and didn't have the good sense to take care of himself, or to consider how his actions were affecting others close to him.

Or, maybe she had just realized there was enough room in the back of the SUV for a coffin so that she wouldn't have to make a special trip back up to get me. She could just take me along home with the luggage.

Jim and Kathy left to attend to some guests and said they'd catch up with us later. I had just lost my accomplice and now I had to face Mary by myself.

"Would you like to sit down?" she kindly asked, sensing that might be a good idea given what my empty glass looked like.

*Bless her*, I thought to myself. That was probably a good idea.

"I'd like to get some fresh air first. Then sit," I told her.

She said she didn't doubt that.

We walked outside and onto the patio. I turned and gave her a big kiss.

"That's from me. Not the whiskey."

She was gracious enough not to question it.

"I love you to the end of time," I said. "And I've seen how long that is."

"I know," was all she said or needed to say.

We went back inside to find our table seats and listen to the music. I got up for one slow dance with her after I gingerly stepped out onto the floor at the first notes of *Moonlight in Vermont*. It was more swaying back and forth than moving in time with the beat, but it would do. I'd hang on for dear life to this woman who dropped everything to stand with me.

As I pulled her close and she pressed against me, I could smell her scented hair. I leaned the side of my face against hers. I didn't recall any other dimension smelling that good.

We rocked from side to side, mostly in a small box that we'd claimed as ours on the floor. If only for that brief moment, with me holding her, I realized that given the choice, she was still the one I'd spend eternity with. Then in the numbness of the medication that brief moment was gone again. But it signified, for whatever flash was there, that I was still here. Still alive. And I said a silent thank you to the universe.

For whatever reason, I had collapsed. I was revived. I had no explanation for any of that as we swayed together. But pressed up against the woman I loved, I promised myself to make the most of it with whatever time was left to me. Or us.

And in some distant echo beyond the jazz, I heard the sound of a cheerleading mother's finger tapping on a kitchen table top.

We sat down after the band paused between numbers and then just listened to the music for the rest of the evening. Forty-five minutes was all I could handle. Suddenly, I was exhausted. Like the bottom had fallen out of me.

*I need to leave before I collapse*, I thought. But I wouldn't admit that to Mary.

I was pretty sure the whiskey was introducing itself to the drugs I took and they were beginning a mixing dance of their own. So we drove back to our room and I thought I'd call it a night.

The next morning was cooler than when we had first arrived less than twenty-four hours before. We stepped out through our room door to go grab a morning snack in the commons. We were invited to a continental brunch provided for the wedding guests but I needed something now. I felt good considering everything that happened at the dance. Actually it was the best I'd felt in a week. I put it down to the medicinal whiskey and made a mental note to try that again.

After stuffing a couple granola bars into my jacket, Mary and I headed out for a walk on the footpath leading away from the motel. I still dragged my leg along although I could finally put more pressure on it without the pain I had before.

The wedding had only been over for a few hours but already that morning the leaves had lost color and began falling. Mary noticed that first as she kicked at some leaves already lying on the ground. Neither of us had ever seen such a quick change in fall color. We walked past our room as we headed for the woods. I noticed an unexpected spring in her step.

Leaves showered down on us as we walked. Then it became a leaf storm. It was like they sensed their time was over and their job finished. Now it was time to, well, literally fall. And it was time for us to leave. We walked back to the room hand-in-hand. I felt like I was renewing an old friendship with her as the leaves seemed to bless each step we took together.

The whole time during our walk Mary had a playful smirk on her face. I hadn't seen that in a long time. And certainly nothing like it that week. She was up to something.

We reached our room door, checked to make sure we didn't leave anything behind, grabbed our bags and loaded up.

While driving over to the continental breakfast, Mary had a surprise question.

We had just left the parking area and gotten onto the highway. Then she turned to me with a naughty smile.

"You're not going to tell anyone about the sex, are you?"

Stunned. That was the only word that could describe my

reaction. I looked up at the windshield and then over to her to make sure I'd heard her correctly. She was grinning.

"What sex?" I asked. Like I wanted to deny it if it really happened.

"The sex you wanted to have last night."

"Me?" I say sheepishly.

"Yes, you." Now she seemed determined to make me confess.

I looked around thinking there was someone else in the car sitting behind me that she was talking to.

"Uh…. You'll have to remind me." I finally said.

"You wanted to feel alive last night. You said you *needed* to feel alive."

"Boy that sounds like an old college line if I ever heard one."

"Yeah. Probably. You don't remember?"

"Umm, no. I wish I could." It was still lost in the cobwebs.

"Well, it was nice," was her reply as she looked ahead at the road smiling.

*Where in the world was I that I can't remember that?* I thought. At my age that's a landmark moment and I missed it.

I told her that I'd have to think about that.

"Please do," was her response as she tapped her fingers on the steering wheel to a beat only she could hear.

We arrived at the main lodge and said our goodbyes after a short visit. Mary had found a brochure at the coffee shop describing an art tour being held in the area that weekend. She said she wanted to visit some shops since we were there. With map in hand, we found four or five that interested her. I got out at the first one but then stayed in the car at the rest because it was easier than try to lift my leg in and out each time we arrived at a gallery.

At one stop I took a call from my cousin who lived in New York but heard about what happened to me from his older sister who had spoken to Mom. The rural grapevine was alive and well.

He led something of a nomadic life and I had often felt a pang of jealousy that he could just up sticks and leave when he felt like it. Not being married most of his life had made it easier for him to move around. He had held a number of diverse jobs but never stayed in one place for any great length of time. He had worked as a semi-truck driver, a massage therapist, a house sitter, and a wannabe beef farmer. And probably others that I didn't know about. He was the free spirit in our family and I admired him for his grasp of freedom in untangling himself from the normal expectations of life.

He sounded excited.

"I'm planning to walk the Appalachian Trail in the spring," he said with boyhood enthusiasm.

Wow, I thought, he certainly had shifted his focus.

"Good for you." I said. Now I could be a cheerleader.

I asked if he remembered that one of our grandparent's cousins had done that while he was in his 80s?

"Didn't you write about that in our family history?"

"Yeah I did," I said, pleased he remembered. At least he read it.

I reminded him that this cousin even made it into a national best-selling book. Sort of.

Fred Luehring was an early proponent and lifetime participant of physical fitness and had pioneered a standard method of swimming instruction in the 1920s. He was ahead of his times. He also had walked The Trail by sections even though it took several decades to complete. When he finished his last section in 1966, he was the oldest person to have completed the twenty-one hundred mile trail from Georgia to Maine, with its five million steps, when he was eighty-five years old. Bill Bryson made mention of his achievement in his book, *A Walk in the Woods*, although he didn't mention Fred by name.

He knew it might be a challenge.

I suggested he consider getting on an exercise program before attempting his walk.

"Medical assistance along the trail is minimal," I reminded him.

He was aware of that.

I suggested he read the Bryson book.

"It'll give you some idea what the trail is like."

He told me to stay well and he'd stop by the next time he was back.

Mary came out of the shop with a bag. She stepped quickly to the SUV. She seemed pleased about something. She had carried a wrapped package over to the car and slipped it behind the luggage. She relented and said it was my Christmas present and, no, I couldn't see it.

"I'd like to make one more stop if you're up to it," she said as she buckled herself in.

She had never been to a cranberry bog and there were several open for tours that day. I told her to pick one. She had already circled two on another brochure she had picked up at the coffee shop.

*No wonder it had taken her so long to join me and the EMT at our table.* I thought.

The cranberry harvest had been over for some time and the bogs had been drained of water for the winter. The sales room was designed to replicate a log house, and a video provided a quick lesson on harvesting cranberries. That was followed by our cursory look at the items for sale. From cranberry candy to cranberry scented candles to artistic impressions of cranberries themselves. I couldn't stand them myself because the juice did funny things to the inside of my mouth. So I passed on everything the place had to offer.

"Ready?" Mary asked when she turned to me after finishing her examination of the displays.

"Ready," I said. I was ready. Ready to get on with my life. With our lives. With all the rough roads that might still lie ahead.

The five hour drive back home seemed to go faster than the trip up. We pulled into our garage and Julia came out to meet us and welcome us back. She had agreed to farm-sit while we were gone. It was early evening and the only thing I wanted was to go to bed. After I gave Julia a hug I said I'd talk with her in the morning.

The Christmas present Mary bought me was hung on my office wall across from my desk. It is a fall scene of a North Woods lake with leaves turned color and mist drifting over the water. It could have been taken from our chairs at the wedding. Every time I looked over at it I remembered sitting next to Mary and holding her hand.

We had a new start. Together. And it felt good.

Now if I could just remember the sex.

# Chapter Eleven

My two-week, post-hospital appointment with my personal physician, Dr. John, began right after he asked me if I remembered how I felt before I collapsed. I said that I never felt any pain,

John had been my physician and my friend since the early 1980s when he arrived on the local hospital staff. He was a soft-spoken man with a dry humor, and with a thin body frame that often made me a bit jealous. He could be gentle but devastatingly honest. That was a good thing for me. He was my go-to person in our local health care system.

I gave him my standard litany of naps, short walks, more naps, early nights, forgetfulness, lack of energy, more naps, and my lack of appetite.

He stopped typing on his laptop that rested on the desk next to where I sat. I had my right elbow on the edge bracing myself. He leaned back in his chair and folded his hands on his lap. He listened. When I finished with my list, he resumed typing on the keypad without saying a word.

Mary was beside me in the next chair because she insisted on driving me to my appointment. Besides, she wanted to make sure she heard what he had to say rather than rely on my faulty memory.

The consultation room was equipped with a cushioned examination table that took up most of the available space. It looked like a compact version of a Swiss army knife with multiple drawers that can be pulled out to reshape its configuration. It had a thin sheet of paper running down the middle that crinkled when I sat on it after he asked me to sit and open my shirt so he could listen to my heart.

My blood pressure and pulse readings had been taken minutes before by an aide, who asked what medications I was taking. She listened to my recitation of the meds although she already knew what those were because she checked them on her screen as I mentioned each name. Maybe she just wanted to see if I knew what I took and that I was taking all of the ones prescribed to me.

She left after finishing her questions and shortly Dr. John walked in with a smile. He said he was glad to see me after what happened and asked how I was doing. He had read my reports from the two hospitals and the ambulance crew and now wanted to know how I felt just before it happened. That question started our conversation.

I then stopped to choose my words.

"It's your fault, you know," I said as I turned to him with a deadpan look.

"Oh, how's that?" he replied as he looked up from his keyboard smiling, knowing I was about to make a comment. We knew each other well enough to appreciate each other's subtle humor. I had his attention even if he feigned surprise.

I said that if he hadn't gotten me to the Wellspring Center, I might have collapsed somewhere else and that might have been the end of it. He wouldn't see me again. So it was his fault I was in the hospital.

He grinned and said he was glad then to be the one responsible.

"They sent me your hospital report and pictures of what they found. You're very lucky," he added.

"Yeah, I get a lot of that lately," I replied with a chuckle.

He was one of two people who had a passive responsibility for my collapse at the gym. In a way, they were the point people who put me on my long conveyor ride.

The day I turned eighteen, I became a Red Cross blood donor my first semester in college. My donations continued regularly for the next forty-five years. I didn't encounter any problems because I was the fortunate recipient of my mother's and her father's low blood pressure genetics.

During the year before my collapse, I began registering slightly higher blood pressure levels with each two-week platelet donation. Not a meteoric rise but the trajectory was on a steady gradient upwards at each mandatory examination that preceded a donation. Then, there would follow several donations when my pressure was normal. Then I'd go through another phase where it would be high again. It was like watching a basketball bounce. It got to the point where I never knew what the numbers would read the day of my visit.

I was allowed two separate readings that could be taken at one visit. The second could be after a ten minute "time-out," when I'd be able to sit and think calm thoughts to try to drop the numbers. If the second reading then was low enough to meet their criteria, I could give platelets. If not, I was walking out the door until the next time.

I began to avoid things that might trigger any increase the morning I was scheduled, such as drinking high octane coffee or tea, eating anything sweet that might increase my sugar level, running late or anything stressful that might trigger an increase in my blood pressure. I didn't want to admit to myself I might have a problem. *It'll go away*, I wanted to believe.

Until I had no choice.

It took a 145/104 reading to grab me by my shoulders and shake me out of my denial. It sent me out the front door of the Red Cross building with an alarm ringing in my ears.

That early December day now had a dark cloud hovering above me and I wondered if I would make it home. Or would my blood vessels burst before I got there.

I failed to realize that my previous four visits had signaled a dramatic shift. But I had closed my eyes to it until that particular morning when the technician removed the cuff from my left arm bicep and gently placed it in front of her on the desk without saying a word.

She reached for my donation card and held it by her left fingers, flipping the plastic from one side to the other to look at the blood pressure numbers written in indelible red ink from my previous dozen donation dates.

She tapped her right fingers on the desk, thinking, and then turned to face me.

"Your levels have been creeping up," she said without waving an accusatory finger.

And now they were staying consistently higher.

"I'm sorry but we can't take you today," she finally said without emotion.

She wasn't allowed to give medical advice but asked that I consider having a talk with my personal physician. She couldn't tell me what to do but the urgency in her voice shook me by the way it was said.

"If this continues there's a greater risk for a stroke. Or worse."

That comment blistered my ears as I walked out the front door to my car. I sat for a moment after buckling in and thought about its consequences.

I had lived in a farming community most of my life. I was aware of farmers who had strokes and saw how that affected them and their families. It was a fortunate person who survived a stroke unimpeded and fully recovered.

I didn't know a single one.

My sample was limited but, regardless, I knew I didn't want to have a stroke. Whatever I could do to avoid that would be worth the effort.

My appointment at the end of December was with Dr. John. I handed him my Red Cross cards from the previous eighteen months as we settled into chairs in the exam room. They looked like a financial report with peaks and valleys but with a steady increase in price share.

He sat stone-cold still as he concentrated on reading the numbers. Then he glanced up at me.

"Your bottom number is my concern."

The frown I saw now had me concerned.

"What's it mean?" I asked.

He said the diastolic number—the bottom one—indicated the pressure when my heart muscle was between beats and was refilling with blood.

"It's really too high. And now seems to be consistently high." He pursed his lips as the weight of my situation formed fully in his mind.

He said a prolonged and sustained high level could seriously damage my heart and could lead to a—here was that word again—stroke.

"Maybe not today. Maybe not next year. But quite likely in the future. And sooner than later." He said it so matter-of-factly that it took me a few seconds to realize he was looking straight at me. I almost felt faint as alarm bells went off in my head again. I sat there blank-faced.

He said that this wasn't the end. Then he stopped, for what I guessed was to let it sink in, and then added, "Unless it comes tomorrow."

I shrunk into my chair.

"We can approach this in two ways," he said. He was now more upbeat as he explained some options I had. "I can put you on blood pressure medication right now which will give a fairly quick response. Or, you can change your diet and start a consistent exercise program."

I thought about what I had seen with my father-in-law's reaction to the blood pressure pills and I was sure I didn't want that. After a few moments, I pushed back, still denying I had a problem. I said that I thought I had been fit because of the work I did around the farm.

"That's a misconception," he said. Farm work was certainly good for muscle tone but it didn't really do enough for cardiac health.

"I know farmers who are some of the strongest people I've ever met," he said. "They are good for heavy work and lifting but most don't do enough cardiac exercise to strengthen their hearts."

I was probably one of them and even my long walks in our pasture simply weren't enough.

"We have a fitness center," he continued. "It's located in the old hospital building. It's supervised. It has good equipment and a very competent staff."

They could help me set goals and monitor my progress. I had the option to choose a different road. Or I could choose to do nothing and wait to see what happens.

"Because it will. Sometime," he added.

I scheduled an appointment at the Wellspring Center for after the holidays. At the beginning of February, a Health Fitness Specialist named Sarah was assigned to me. After a basic physical assessment and setting target goals for the first few weeks, she led me to each machine for explanations and instructions.

I was familiar with most of the mechanics because I had taken a weight training course in college. There, my instructor was a five-foot five-inch human dynamo. Although built like a cement block with hard, bulging muscles to match, he was a garrulous man with a terrific sense of humor. He had survived a construction accident earlier in his life by holding himself up with his hands and arms to keep from being completely impaled by the steel rod he fell on until help came to lift him off.

I thought of him as I restarted what he taught me over three decades before. My intent was not to get myself into a shape where I had to extricate myself from an impaling object. I just wanted to get my blood pressure down to a less serious level.

During that spring and summer I spent three hours a week developing my intensity in small increments on the machines. I altered my diet to include more fruits, vegetables, yogurt, and reduced my fat intake. I had worked with dairy cattle most of my life but I even relinquished my cherished whole milk for skim.

Dr. John had asked that I report back with him in two months so he could check my progress. He cautioned me that it would take about three weeks to alter any habit. I likely would see progress in a couple of months. But I'd have to stick with it.

I was pleasantly surprised. After a three weeks absence, I found I didn't miss many of the things I ate before. It became easier to avoid sweets altogether.

The Wellspring Center fitness area wasn't the biggest exercise room I had ever been in. The equipment was packed closer together than what I remembered from my college fitness room and I only needed to take a step or two before I was at the next machine.

A small walking track was laid out around the room perimeter making it close to the pedal machines and leg press. The equipment was adequate but if too many people were in the room, a time limit was applied to each machine. The treadmills faced south so I could look out the large glass windows to the street and across the lawn to the Sauk Prairie Ambulance building. I often joked with Mary that if I ever needed them, they were right across the street.

My weight and blood pressure slowly dropped over the next six weeks. Like a couple walking hand-in-hand down the same sidewalk. But the damage already had been done and I didn't know it. It all came to a sudden stop the morning of October fifth.

If I hadn't taken that road to the fitness center, if I hadn't listened to the advice of the Red Cross nurse, if I hadn't chosen to work with Dr. John and Sarah, I wouldn't be on any road at all. It would have ended sometime, somewhere else.

Because of all that, I was directed to another road, going in a different direction.

# Chapter Twelve

———————

The physical distance between Mary and me, and our son and daughter and her fiancé, provided few face-to-face opportunities to talk about what happened the morning of October fifth. It was a month before I had a chance to sit and discuss with Marcus, Julia and Victor, their perspectives of my collapse so that I could understand what they felt. They were told I had had a heart attack but that would be clarified later to a sudden cardiac death. Pick your own choice of a description.

At the beginning of November, we gathered at a restaurant to celebrate my birthday and Mary and my anniversary, both which, only a month before, were close to never being celebrated again. I would have missed my sixty-fourth birthday and our twenty-ninth anniversary.

Before our gathering, I could easily have acquiesced to the idea of letting this life go without regret because I realized how temporary everything seemed. But it wasn't a resignation that the end was inevitable, it was a realization that my striving to live a few more hours—as noble as that might seem in the moment— wasn't the entirety of my existence.

Until that attitude changed, as well, after meeting with them and celebrating my life here.

When I finally was able to talk with Marcus, Julia and Victor about what happened and their feelings, I realized I was being extremely selfish. I had ignored—no, not ignored, was completely oblivious to—what they and Mary had gone through on their own, on my behalf. It re-framed for me what part I played in their lives even if I didn't think it mattered to me that I stayed or not.

But it did to them! And I hadn't realized how much. A month later I still failed to appreciate the fact that I would, indeed, be missed from their lives.

As we settled into the circular cushioned restaurant booth which made for easy back-and-forth conversation, I became aware of how grateful they were.

We waited until our water glasses were set around the table before I dove into my questions. That was the first chance since I escaped the hospital to listen to them.

Small chatter weaved between us as we sat examining our menus. After the waiter left with our orders, Julia started by saying she and Victor had arrived in Madison by mid-afternoon.

"I was at the bank when Mom called," she explained. "I was working at my teller station. It's kind of funny now but I never had my phone next to me because they didn't like us to have them near us when customers come in. But that day I had it next to my computer.

"As soon as I saw it was Mom calling, I knew something bad had happened. She never called me at the bank unless it was something really important. Then when she told me, my heart just sank."

As Julia fingered her engagement ring, she reminded us that she had a similar experience a few years earlier.

"It was the same feeling I had when you called me in Belgium during my year as an exchange student and said Grandma had died. You didn't even have to tell me what happened because I knew."

Her two bank co-workers said she could leave right away. They would arrange for everything to cover her place and would contact the manager. They would close out her cash drawer and count the money.

"At that point I didn't even care if they counted it correctly! On my way out the door I called Victor to tell him what happened."

"I was still at home," Victor said. "I wasn't working that day so when I got that call from Julia, I said I would drive."

They were quickly on the road for the hour and forty-five minute drive to the Madison hospital.

"Victor calmed me down during our drive to Madison," Julia continued. "He kept saying everything would be fine. But I wasn't sure because at that point we didn't have any other information about you."

They paused. We all sat in silence while we watched salad plates being set down by the waiter before each of us.

There was some confusion about where I was until Victor got a call from Mary.

"We started out for the Sauk Prairie Hospital because we thought you were there," Victor continued. "Before we got to Arlington, Mary called again and told Julia said that you were in UW hospital in Madison. So we changed direction and turned south and headed there."

Julia said she got the call from Mary at about 12:30. "We got to the hospital at about 2:30 but you were still in the emergency room. Or we thought so," she added.

But Victor couldn't find me.

"We waited at the front desk because they didn't have your name," he said. "We told them that you came in with a heart attack and they had brought you by ambulance. Finally they worked out who you were and then showed us where to go. The first person we ran into said you were doing better. That was really the first information we had about your condition."

Julia was upset with me.

"One of the first things I did was to warn you to stay alive for our wedding," she said. "Or I'd bring you back from the dead if you didn't! And then you laughed."

Victor was concerned because he noticed that I seemed awfully confused.

"You did recognize us. Then you asked why we were there. You didn't seem to understand what happened. You said, 'It's nothing. Why are you crying Julia? What's wrong?' Then Marcus came in about an hour later."

However, I seemed to have provided some comic relief, especially for Victor.

"When they sent you to a second room, they took you up to the second floor and the Intensive Care Unit," he said. "We were allowed in there too. And that's where they had your name as Puerto Rico XXX because they didn't know who you were. That was funny."

The waiter stopped to ask how our meals were and refilled our water glasses before he left. As we paused, Victor had a chance to mention that my condition seemed inconsistent with how I acted.

"That was the one interesting thing," he said. "You were quite talkative. The doctors kept asking you questions like how are you feeling or if you knew what day it was. Those things seemed normal. There were times when you may not have seen us because of the curtain in the room that surrounded you. We would move in and out as the doctors or nurses needed us to. So in one moment you may have thought we weren't there, and then in the next we were there and you could see us. And then we were gone again. So it might have been confusing."

I must have appeared incoherent to Julia.

"You kept repeating that you couldn't understand how Marcus got there so fast," she said. "You kept saying you had just been working out. One of the other things you kept asking was 'what are you all doing here?' Then you said you still had your contacts in. I got a nurse to help and they gave you a case for them. But you took them out yourself. It was about that point when Victor and I left but I wanted to stay the night to make sure you were ok. I was so scared."

Victor wasn't as concerned, or didn't let on if he was.

"While you were in the ER you sounded perfectly fine. If I hadn't been told you had a heart attack I would never have guessed just looking at you. You sounded happy."

Victor said that was when he and Julia finally left.

The waiter came to collect our plates after we had all finished our meals. We waited in silence while he cleared them before Julia continued.

"It was about nine or so that night and Mom and Marcus said we should go back to Ripon because I needed to be at work the next day. Victor and I felt much, much better after we saw you. It made the ride back a lot easier. You looked like someone—like when they have their wisdom teeth out—they're happy. That's what you looked like."

Maybe I was, maybe not. But Victor noticed something else.

"You were making a lot of jokes with the doctors. But you would forget what you just said and then repeat the question. You did that a lot. That's what concerned us the most. Your memory. Your short-term memory wasn't there. I mean, it was really short.

You had no idea that you were repeating yourself. But still, you looked so normal. That was really surprising to us."

Julia said she had one last comment before they left that night. "The first thing you said to us when we saw you was 'I'll be at your wedding.' Looking back on it, that's not a phone call I ever want to get again. But I said, 'don't do that again!'"

Marcus had arrived at the hospital last because he had the longest drive.

"Mid-day I received a call from Mom," Marcus said. "And she said that you were in the hospital. I had literally just driven back to Minneapolis that morning having completed a week-long business trip in Madison. I was dropping off my rental car at the dealership and was on my way back to my office when I got her call."

He didn't have much information to go on.

"She said you had collapsed while exercising and you were taken by ambulance to the UW Hospital. That's all the information I had because she didn't know how you were. She hadn't seen you yet."

After a quick turnaround, he was back on the road.

"I drove back to my office to gather my things and explained that I had to leave again. But everyone was supportive of that. I was there for about five or ten minutes before I packed up and headed straight back to Madison.

Marcus still had all his laundry from his trip in the trunk but he figured he had enough clothes for whatever time he would be back.

"I will say that it was a very long drive, even one way. I had a lot of time to think while I was driving during that four-hour trip. I tried to not focus on negative thoughts or distractions during my drive, so I would randomly pick topics to remind myself to think about."

Little things to help stay awake.

"I tried to keep my mind off worst-case scenarios for you. I found myself thinking about the trucking industry. Random, I know. I guess perhaps it was because I was one of the only cars driving on the highway, since it was a business day afternoon and there were many semis driving. It also seemed like the drive was taking forever."

As the dessert menus were handed around our table, Marcus said the miles back down seemed to inch along.

"More than anything else, I kept reminding myself that I was grateful because you were in good care. I knew I needed to focus on that the most. Mom had said you were alive but that was all I knew at that point. But I was thankful for that.

"Thinking back to it now, there was also the emotion of being angry simply because you were in the hospital. It's a bit weird to think of it in that way, but I was angry. Or at least frustrated about the situation and not having control over it. And also I wasn't thrilled that I was now driving four more hours back the way I had just come a short time before. But it was important for me to see you."

I passed on the dessert and ordered a hot tea instead.

"Another emotion I had at the time," Marcus continued, after ordering coffee. "Was more of a philosophy, or a commitment I guess. I wanted to be there for you. And that kept me going while I drove. So it was a mixture of different emotions that's hard to describe.

"I finally got to Madison somewhere between four and five o'clock. When I came into the room where you were and first saw you, you actually looked somewhat refreshed. It was a bit weird. You had good coloration and looked alert. I wasn't sure what to expect while I drove down but I have to admit that the way you looked wasn't what I expected. You seemed very comfortable."

He said that I must have been surprised in my own way.

"When you first saw me, your eyes got really big and it appeared you were surprised I was there. You talked to me but the thing I recall the most was that you were surprised I was there and that I must have made quick time. As if you didn't realize four or five hours had gone by."

By that time night was settling in over the Madison hospital.

"I stayed for a few hours and it was dark outside when we left," Marcus said. "I think it was about nine o'clock when Mom and I finally left the hospital. I had told Julia and Victor to leave earlier since they had a long drive to get back to Ripon. By that time you seemed ready to relax for the night and we said goodnight."

I sat looking down at my steaming tea while I listened and admitted to them that I couldn't recall them being there at all or of their leaving.

"On Tuesday," Marcus continued. "We visited you in the second hospital they moved you to and talked about different things and the sequence of events from the day before. I wasn't sure you understood any of it though. On Monday night you had told me that the key to your locker was in your workout pants and someone would need to retrieve your bag and clothes. Then I took Mom out for dinner afterwards. It was a quiet and weird night on the farm. It's not the same without you there."

Mary set down her fork. She stepped into the conversation with some clarification. "We did go back to the farm on Monday night with both vehicles. The next morning Marcus and I drove together in his car to town. Marcus retrieved your clothes and we picked up the car that was still in the fitness center parking lot. I drove it over to get the tires changed and Marcus followed. When they finished, we both drove to Madison again but separately.

Marcus was glad I had put the key in my sweat pants while I worked out.

"I went to the fitness center and I explained to the staff at the front desk why I was there and they asked how you were doing. They were glad to hear you were OK," he said. "I asked if I could get to your locker and pick up your clothes since I had your key. They explained where the locker room was and then I packed up all your clothes."

"So Tuesday morning we came to see you at the hospital again," Marcus said. "After seeing you in good spirits, I decided I would head back to Minneapolis. I didn't know yet that you would be scheduled for a procedure but there wasn't anything else I could do for you. But I made Mom promise that she would stay in Madison overnight so that she didn't have to be on the farm by herself, alone."

Marcus said he was thankful for several things.

"Looking back, there are three reasons why I'm glad things played out the way they did. Having a heart attack is not an ideal situation or life event, but the result was the best I could have hoped for. First, I am happy you are alive and still with us. I haven't given much thought to what I would have felt if I had to go through life without a father.

"Second, I was happy that you had great care. You were surrounded by good people the entire time, whether it was while working out, or while you were in the hospitals.

"And third, I was relieved that what happened to you happened where it did. I am extremely grateful that it didn't happen in the barn four days earlier when you and I were arguing while trying to corral a steer to be loaded out for the market. I am relieved you didn't collapse then and land face first on the cement and in the dirt with Mom and me standing there not knowing what to do or to be able to get you help. That would have been traumatic for all of us.

"Looking back now, I didn't realize it at the time but all three of those things were important. It could have turned out a lot worse. I'm thankful that you have made a good recovery and that you are still part of my life. You cheated death and I'm so happy you did!"

I picked up the check as we got up to leave. It was a bill I didn't mind paying.

# Chapter Thirteen

Gratitude. The word hardly encompassed all the feelings I had after returning home from the hospital. And each day after put an exclamation point on it. I breathed in the fresh air. I watched the morning sunrise. I felt the warmth of the noonday sun and the touch of Mary's hand, which often felt the same. I talked on my phone with Marcus, with Julia and Victor. I heard the voices of my mother, my brothers and sisters. All things I might not have had a second chance to do.

I decided it was time for a *Thank You*.

Our parents brought the six of us kids up to be thankful for what we had. Much or little. Wanted or not. We still had more than many others. Be thankful.

In current-speak this was almost a mantra in our farm household. Or would have been if we had known what a mantra was. Did we kids complain? Sure. Were we always grateful? Probably not, especially when told we couldn't do something or have something. But the seeds of gratitude incubated. Until they eventually broke through the surface and we found the fertile soil they were planted in later sprouted blooms that Mary and I tried to pass on to Marcus and Julia.

After my two-week check-up with Dr. John had finished, I told Mary I wanted to go to the fitness center. I still didn't know who the people were who came to my rescue.

Sandy was monitoring the fitness floor and came over when she saw me walk in. She asked if she could give me a hug and then asked how I was doing. She said I had given them all a scare that day but I looked really good to her.

I explained that I was on a mission and wondered if I could find out who had been involved with rescuing me? She said that she could give me names but not any contact information.

I said that was fine. I wanted to write a card of thanks and leave them here for her to hand out. I wouldn't be back for a workout for quite some time yet, although I said I had been scheduled for a rehab program that began in a couple weeks. I'd see after that what the next step would be.

She wrote out four names on a slip of paper. I asked her to tell everyone hello from me and then Mary and I left.

We walked across the street to the ambulance building and found Kevin sitting in his office. He got up from his swivel chair with a beaming smile. I introduced Mary who had never met him. I said thank you again and that I'd like to express it to those who responded.

He could give me names but not addresses after I explained that I'd like to mail each of them a card. He said eleven EMTs had responded and even one with a fire truck who was at a school demonstration. Some EMTs were hands-on, some moved equipment, while others arranged pathways to move me out or helped move people away from the scene. He said they all were vital to my survival but he specifically mentioned those who arrived first after I asked.

Then he laughed as he thought it might take me some time to write that many out.

"Better yet," he suggested. "Why don't you come to our next monthly meeting, if you feel up to it?"

It would be held the next Monday evening at the station. I then could thank everyone in person. He said the EMTs would appreciate hearing from me and to see a person they had helped reach a successful outcome.

"It would be good therapy for them," he said. "They need that support too."

Over the next few nights I wrote out my cards from a pack that Mary had gotten especially for that night. They were blank on the inside so I could individualize them even though I didn't know the person I was addressing. It felt like sending out early Christmas cards.

Mary and I arrived that evening shortly before 6:30. A group potluck was in progress as we stepped into the room. It was arranged with emergency equipment along the perimeter walls and with tables and chairs placed in the center for their meeting after the meal. Kevin saw me first and came over to shake my hand and said hello to Mary again.

Several EMTs knew I was coming, but many didn't. I couldn't make much small talk because I didn't know anyone else except for one EMT. I had played local intramural basketball with him forty years ago, in what seemed like another lifetime for both of us as we reminisced.

When everyone was seated and the talking ceased, Kevin introduced me to those I only had met in an unconscious state, and to those who hadn't responded to my event. He then turned it over to me and I stood there for a moment simply looking at the group as I tried to formulate my thoughts. I glanced down at my note card on which I had written four words to help me remember the points I wanted to say.

"How can I adequately say thank you for such unselfishness

on your part?" I started. "Particularly that you didn't know who I was. Only that I was someone who needed help."

I explained that their actions gave Mary and me the chance to celebrate our anniversary yesterday, and I'd be able to celebrate my birthday in a few days.

I said the best I could do was hand out thank you cards to each of those who helped. I knew there were some whose names I didn't have that may not have been on call or couldn't attend.

"But I want each of you to know I appreciated your service and didn't want you to feel neglected. Thank you as well."

I went down the list of names Kevin had given me and asked that, if they weren't embarrassed, I'd like them to come up so I could thank them individually. Most were wearing a t-shirt with the logo of the local service and as each received their card, I was finally able to put a face to the name I had written out. First a hand shake and then an unashamed hug. Then a second hand. Another hug. Then another.

It was a moving moment for me because I was shaking hands with a person who literally helped bring me back to life. How many people get to do that or say that? I came to the last card and handed it out.

Then I said that although my hands were empty, they all had filled them many times over. I thanked them for allowing me to come to their meeting. I said it was important *for me* to say thanks because that was all I had to offer them in return.

Dean stood up.

"It means a lot to hear from you," he said. "Because we don't always get such a good outcome. And we don't often hear from survivors later. That's not required but we do appreciate hearing from people we help. We're grateful you took the time and made the effort to come. It can't be easy during a recovery like yours and considering what you went through. Well, it's just very pleasing to all of us."

My voice finally cracked when I said thank you again.

Mary stood up to thank the group. She told them that they had given her husband back to her. She was grateful for that. Then we turned and walked out the door.

It was another ten days before I was able to return to the fitness center with my cards. I was surprised as it had been transformed since Mary and I had been in less than two weeks before. Most everything had been moved upstairs to the second floor into a room with three times the space and twice the amount of equipment, most of it new. With its high ceiling, it now had an open-air feel that wasn't in the former room below. Their move was planned long before my incident and the former exercise room below was now fully dedicated for rehabbing patients.

Diane, Sarah, Sandy and Josh were in the room and I thanked them as I gave each their card. I said my plans were to be back.

Sometime. At least now it was possible because of what they did for me.

# Chapter Fourteen

A trip outside the halls of a hospital ward, the joy of a single dance at a wedding, and the gratefulness of being alive. All that euphoria quickly slammed smack into the reality of everyday life in just a few weeks.

I realized that the world would still exist without me. That's not a bad thing, but it places me in a different context when I don't try to be bound by it. However, my presence—anyone's presence—is a unique expression born in value and a consciousness of the preferences or idealizations that make me—well, me. What I like may not be what someone else likes. What I abhor, may be what others wish to embrace. But it is still the same object of, perhaps, desire or rejection, just viewed from different perspectives. Both can be beneficial or learning experiences for each way they are perceived. I was still trying to understand what to learn from my experience.

Mary had returned to work but she was hesitant to leave me alone. She worried that she would come home to find me in some ungodly position, like being face down in the pasture by our cattle, or that I had slipped and drown in our bathtub shower, or that I was lifeless sitting in my recliner from another sudden cardiac death. Or worse. I could be mangled in a piece of farm equipment that I carelessly had used and be disabled the rest of my life. The mind reeled as to the number of ways I could injure myself in the stumbling, tentative and less-than stable physical state I found myself.

Mary didn't want to come home to find a dead body, she repeatedly told me. I tried to reassure her that it wouldn't happen. I'd be careful. But we were at an impasse as that went on each day for the next two weeks.

After she had left in the morning, I used my time to step outside and stand at the fence looking at our cattle milling around in our smaller pasture. I would count. Twenty-five.

*That's way too many for me to care for*, I thought. I could hardly lift the handle of a hay fork let along try to take care of all these animals in the coming winter months.

One night Mary and I were sitting at our kitchen table. Both of us were dog-tired. Our plates were empty after finishing another late meal, long past when we normally eat. We sat silently at opposite ends staring at the stack of mail piled up between us in a mound of envelopes. Neither of us made a move to lift the newly arrived ones to see what was on deck.

I was about to get up from my chair but just fell back down into it. Mary lifted her head from her two hands which propped it up to look over at me. I said I was ok. I was just thinking.

"About what?" she asked.

"About our cattle," I said. And what we do with them. There were twenty-five head out there.

I paused.

"Who is going to take care of them this winter?" I finally said. It may have come out as a rhetorical question but it was also a statement.

Her answer was to just shrug her shoulders.

"Do we keep them?" I asked. "Maybe we sell them? What about the farm? Sell it?

"And what about us?"

My questions floated between us like silent companions but they never landed on the table to join us out in the open. Mary said she was too tired to discuss tomorrow let alone three or four months down the road.

"Well, the pastures are still green," I said. "There's enough for them to eat, for now anyway. They just have to go out and get their own meals. It's what happens when the snow comes that I wonder about."

Mary was silent. Now I had tossed another concern onto her lap.

We had enough hay stored in our barn to feed all of them during the winter and get them to fresh grass the next spring. That wasn't the problem. It was the time between now and spring that I was concerned about. I could probably handle the skidloader that I used to put out a round bale when it was needed but I wouldn't be able to stay out in the cold for long periods.

I got chilled easily, even more than I ever did before. The blood thinners did an excellent job. I bled like a fountain when I scraped or cut myself. I was sure that medication was keeping my blood vessels open to avoid clots but I also got so cold I couldn't stand it. I put on double socks, double flannel shirts, double gloves and would even have used double coats if I had an extra large to put over my regular outdoor one. And I still was cold after all that.

I couldn't seem to warm up once I was chilled. I took hot showers until my skin almost blistered from the heat. But my fingers were the worst. One cold day and they felt like they might just break off like icicles if I hit them. When they became cold, I couldn't feel them. And it wasn't even below freezing yet outside.

That was still the least of my concerns. What happened if

I collapsed again? Or the cattle waterer lost electricity and the unit froze solid? What if there was an early calving that became a problem? Who would assist?

I explained to Mary that I wasn't in any shape to handle any of that. And if I couldn't do it, that meant she would have to.

She pulled both arms up from beside herself and placed her elbows back on the table. She raised her hands to the sides so that they framed her face.

It was early December. I suggested there was still time to make some adjustments. But we'd need to do it soon.

"Ok. What are our options?" She finally asked, tossing the ball my way.

I said that it was not just my decision to make. So I asked if she thought she could handle all of that?

"You're kidding right?" she replied as if I was making a joke.

"Then we need options," I said. "We have options!"

"Tell me what you're thinking," she said.

I had my opening.

I ticked off the mental list I had made over the past two days while she was at work. I said that if we could sell all the pregnant cows and heifers, that would significantly lighten the work load. It would take less feed to carry the rest through winter. I wouldn't have to worry about any calving problems in the cold weather. And we could still keep the young steers and unbred heifers and female calves.

"Then we could start over and build up our cattle numbers again."

With that I had finished my case and I was also physically depleted from that discussion.

Mary asked who would buy them.

I said I knew a couple of people who might be interested. No guarantees. But it would be worth a call or two to find out.

Mary is the chief financial officer for our household and I could tell she was beginning to run some numbers through her mind because she relaxed and eased back in her chair. She was warming to my idea. She said she didn't mean to sound harsh but she had a full plate at work that week and wasn't expecting to make such a monumental decision that night.

I agreed that selling most of our herd would short-circuit our future plans for them. But that was a discussion for another day.

"The time is right for us to downsize. It makes sense," I said. "We just need to take that step and see where it goes."

Mary said she was willing to let all the cows go except for her favorite one.

I said that's fine, "One it is. That leaves us with ten animals if we sell the other fifteen."

I made two phone calls over the next three days and got two buyers to visit later the next week. And just like that, we cut our herd down to ten head.

I breathed a sigh of relief two days later as I watched the two cattle trailers leave our yard, loaded with the cattle they had bought.

The pile of bills on our kitchen table had just gotten smaller.

# Chapter Fifteen

It was time for some fun! It seemed a long time since Mary and I had anything to celebrate. We needed to find something to celebrate in a tangible way. Thanksgiving had arrived and Christmas was just behind it. Thanksgiving dinner was to be held at Bob and Jane's farm house that year, sixteen miles from ours. Bob was Mary's older brother and, along with his wife Jane, we had shared that dinner with them many times.

Bob's son and his family joined us. Marcus brought Paige, the sparkling young woman he had become more than friends with. We gathered around the large wood dining room table. Jane's culinary skills were legendary in our family and I broke my diet during the meal with no regrets. I tried everything. But the small portions positioned around the edges of my large plate to make it look full now seemed anemic compared to others who had heaped potatoes, turkey, dressing, gravy, steaming Brussels sprouts, cranberry sauce, and salad onto theirs.

I wasn't there for the food, really. It was the company. The family gathering. The touch and conversation with another human being that reminded me how good it was to be alive. To stop and take account. To slow the pace for just a short time. That was my reason for being there.

While we were eating I caught Julia glancing over to me. She thought I had my head down and I wasn't looking but from the corner of my eye I saw that concentrated concern on her face as she momentarily checked to see if I was alright.

I looked up and winked at her. I laid my fork down and took in the scene around the table. The quick jokes. The constant chatter. The questions of how the twin girls were doing in school. The answers which then brought more questions.

That long-ago memory I had in the hospital resurfaced. Suddenly my grandfather came back into focus. I could feel it now like I could years ago when he came home from the hospital after his heart attack. Only it was a Christmas meal instead. He had been in the hospital over three weeks and I only recalled one instance of going to see him. That was a time when children were not encouraged to visit patients. Maybe we were seen as a nuisance instead of real, grown-up visitors.

When I entered the room, Grandpa was cocooned under a canopy of clear plastic sheeting, called an oxygen tent, to help him breathe. Nasal tips were still far into the future. We kids weren't allowed to lift it or touch his hands under it although he seemed to slightly reach up with his hand as if he yearned for a human touch amongst all the medical gadgetry.

When he finally returned home, my parents and grandmother had transformed one of the rooms on the first floor into his new bedroom. There would be no more slow ascents to his second floor bedroom aided by his cane.

They set up a bed, two chairs, and a pedestal on which sat a small black and white television. That was his new companion during the quiet times when his grandchildren were at school, and while Grandma was out helping with morning and evening chores. My mother became an unintentional sentry, performing watch duty while attending to her housework.

He seemed to get stronger in the days after his return. Perhaps the familiar surroundings of home and family had aided his recovery. Perhaps it was his response to home cooking. I couldn't say. But he never made a return to the hospital and by spring he was outside, slowly moving step by tentative step from the house across our farmyard to the barn where he had labored for over sixty years.

Grandma liked to sing and was especially partial to church choir and our county's homemaker chorus group. The chorus had been invited by one of the early Madison television stations to sing during their noon program broadcast a week before Christmas.

I wandered into his bedroom to check on Grandpa just before the program started. He asked me to turn on the little black and white picture. He was sitting on the edge of his bed to watch the program and motioned me over to join him. I climbed up, my short legs dangling over the side like his. Even at my age at that time, he wasn't much taller than me but he had thick hands and arms from years of handling his massive Belgian work horses.

Showtime arrived and the chorus was announced. They launched into a medley of Christmas songs and I saw Grandma standing on the left side of the screen in the front row because she, too, was not much taller than Grandpa.

Suddenly I noticed that the bed was shaking just as I pointed to Grandma. I turned with boyish excitement to smile at Grandpa. At first I thought the anguished look on his face was from pain. I almost yelled for Mom but stopped when I saw the first tears start to glide down his face. I was surprised because I'd never seen my grandpa cry before. But he wasn't paying attention to me. He was looking at the television and quietly sobbing while his shoulders gently shook.

When the singing stopped, so did his tears. He wiped them away with the flannel sleeve of his checked shirt. I touched his free hand and looked up into his eyes with a little smile. I slid off the bed and walked out of his room. I probably could have hugged him instead but I felt like an intruder at his private moment and decided not to say anything at supper that night.

He and I never spoke about that moment when we were together after that. What was there to say? That the woman he spent his life with could still move him? That he was grateful to have survived his heart attack to see that chorus sing? To simply have another day? Or was it an emotional release of all the pain, dislocation, and the uncertainty of mortality he had experienced?

I understand his mix of emotions as I sat there at Jane's dinner table. I'd been there too. But that insight was still decades in the future for me when we sat around the dining room table with Grandpa for our Christmas dinner.

Halfway through the ham and turkey, I glanced up from eating my gravy-covered mashed potatoes and saw my grandfather sitting quietly, just looking and taking stock of each of us in turn. Was he contemplating his good fortune at still being alive? Or was he simply grateful to be granted a glimpse into his legacy with his grandchildren close at hand?

Amongst the clatter of the dishes, platters, forks, and knives, Grandpa continued to study each one of us without them noticing until he saw me looking back at him. With a quick half-smile and a slight nod he acknowledged the secret we had shared in his room.

I never asked him and perhaps it wasn't important that I did. We all have our special memories and we make of them what we want. Perhaps we simply try to mold those memories into what fits most neatly into our life narrative. In recalling that moment while sitting at Jane's, I wondered if he was remembering his own childhood Christmas, and the longing for his own father who had died when Grandpa was four years old and never got the chance to know him.

I viewed those events differently since it had happened to me, in ways I couldn't possibly understand before. Maybe in his own way Grandpa did see his future before him much like I was trying to understand mine that sat before me.

Over fifty-five years later I shared his vantage point at Jane's Thanksgiving dinner. I was seated at a table with our children, and the children and grandchildren of Mary's brother and his wife. I took my moment to survey the table unnoticed as everyone else was in conversation.

Then I realized Julia was observing me and acknowledging my observations, and she gave me a quick smile. I nodded back to her.

I would recall sharing that table moment with my grandfather eight years later when I said goodbye while leaning over his casket and whispering to him. Ironically, he died from cancer not from the effects of his heart attack.

That long-ago dinner, and seeing his smile across the table, stayed with me through the years. It was like I was shaking an invisible hand that reached across the six decades to find my grandfather attached to it.

But that was then. This was now. If I reached across this table, in this life, I still *can* touch Marcus and Julia, and Mary.

It was a time to be thankful for all that.

# Chapter Sixteen

Down Time.

I had lots of it.

Like when I couldn't do any kind of physical work around our farm. Or when I often—more often than I cared to admit to myself—had to lie down because I simply couldn't stay awake.

Two weeks after returning home from the hospital I was fully responding to the medications, but in unexpected ways. I originally had thought they'd be helpful, not debilitating. I developed a new routine that was more emotional-editing or habit-editing than anything else. Like taking one thing out and inserting another.

My eating habits had changed. My sleeping habits had changed. My life had dramatically changed, all because I had no energy.

I woke at eight in the morning. I had usually been up by six. I dragged myself out of bed to go pee. It was a relief to be without assistance, without someone holding a jug, without anyone hovering to expect a certain quantity. I could simply let it go, straight into the toilet, no questions asked. I usually stumbled to the bathroom because once I got out of bed I floundered from the disorientation of my surroundings.

I had to force myself down to the kitchen to make something to eat because it was easier to lie in bed, half comatose. I would grab a plastic container of yogurt. Plop four heaping tablespoons into a cereal bowl. Pour some maple syrup over it and sprinkle a cup of six-grain granola on top. Mix it with my spoon and then have at it. I had no appetite so that was filling enough until I found some fruit for lunch. I could tell I was dropping weight because my pants fit looser than before. Then I'd sit at the kitchen table to stare at what became my full breakfast.

Alone.

Mary was back in her daily routine and had usually left for Madison by the time I placed my feet on the floor next to our bed and tried to stand up.

I knew she would call about two hours after she left to check in that I was ok, or had made it out of bed. She had now become the sole income earner in our household and the financial pressures were slowly mounting. The bills seemed to flood in with each mail delivery. Most were taken care of by our insurance but the paperwork still had to be confronted and since she was the most adept, she handled them. If I made a mistake it would take an inordinate amount of time to correct it, so she felt it was easier if she handled it herself. Who was I to complain?

The bills not covered by our insurance clawed away at our dwindling savings that had been unexpectedly tapped into. Mary tried not to say anything but I noticed each time she dropped the pile of mail on the kitchen table and walked away from it, that she was probably thinking that if she ignored them, they might magically disappear. I ached to see her feel that way. That wasn't us. We'd shouldered on together through the tough times before. But that was when I could contribute. Now I felt like that millstone.

I tried to answer when she called or she'd probably go crazy wondering if I was still alive. If I missed her call or couldn't get to my phone before it kicked into voicemail, I'd call right back to let her know I was fine.

By ten in the morning, I was exhausted after being awake only two hours. I needed to sit and take a nap. Then I was up again. Maybe I'd go to my desk thinking I'd do some work on a book that was due to my editor in a month. I'd stare at the papers. But nothing came. My mind couldn't focus on anything. I'd toss my pencil down and get up. I made some tea and walked outside with it to the table in our back yard. Plop down. Hope something clicked. Then listened to the silence. I often wondered what was next and what I was going to do. I knew I had reason to be grateful but I couldn't even conjure up vacant emotions. I was emotionally depleted, while Mary was physically. I was numb. And if I was, could Mary be far behind?

My greatest late morning achievement was to make myself a salad for lunch. And I was extra careful when cutting some fruit. I held everything by my fingertips so I wouldn't get the knife near my skin. After all that strenuous activity of making lunch and then eating, I couldn't keep my eyes open any more so I'd go take another nap.

What a daily routine that was!

I had accepted the idea that each time I sat or laid down, I might not get up again. But I was too tired to even care one way or the other. If tomorrow never came at least I'd get a good, long sleep, with no interruptions. When I did lie down, I was gone in seconds after I closed my eyes. Was that really a life I wanted?

I'd wake up and for a split second I would often be disappointed that I was still here. *It might be easier if I simply left again.* I thought. So I would try to do some reading. Words that were once second-nature to me became a mystifying configuration on the page I'd be reading. I would try to decipher their meaning but then realized it might not make any difference even if I used the dictionary at the edge of my desk, because I couldn't spell them anyway. My word memory, let alone their spelling, was lost to me.

With the day then half gone, I ventured out to get any eggs from our fifteen laying hens. It was only a short walk across our lawn to the chicken coop. After collecting what they decided to contribute to our farm economy, I'd place them in the small wicker basket Mary had converted from her flower arrangement supplies.

Then it was to the mail box, if the postman wasn't late. I opened the lid with some trepidation because there would likely to be more bills arriving now that enough time had passed for the hospital charges to get processed and sent through the labyrinth of the medical system before being spewed into the postal system that was quite punctual with delivering those envelopes to us. Now I hoped they wouldn't be so efficient.

Tracking back to the house, I'd head to the recliner to sit down and find myself awake again half an hour later.

*How can I sleep so much?* I thought as I pushed myself out of the chair. I'd never slept this much in my life.

I stood and sarcastically considered what next to do during my hectic day. My left knee felt better. Two days after we got home from the wedding the pain had left just as quickly as it had arrived. It felt odd that Tuesday morning when I got up. It had become routine to anticipate the pain in the morning when I stood up and just like that it was completely gone.

*So how did that happen?* I asked myself. I tested it again. Nope, the pain's gone. *Well, how about that.* I thought.

My new medications probably had something to do with it. I had been fed lots of stuff through my IVs and I imagined that pain-killers were mixed into the brew I had received from the suspended bags.

When I left the hospital pharmacy, I was handed a clutch of plastic bottles filled with pills that rattled each time I shook the bag. The pharmacist painstakingly went over each one, literally reading off the typed labels as if to make sure she didn't miss anything. Or that I didn't and that I fully understood the pharmaceutical journey I was about to embark on.

After I got home, I spread them out on the kitchen table and examined each labeled container. There were three new medications with names I couldn't pronounce. *Does someone actually have a job thinking up their names that no one can spell?* I wondered. Was it the industry's inside private joke on the patients to make these drugs sound and look more impressive than they might otherwise be?

One was a blood thinner. Another for blood pressure. The third a cholesterol. Plus an aspirin to top it off. These four were to be taken daily at a regular time and until further notice. That sounded like an awfully long, indefinite time to me.

Mary bought me a plastic seven-day pill tray with the day labeled on top of each flip-up lid so I wouldn't miss a single day. On Monday mornings I refilled each compartment for the next week. Each tiny cubicle got four pills and I snapped it shut when I finished. We now had a "pill drawer" in our kitchen cabinet for the first time in my life. I didn't know what to do with the nitroglycerin pills because I'd need them only in an emergency. I hadn't yet worked out what difference it would make to have them in a bottle. *If I collapsed again and couldn't open it, what good would they do me then?* I thought as I rolled the small vial from side to side in my fingers, looking at the label, as if that would give me an answer.

These would have to stay in that bottle because I drew the

line at wearing a chain necklace with a dangling pendant that could hold three of those small, white nitro pills. That sounded a lot like having an AED box strapped to my chest. I did acquiesce to Mary's request that I at least kept the small stainless steel vial she had purchased for me. It was a third of an inch in diameter and two inches long that I could easily keep in my pants or shirt pocket. "Just in case," as she put it.

I've never liked wearing jewelry although there were times when I seriously considered getting one ear pierced. That was before I was married to Mary. But lately this thought had come around for reconsideration. It would have to wait at least another year because with the blood thinners I was taking, I'd never get the bleeding to stop from a puncture. I wore my wedding ring only on special occasions or when out I was out with Mary. I never wore it when I worked outside on our farm.

My aversion to wearing rings developed when I was about eight years old. I had noticed the stubby left half of my great-uncle's ring finger and asked my dad about it. He said his uncle had gotten his hand caught in the gears of a silo filling machine. It caught his ring and pulled the top half of his finger off as he yanked his hand out. I cringed because I knew what that entailed. But it might have been worse. While he may have lost half of his finger, at least he didn't lose his whole hand or arm. Or, he could have been killed by being pulled into the grinding machine. I didn't think wearing a ring was worth it. Besides, I figured that if I needed a ring to know I was married, I had other problems with my wife.

I decided I'd keep the stainless steel pendant, if for no other reason than to keep Mary happy. I stuffed it into my blue jeans pocket when I went outside. *But no ring*, I said to myself as I wiggled all five full-length fingers of each hand, palms down, in front of me.

I'd putter around during the day until Mary came home. She was usually exhausted from the drive, the traffic, the pressure of deadlines, and the multitude of issues she dealt with during her day at the church. She loved the part of her work that supported a ministry with the homeless, the disadvantaged, and the ones forgotten by society. That was the energy she drew from those days. It certainly wasn't me. I didn't have any to give.

I tried to fix a meal for us as best I could but always kept it simple because I was constantly cautioned about using knives. Marcus gave me an electric shaver so that I no longer needed to use a razor because with any slight nick I might end up at the local hospital's emergency room with a gushing vein. I once looked like Niagara Falls after I had cut myself.

Meals became simple affairs and after she ate, Mary sat down as exhausted from her day as I was from mine, although I felt guilty because I hadn't really done anything. There was no impulse for either of us to check how our day went. Other nights she worked until it was quite late, trying to catch up on paying bills, making delayed phone calls, washing clothes, and fixing meals ahead for me so I didn't have to use any knives.

By this time I knew she was frustrated more because of my collapse upsetting her world than she was with me. But from my view it was all rolled into one and whether it was intentional or not, I felt it was all focused towards me.

Sex was the farthest thing from our minds. At least mine because the blood pressure and blood thinner medications have made me totally numb where it most counted. If you had shown me an erotic photo, I'd likely yawn and then ask if I could just go take a nap. Suggest some wine to get me in the mood and I'd ask for the whole bottle and still skip the sweeties. I didn't have the heart or the courage to ask what Mary thought. She was already dead asleep by the time I made my way to the bedroom. I'd lie down and melt into the mattress thinking about the riveting day on tap for tomorrow that probably would be no different than today. Or next week.

I felt like a shell waiting to crack.

I had been told the blood thinner would be discontinued after one year because there was no added benefit to continue it past that point. The blood pressure pills, however, didn't have a sell-by-date and I would continue taking them into the foreseeable future. That's a long time, and it was still only October—less than a month after I had collapsed.

I walked outside to the table that morning, soon after Mary left. I sat under the shade tree. The cranes were trumpeting across the smaller pasture near our house. They called to each other. Or were they arguing? I didn't speak Crane. Since they mated for life, I wasn't sure whether they were just having a marital tiff or discussing how their morning was going.

The dead remnants of the tree trunk towering next to me was a shade tree in memory only. In its prime it was a one hundred twenty-year old Elm with an eighteen-foot base. Like millions of other Elms, it was alive one fall and dead by the next spring. Here today, gone tomorrow. I thought there must be some metaphor in that but let it go.

I had trimmed off the dead branches of that elm myself long before my collapse. It took me a month. Its two- and three-foot diameter limbs had to be dropped so I missed the house porch, the clothes line, the garage, and Mary's flower beds. Those branches once spread a canopy over sixty feet but had become bare skeletons of their former selves.

*Nothing lives forever as it is or was. It all changes in time.* I thought.

The chilly air made the steam rise up from my tea mug. Birds flitted around from tree to tree, chasing each other in a game that resembled tag-you're-it. For the first time since I got home, I could try to think about what happened at the fitness center.

It didn't seem like such a big deal to me as it did to Mary, or Marcus and Julia, or my mom. I had been told numerous times that I was very close to the end. But that didn't really mean anything to me. I couldn't put myself in their shoes to understand what they were going through. I could only stand in mine. And they probably couldn't understand the full scope of what I experienced while dead.

*How could they?* I thought. Maybe I could *try* to explain to them something of what it was like, something I had never experienced before, and likely something they hadn't either. It was all new territory.

I hadn't brought up my visit to another dimension to anyone yet because they had their own things to deal with every day. I didn't think they needed to listen to me explain something I couldn't yet put into words myself. Besides, that wasn't the first time I had approached dying. It occurred to me that I seemed to be inching closer to death every time I had another near-fatal encounter with it.

I leaned back in my chair and folded my hands behind my head. I closed my eyes to block out distractions and silently counted with my fingers the number of times I'd had a serious brush with death in my sixty-three years but survived.

Five. Not including the one that happened two weeks before at the fitness center.

The first time was at a summer camp with several grade school classmates while in my early teens. I almost drowned. Had I not been able to grasp a person's arm who reached out to me, I would have been towed under by the churning water. The second involved my older brother and, although I wasn't present at the time of his accident, I was *supposed* to be in the car with him that night when he hit a bridge railing that impaled the passenger side where I would have been sitting. Because I wasn't there then, I was here now.

In college I worked in the kitchen of the housing unit where I lived to help serve meals in return for part of my monthly room and board. At one dinner time I had gotten a piece of meat stuck in my throat while in the kitchen with only one other person, who then slammed me on the back to knock it loose before I fell down. If he had not been present the outcome likely would have been much different. A similar thing happened while eating popcorn one evening at home when I completely blacked out after I got some stuck in my throat. I came to only after Julia had rushed over from her chair and slammed me in the middle of my back with her fist to force it out.

But the closest encounter I had with confronting the possibility of imminent death until the fitness center was when I came face-to-face with a 1,600-pound, three-year-old Holstein bull on our farm, who pinned me down in a pen. Had he been mean instead of playful, I would never have been able to retell the full story. I extricated myself without any serious physical damage, although my hurt pride at letting an animal I had raised get the better of me took longer to wear off.

Those near-collisions with life's end were probably no less or no more than anyone else's experiences in their own circumstances. I probably was lucky then, just like some said I was lucky just three weeks before.

But I wasn't sure.

Was it luck like Dr. Alan seemed to believe? Or was there more to it so that I was *moved* by some force to go to town when I partly resisted? I'd never won a lottery so if it was purely by random luck, then I had selected all the right numbers for the first time in my life. If my collapse was to happen at that precise moment, at that most opportune place, among those most trained people to help, with an ambulance so close by, *then surely more than luck was involved, wasn't it?* I thought while I looked out to the east pasture and our cattle.

When would I get an answer? Or would I ever get one? I had no idea.

I stood up from my chair and went back inside the house to take a nap.

My questions persisted and I woke up later with the same ones. Maybe the answers were simply a re-articulation in different form from what I intuitively knew already.

Then another question elbowed its way in.

What would have happened, say, if I had collapsed in our pasture earlier that morning? I immediately thought of my grandfather. There *was* a parallel between him and me so I decided to play a game of 'What If?' with myself.

I thought it probably took a long time for that young doctor to drive the eight miles to our farm to help my grandfather. Being new to the area, he probably wasn't familiar with the roads or the farm families. And it was dark. There were no all-night lights like there are today. Farm yard lights were typically left on if that family went out for the evening so there'd be light to see the farmyard when they got home. It seems counter-intuitive now but made perfect sense then because every farm family in our area did that. We could tell when a family went out for the night by looking across the fields to see whose light was on. It wouldn't be turned off until after they got home. The light Dad put on must have served as a beacon for the doctor to zero in on our farm.

What would the possible scenario have been had I stayed home that Monday morning and walked out into our pasture and collapsed there instead of going to town? I realized I most certainly would have died there because I would have been by myself.

But let's say there was a person with me who had a cell phone and got a good connection. That in itself is laughable at times in our rural area. But let's say they could place a 9-1-1 call and it connected. The dispatcher then calls for an ambulance and alerts a county police officer. Because this is a rural area, a county officer out on patrol would most likely attend to the emergency rather than one from a village or city.

Our farm is grassland and our pastures are some distance from our buildings. To reach the gate opening into the field, they would have to drive through our farm yard and then go another four hundred feet before they reached the field entrance.

The closest EMT service is eight miles from our farm. Let's say they were the first ones to respond. Volunteer EMTs who live in rural villages are often at jobs or away from the station. Once alerted they would need to drop what they were doing to go to the ambulance building which may be several blocks away or miles from where they received the call. Once an ambulance is dispatched, they would need to drive to the scene.

How much time has passed at this point?

Fifteen minutes? Twenty minutes? This still hasn't included the drive time to cover the eight miles to our farm. Add at least another ten minutes, minimum.

They may not be familiar with our rural address so likely would need to use GPS. The county police car may be patrolling dozens of miles away and could now be speeding on its way after it had been notified.

The ambulance crew would finally arrive at our farm address but would still need to locate me. Say they were given help and knew I was positioned somewhere out in the field. They first would have to open gates to get into it. Then, depending on the weather—remember this is not hard pavement, its soft ground—the fields would be difficult to navigate with a heavy-body ambulance loaded with equipment and slick wheels. Grass pastures would be better than open, newly-tilled soil, but in mid-summer or late fall, they might not be able to locate my prone body in the tall grass. They then would have to drive around to survey the entire field and search because I wouldn't have a GPS tracker attached to myself.

Now how much time had elapsed by that point? Half an hour? Forty-five minutes?

And all that time I would be lying there either alone, or if someone was with me they would likely be completely exhausted from trying to resuscitate me.

Perhaps the EMTs find me. At that point, with all the time that had elapsed, what would be the percentages of survival, or any kind of good outcome? And what about the person who may have tried to give assistance? What feelings of guilt would they experience, perhaps later thinking they *didn't do enough*?

The logistics in a rural area are significantly different and more complicated than those in urban settings. That's not to say there couldn't be positive outcomes but this would explain why it would not be a statistically high percentage. Add to this a heart attack that may have happened during the evening or in a thunderstorm, and it becomes easier to understood just how fortunate I was that my event happened when it did, where it did, and not in the middle of our pasture.

Chris had said he was glad I chose to come in for a workout rather than work on our farm that morning. At the time I didn't think much about it one way or another.

But now, looking at the earthly world spread out before me, so was I.

# Chapter Seventeen

No one handed me a form that I could fill in with my questions, and I was on my own in finding the answers.

The medical explanation was buried somewhere in front of me. A six-inch stack of printouts, graphs, timelines, pictures that I had requested from each hospital, my local EMT director, and my local police department, were piled atop my desk. They may answer some questions but I wanted an explanation that would help me understand what I saw while in another dimension, and why I felt much different inside than before the morning of October fifth.

But, finally, nothing in that heaping mound of papers and reports gave it to me.

The medical answer was pretty straightforward. I had two blockages and they had disturbed the blood flow which then triggered a disruption in my heart's rhythm. That happened in a split second, not over minutes. The instant my heart lost its natural rhythm, I collapsed. The chest compressions bought the Wellsprings staff, the EMTs, but especially me, time to get the AED set up and rolling. That it was handily available and quickly applied lessened the time my heart wasn't working. Then, several shocks later, my heart ions reorganized as if shaking themselves awake from a long nap, recognized each other, and began their exchange and danced together once more. It also helped that my brain was awake enough to remember to alert my heart that it needed to wake up and do its job too. Then my heart started beating again after everything was reset with the electrical shocks.

That was the basic technical explanation. But I wanted more. I wanted the metaphysical one because I knew it was there. Somewhere. Just waiting for me to discover and understand it. It *had to be* there, otherwise none of what happened made any sense. How could I go through all that trauma and come out almost completely unscathed and without any heart damage? If I simply had won a physical lottery, then maybe I needed to run out and buy a real ticket and hope that the same luck rubbed off on me.

I could choose any path I wanted. I could stop thinking about it completely and simply be satisfied that I had an unusual experience. I could walk away knowing that my heart had been fixed for the short duration and likely give me a few more healthy years and maybe even escape major problems for an unspecified period into the future. Or, I could grab my future by the shoulders and make the most of it. I probably could live with what I experienced and toss it aside, ignore it, dismiss it, or I could explore and try to understand it.

I felt certain there was an explanation that far exceeded the medical one of why I survived, why I looked normal even though I went through a physically traumatic event, why I recovered so quickly to leave the hospital after only four days in their care, and why there was no residual damage to my heart.

*Why?* That was my burning question.

But, deep down, did I really want to know? Maybe it would be better just to forget the whole thing, agree with Dr. Alan that I survived simply because I got lucky, accept that and get on with my life. However, the researcher within me said, no, I needed to look into it. I needed to understand it.

But first, I had to deal with life here, yet again.

Mary wasn't mentally absent from her job. I was absent from being alive in mine. I realized that only weeks after my hospital stay. My attitude of nonchalance, my seeming indifference as to whether I wanted to be alive, whether I cared to be or not, after what I had witnessed was beginning to erode her own sense of worth. It seemed that she was doing things that she didn't feel were appreciated by me. That somehow all that she went through on my behalf was for nothing if I didn't want to stick around.

Why would she care if I died, if I didn't? She could take the insurance money and start a new life. *So what?* I could think. I could die on my own and be comfortable with that. I knew what to expect. I knew what happened next after I left here again. It really wasn't that bad. In fact it was so great that I found myself often thinking about how I could get back there. Many times it felt much better than being here. At least there I didn't hurt or have to deal with daily problems.

Maybe I thought Mary didn't need me. Maybe I didn't need her. Or maybe deep down I wanted to leave again because it would be so much easier. But that was a wrong conclusion about where I was in my thought process.

I had to admit that my thoughts were pretty scrambled for weeks on end after I returned home. I couldn't remember things I had done ten minutes ago. If I was reminded, I simply shrugged as if it didn't matter. I couldn't remember people's names. I couldn't remember dates or times I was supposed to be somewhere. And that was the current stuff.

Simply put, I had a difficult time reintegrating myself into life here. My time away in the other dimension was so fresh that when I looked around and saw the mess of this world, it was all I could do to convince myself to hang on to be here just a little longer and that feeling might pass.

By then it was a month after my hospital stay and our discussions didn't extend to any significant length. Mary was tired. I was tired. Tempers flared. Mostly hers because I couldn't find my anger spot anymore, perhaps because of the blood pressure pills. I referred to them as my decompression pills. They took all the wind out of my sails. Our conversations were short. Disagreements over the slightest thing would set off a one-sided argument. We both walked away in different directions. We had been handed a booklet about heart surgery recovery, and how to deal with a post-hospital stay. But for me, there wasn't anything that touched on a post-cardiac death and how to deal with the feelings one would have from experiencing another dimension.

No one had written any chapter about that.

A long, long time ago we had promised that we'd never go to bed angry with one another. That promise seemed buried deep in the past during those weeks. I wouldn't be able to find it without a metal detector. There we were, striking back at each other over things we hadn't caused, with words sometimes laced in sarcasm or shot as arrows that caused the most pain. And for what purpose? To one-up the other? To salve our hurt pride?

I'm sure my parents had disagreements but I didn't recall it ever being in front of us as kids. Maybe they did and I just didn't remember it, or didn't want to, or them in that way.

I was pulled up short one time by Marcus and Julia after I had a loud disagreement with Mary when they were young. They demanded we stop. Stop It! Stop It! Stop It! And they made sure we apologized and gave each other a hug before they let us off the hook. It was a humbling experience having one's children being referees and the only adults in the room at that moment.

Now we were without our referees to send us to our corners. *Maybe Mary could live without me.* I thought.

I wondered. Maybe we could walk away and be comfortable with that.

I then realized that it might be a subtle form of arrogance in my having been gifted with an extraordinary experience and it was projecting something of a *holier than thou* attitude that was never intended. I'd been there, you hadn't. I knew, you didn't. All while she'd been trying to hold our lives together financially and professionally.

I knew I was in a fog most of the time but I needed to try to explain my side of it. Not only for peace in our household but to explore out loud why I was still there.

So how do I explain it when I still didn't have answers? But I needed to try.

I asked Mary to sit. It was Saturday morning. Mornings were best before the rest of the day's challenges presented themselves. It was a cool morning but we headed to the porch and settled into two of the tan-colored, metal patio chairs that surround a small round table. Mary turned up the portable heater to take the chill out.

I started by saying that maybe none of this had been easy for her.

Mary rolled her eyes to say, *Oh, really,* even though she didn't say it out loud.

I said it wasn't a competition. I was trying to find some connection with her. If she wanted it.

"Should I leave?" I said it point blank. I was tired of euphemisms and tip-toeing around everywhere I went in the house or in our conversations.

"Why?" was her response. I took it as a positive that she didn't take time to think about it.

I said because she was always upset.

"Wouldn't you be?" she asked, facing me straight on.

"Ok, maybe I could understand her anger and frustration a little bit. But what was I supposed to do about?"

I said that if I could change it I would. I knew I looked like I was just sitting around all day. That was frustrating for me too. I would do more if I could, but I couldn't.

Finally she said, "I know."

Any upbeat assessment of one's survival needs to be tempered by the reality of what is experienced by the rest of the family. Those who witness a stroke, a heart attack, a sudden cardiac death, or other physical impairment of a family member are likely often the ones left with the memories of that traumatic scene while the person to whom it happened may have no recollection of it at all.

Like me. Mary mentioned that.

"It's been an on-going thing. I'll mention something that happened because I want to talk about it or the name of a person who helped and you don't remember."

But she recalled it clearly.

"That's been hard. Because you're completely oblivious to a lot of what the rest of us went through emotionally, or what we were experiencing because it wasn't something you remember."

Like when I didn't recall being in the ER when Julia and Victor came in.

"You don't remember the strained look on their faces when

they saw you," Mary said. "But I do! I still can see their pained looks. You didn't hear their concerns but I did! Because you didn't remember then and you don't now."

"How could I know?" I asked.

"I'm not saying it's your fault. But our pain was real too. Even if we didn't show it or didn't want to."

Collateral damage.

"Everyone in the ER was focused on you, which is what they're trained to do. But there wasn't anything for us. We could only watch. We were helpless to do anything. Do you have any idea what that's like?"

That feeling hadn't gone away for her either.

"It may be easy for you to think nothing much happened because you can't remember it. Even today. But it's still very real to me."

There was a l-o-o-o-o-o-n-g silence.

I said I'm sorry. I never meant it to happen.

"But it was better than somewhere else," she finally replied.

*That's an opening.* I thought.

"Ok. Remember your appendectomy?" I said.

I said I had a call on our answering machine and she had asked me to come to the hospital. I had just gotten home from a four-hour drive for my work. I ended up taking a taxi to get to the hospital near where we lived in Minneapolis so I could retrieve her car. She had left the keys in it in the parking lot. I paid the driver, found the car, grabbed the keys, locked the door, and went in to try to find her. Then when she got home, I gave her that tinkley bell and she drove me crazy for the next two days with it, as if I was employed as her personal butler. Even the cat expected to be catered to on her bed!

We both had now reached the absurd self-flagellation, self-pity plateau that had been building over the past month. How do we get down off the top of that mountain?

It happened in that instant. It was when I realized I wanted her more than I wanted myself. I could live with myself in Eternity. I had seen that. But I *couldn't* live without her in this dimension, not in this life, as long as I was here. And it appeared that I was going to be here for some time yet.

I stepped back from the edge of that chasm. My pride dissolved and I leaned over and kissed her as the only woman who mattered to me.

I had received an answer I didn't know I needed to ask.

Maybe now I had enough time to find the rest.

# Chapter Eighteen

---

Before I left the St. Mary's Hospital Cardiac Care Unit on Thursday afternoon, two nurses walked into my room carrying bulging packets and folders. I was to be prepped for my post-hospital/surgery/cardiac collapse life before I could be discharged. A sheet with my new and specially constructed diet was pulled from one packet and handed to me. The discussion that followed highlighted what I needed to consider after I got home. Every line was gone over as they checked to ask if I understood what was just explained. Then a second folder that contained the list of medications, their dosages, times to be taken, and various other directives I couldn't remember two minutes later was discussed. Mary diligently took notes and asked a few questions for clarification—more hers than mine—and when they were satisfied that at least one of us understood what they were explaining, they moved on.

"Lastly," one said, "You are also scheduled for a cardiovascular rehabilitation program at your local hospital."

*This was not optional*, they emphasized. I was told there was no wiggle room for discussion on that point. Although once I had completed my rehab, I could continue on a fitness program or stop. That was my choice but they hoped I would continue with some exercises.

Their directive was part of the insurance coverage to decrease my risk of collapsing again. I was to report to my hospital's second floor rehab room in two weeks. They handed me two packets and then I was officially released after signing papers saying that I accepted their discharge.

*Why wouldn't I sign it?* I thought as I shakily wrote out my name on the form.

Our local hospital overlooked part of the Wisconsin River Valley, and the twin villages of Sauk City and Prairie du Sac spread out along the river bank for three miles. It was constructed in a beautiful setting with an exterior that felt like a scene depicted in a Frank Lloyd Wright prairie post card. The campus is surrounded by tall prairie grasses, trees, and there was a lot of open space between the building and the nearby highways. Tall pine trees, planted long ago, buffered the noise from the busy state highway on the west so that when standing in the parking lot, only low and muffled traffic sounds could be heard.

That new site had shifted from the downtown old community hospital, where my dad had died, and was constructed in uninhabited space that allowed for a major expansion in the number of available rooms, each with state-of-the-art equipment, and for a gigantic parking lot. Mary had taken the open house tour several years before and thought she'd like the new spacious birthing room, but I hoped her thinking was only as a *grandparent.*

The rehabilitation wing I was sent to had two floors. Mary went with me on my first visit to watch. We took the elevator up from the front entrance hallway, then turned left after we stepped out. We walked down a long carpeted corridor to find the room where I'd been assigned to appear for my first session. No one else was in the hallway and the sounds of our footsteps bounced off the walls and ceiling as we walked. We found the room number, pulled open the heavy door and stepped in, only to be surprised by whom I saw.

Laurie greeted us with a big, bright smile. Her light hair framed her freckled, beaming face from behind the reception desk.

"You look better than the last time I saw you," she joked. She had been working at the fitness center's reception counter when I collapsed and had helped move people out of the way. She introduced herself to Mary, who had never met her.

I said it was good to see her again. She was a familiar face from my recent past. We had usually exchanged greetings and briefly chatted before I entered the old fitness room, and now she directed me to the rehab room.

"Through there," she turned and pointed to a wood-framed glass door. "Turn right, then straight to the room. You'll see others in there for their session. They'll be waiting for you."

Julie and Marnie were my therapists. They welcomed me as if I was a long-lost friend even though I had never met either of them before. I quickly glanced around the square room where equipment was already in use. Julie said to follow her as she headed to the men's small changing room while Mary took a chair next to their desks at the front. Julie handed me a t-shirt with the hospital's logo imprinted on the front and said I could work out in street clothes or I could use my gym outfit.

"Either works for us," she said.

I was handed a card printed with instructions on where to place the patches she pulled from a drawer under the counter. I would be putting five round patches the size of silver dollars with a peel-off, self-adhesive strip onto my front torso for every session. No one had bothered to tell me before I came in that I needed to shave parts of my chest. I mentioned this to Julie but she only smiled and shrugged her shoulders, and then pointed to the spots where I attach them to my skin. I could use the card if I forgot.

At first this seemed too much like what happened in the fitness center. No one bothered or had time to shave my chest before they had attached the AED patches. When they pulled them off later in the hospital, they also ripped a clump of hair. I was about to be subjected to that medieval torture again.

I placed the five sticky patches on my upper chest, just below my clavicle, on my rib cage and on my abdomen in the designated spots.

"These patches will stay on during your entire session. Each time you'll put on new ones," Julie said. "I will be able to monitor your condition while you're exercising."

She handed me a monitor pack that was as large as my hand. Five different colored wires dangled from the bottom of it but drooped like wilted flowers when I turned it upside down and slipped it into my t-shirt pocket. Each color corresponded to a specific site shown on the laminated card. Like a treasure map. The monitor wouldn't work if any wire was attached to the wrong patch. That portable unit freed me from any need for monitors on the stationary machines and transmitted signals to their desk computers. My heart rate and blood pressure would be constantly monitored while I exercised.

We were ready to walk into the rehab room that was located twenty steps from where I changed my clothes. I trailed behind Julie as she led the way into where several rehabbers were already puffing their way to the end of their individual session.

Julie began with the equipment and quickly ran through those I'd be using, how much time I'd spend on each one, the maximum stress level I was allowed with each, and the speeds I could reach on the bike or treadmill.

*That's a lot to ask of a first-timer*, I thought.

"You're scheduled for thirty-five sessions," she explained. If I progressed to a level they believed was safe to release me, I'd be finished. Julie said they didn't want me to exercise outside of this program except for light walking.

"This is still a critical period for you," she added. "We want you to do your strengthening under our supervision."

It wasn't exactly a drill sergeants' command but it was darn close. Although I towered over her small frame, I instinctively believed she'd be capable of taking me to the mat with one hand if I caused any problems. So I meekly listened because I knew I wasn't able to get myself off any floor yet.

The list of don'ts got longer as I stood there. They couldn't stop me from doing what I wanted outside of this room but they hoped I'd follow their suggestions.

It was an overlapping patient program. Some who were in rehab at that moment would leave after they completed their program, while others would join the group as they entered theirs.

Most of those I encountered had had open-heart surgery. Theirs was a planned event while mine wasn't. Besides Julie and Marnie, one other person had heard that someone collapsed at the fitness center. He was surprised to find out it was me because he'd heard they didn't think I'd survive. He said it as if mentioning the latest local gossip. I simply smiled and said I was glad I could still surprise someone.

I was scheduled for forty to forty-five minutes for the first nine sessions, if I felt alright. The first session barely lasted twenty minutes before I had to stop. My vital signs looked fine, but they said I looked strained and released me for the day.

After watching my session, Mary had a different take on it. She sat quietly through it and watched every move I made like a hall monitor. She took notes to discuss with them later while I changed.

*This is going to be a long road back*, I said to myself while sitting on the bench in the changing room.

As we walked outside, snow covered the ground. The weather was cold. I was freezing as I cooled down from my abbreviated workout and headed to our car in the front parking lot. I assured Mary I was fine to drive but she got into the driver's seat before I had a chance.

I was miserable during the drive home. And depressed with it all. *I'll never get back to normal*, I thought. That was the first time I acknowledged to myself that what happened to me at the fitness center was of greater impact than I would ever have admitted before. I no longer could feign ignorance at my condition.

My second session was the next afternoon and it was even shorter than the first. Two consecutive days of exercise and I was exhausted. I wasn't in any condition to continue. *Maybe I never will be.* I could barely dress in the locker room.

"The next time you're here we'll restructure your visits," Julie said with a sympathetic tone before I left. She was concerned that I'd already taken on too much, too soon.

*I have to restructure my life too. Especially on our farm*, I thought as I drove home alone with the heater cranked high and at full blast. I didn't have any energy to perform even the simplest work outside. *I still had a hay bale to put out for the cattle*, I remembered. And Mary wasn't around to monitor me. I really was on my own. I supposed I would soon find out if I could walk-the-walk about handling things by myself, rather than just talk-the-talk about it.

After I arrived home, I dressed for the outside cold, started up the skidloader, and got the hay bale placed into the feeder without any trouble. But I was in bed early by the time Mary got home late that night. The next morning she asked and I explained what happened. She nodded in understanding and said it was good that I had a few days to rest before the next session.

When I went in for it at the start of the next week, Julie and Marnie presented their new plan.

"We're going to stretch out your visits over a longer time," Julie explained. She was reading the sheet in her hand while I sat across from her in the glassed office overlooking the rehab room. After watching how I had struggled during the first two sessions, they both felt I would benefit from a longer time frame to fulfill my rehab program. Besides, she said, by stretching it out over a longer period it would be better for my recovery than using up all my sessions too soon and before they would be comfortable with sending me out on my own.

With an air of support she added, "We know it's hard the first couple of times. But it will get better. We know your heart can take it because we can see the numbers."

They saw the numbers but they didn't feel my body like I did. I bit my lip from saying it as she explained that the next month would consist of twice-weekly sessions, not three. Then they'd reassess my program once again.

Julie cautioned me at my beginning session not to exceed a workout heart rate over one hundred twenty beats per minute. "At any time," she said.

After two weeks in, I was frustrated by my lack of progress. It seemed that none of what I had done to that point made any difference in how I felt. I didn't have any energy. I was always tired. It was really frustrating to see no progress.

So one afternoon I decided to go for broke just to see what

might happen. I pushed my work on the stepping machine to reach one hundred forty.

Julie instantly jumped up.

"Please slow down!" she yelled.

An alert had flashed on her screen that I exceeded their target level.

She raced over to take my pulse.

"Please don't do that again," she said nervously. That was the sternest rebuke I had received. Everyone in the room looked over at us, alerted by her loud command.

In my defense, if I had one, I figured I would push myself to see how it felt to get up to that level. If I collapsed again, it would be better to do it there at the hospital rather than somewhere else. Besides, it would give them a reason to use the gurney that was always standing empty in the corner.

"You haven't reached a point where it's safe to go that fast yet," she said after she was sure I was alright. She just might have thrown me to the mat that time if the look on her face was anything to go by.

*I can't even cheat at my age*, I thought.

But eventually over the following three weeks—little steps by microscopic little steps—to my surprise, I began to build up my strength and stamina again. But every session seemed like a mountain to climb. I was beginning to understand how cyclists must feel while racing in the Tour de France with everything seeming to appear all uphill, all the time. It certainly did to me in that little room. And I still had a long way to the top.

Each rehab session ended with a five minute cool down by walking around on the carpeted track that circled the perimeter of the room. My blood pressure was checked against what it measured before I started and she noticed both readings were low each time but didn't offer any further comment. I passed it off as a likely effect from the medications because I said I didn't feel I had been at rehab long enough to make any difference. But Julie said, no, it was a positive sign that my heart rate recovery after exercising was now quicker. She said that meant my heart was in better shape than they had thought. That was the first sign that I might actually recover. At least at some point.

My final session was at the beginning of March. Before I left their care, I was given a certificate for completing their rehab program. I took that to mean I had graduated without collapsing on their watch.

During the eight weeks I attended rehab, the number at any one session had varied from three to six men and women. Except for one person when I started, I was the youngest who passed through the room during my stay. The patients had turned over when I left the rehab program. There was a completely new set from when I had started. The earlier ones had moved on while new patients arrived. And someone else would take my place.

Julie and Marnie asked me to return in two months for a final follow-up and to recheck my vital signs while I exercised there one last time.

As I walked out the rehab room, down the hall to the stairs, and finally out the front door into the chilly afternoon air, I was on my own again. I was stepping into uncharted territory. On my drive home, I calculated that I hadn't been out from under the medical support umbrella since I left the hospital in October.

*Would I be ok?* I wondered. *Or would I be back here again in a month or two? Or never?*

I was given a three-month membership at the Wellspring

Center. I could continue my exercises there or I could stop. There was no one to tell me what I should do. It was my choice.

It was obvious to me. I returned to the Wellspring Center at the beginning of April. As I opened the door and headed for the locker room below, it *seemed* I was there only a short time ago.

When I returned up the stairs and entered the fitness room, it *felt* like it was in another lifetime.

# Chapter Nineteen

I was ready for a cleanout.

At first the feeling surprised me because I'd been a collector most of my life.

I started young with stamps because they were readily available. And I could buy new sets from our rural mail carrier if I happened to catch him when he stopped at our box along the country roadside or if I left a note in the box with coins to cover the cost of the latest issue. When I started the stamps were three-centers and I eventually got to first-day covers until I stopped collecting when I reached high school and sports became my interest.

I collected baseball cards at the same time. Each pack of tightly wrapped cards contained five player cards plus a flat, rectangular stick of pink bubble gum. None of us who collected cards could chew that much gum without rotting our teeth, so mine often got tossed or fed to my dad's pigs, which seemed like the sweet taste as they quickly snarfed them down. I collected baseball memorabilia that included score cards, Milwaukee Braves yearbooks, baseball statistics of all the former and current players, and autographs from former players whose addresses I could locate. In my youthful naiveté, I would send a letter to a former or current player requesting his autograph and enclosed self-addressed, stamped envelope so they could return it. How was I to know that Brookfield, the Milwaukee home of Hank Aaron, was too big for the post office to find him when I simply addressed it with his name and city, not having his home street address. I figured everyone must know where Hank Aaron lived! I was sorely disappointed when my envelope returned to me marked as undeliverable.

I also had a coin collection that was largely made up of pennies, nickels, and dimes, with an occasional quarter tossed in. On a pre-teenager's farm earnings in the late 1950s that was all I could afford to collect. Pocket change. I checked my parent's wallets every time they returned from shopping. My coins weren't kept for their future investment value, I collected them simply because I enjoyed it. I strove to fill all the empty coin holes one-by-one in my cardboard holders.

Those two collections sat in boxes that moved every time I did. They went with me to Minneapolis when I moved with Mary after we got married. They moved back with us in 1992 when we returned to the farm. They moved around so many times in our attic during the next two and a half decades that I thought they'd qualify for travel reward miles.

The time had finally come to move them on. After my hospital stay, I no longer had feelings of attachment to any of the things I had collected. Any meaning they had for me was completely gone. It had dissipated like the fog. They were of another time. I realized more than ever that I wasn't going to take any of my things with me after I left again, so I decided to let them go. Mary said she didn't want any of the things I had spent years collecting. Neither did Marcus nor Julia after I asked them.

Well, if they didn't want my stuff then what would happen to it if I wasn't alive? Likely it would get tossed onto a burn pile. I figured it was time to do something about my collections while I still could. I wasn't preparing to die again, it was the recognition that *I* could dispose of them as *I* saw fit. I wouldn't have to rely on the discretion of anyone else, or Mary as my executor, to find a home for my things, which, if you think about it, was going to happen sometime in the future regardless. I could postpone it but the inevitable would happen anyway. Plus, this way I would have total control over what I kept or disposed of in order to down-size and I could live with that. It was my choice.

I sold all my baseball cards and memorabilia, along with the autographs of famous major league players, all long-since dead. It was time for someone else to enjoy them rather than sitting closed up in a box, lost to the world. Besides, that was their pur-pose—to be looked at and handled. Why would I want to hide the stuff away for some future day that may never come? I had enjoyed having them for decades but I hadn't looked at them in years. What was the point in having a collection of anything if I stored it away, never to be seen by anyone else? Simply to say they were "mine" at that point seemed totally irrelevant. It now was all transitory to me.

I realized that that feeling was one of the first three things that changed after I left the hospital: my gratitude to still be alive; my desire to connect again with family and long-lost friends; and the sense that the things I owned had less importance to me than they did the day before I collapsed. It was like releasing the air from a balloon. There was nothing inside me anymore to support what I had collected. It wasn't that I had to let them go, I chose to. I simply lost my desire for collecting anything.

Besides, those things were only luggage that wouldn't fly on the same plane with me. Once I understood that new reaction to my stuff, I released myself from all the expectations I had for them in my future. And, instantly, they no longer had a grip on me. I wasn't tethered to my possessions any longer because I didn't have to invest myself in them like I did before. What would I miss if I let them go?

I found that I missed absolutely nothing.

After that I was determined to find my plastic storage tubs. I dragged three large ones from a back section in our one-hundred-fifty-year-old granary that stood below our house. The wind whipped through the doorway as I dragged them towards the front steps. The interior smelled of ancient oats and barley, crops that were raised at one time on our farm, but not for the past forty years. After Marcus took it upon himself to spray paint the once-weathered exterior boards red, to give it the rustic, traditional Wisconsin farm building look it originally had, it appeared again as an old-fashioned granary from the outside, and it still smelled like one inside.

The three wide-board partitioned bins that had been built along each side of the center alley were long-since empty of grain that was stored after harvest for feed or to market for cash. They now served as storage areas for our kid's early bikes, old furniture, and other stuff I didn't want to carry up to the attic in our house.

I pulled each plastic tub out of their cloistered corners to the light of the doorway. I had shoved them in those divided sections several years before and they hadn't moved an inch since then.

It was work to pull them out. *What was I saving these for?* I thought as I puffed my way to the entrance.

I plopped down on the cover of the first one to catch my breath. My cleanout began with the tossing of old drafts of manuscripts and research materials that I had used for constructing chapters in the books I wrote for a publishing company in Minneapolis. I'd written nine for them over the previous decade and each draft was dutifully stored in separate tubs. Then I remembered a one-time fleeting fantasy that maybe, just maybe, when I was famous, some library would be clamoring for them to house in their collection to allow others to study how I processed my writing.

Brother. *Is that a description of self-indulgence or what?* I said to myself. Maybe it was other writer's fantasy as well. I didn't have any way to gauge that. But it was no longer mine.

I struggled to drag the other two across the thick planked wood floor. At least plastic slid over dusty wood easier than a heavy metal trunk. I hadn't told Mary of my plans and I was down there alone, so I took a break after struggling with each one. Those tubs were heavy and weren't worth dropping over for as I wiped the moisture from my forehead. It would be ironic to rid myself of me while trying to rid myself of them.

I had parked the skidloader outside the door and raised the bucket to the level of the granary floor that was thirty inches above the lawn. I could slide those twenty-gallon tubs without having to lift them into the bucket. Then I'd take them up to our garage so I could sit and go through each one. There was at least one hundred fifty pounds of papers, books, magazines, and folders in each tub to sift through. I wondered how many trees had been sacrificed to produce the paper in them which I would later incinerate.

By the time I finished wading through all three tubs, one folder remained with three single sheets stuck into it. Why was I thinking of hanging on to any of it? The joke was on me.

I came to writing as a career later in life than many, not having anything professionally published until I was in my early 30s.

I could look back and see where it really started. It was eighth grade and Mrs. Perry. She made me feel that I had something to say.

Because she made me believe it, that's all it took. I won one writing competition in high school and worked as sports writer on the school's weekly newspaper. In college I wrote short stories for my amusement and shared them with friends because I never felt they were good enough to send to an editor. Mrs. Perry was probably frowning, shaking her head and folding her arms under her ample chest like she always did when she was disappointed in someone's lackluster efforts.

I wrote poetry, some of it decent even by my standards today, in a vain attempt to dazzle women of my acquaintance, including Mary, although I worked at it for something to say. It apparently did when I showed her one poem on our first date. She said she'd never forgotten it, although I hadn't the faintest idea where I finally put it. She said it captured her heart although it would be years after college before our lives finally intertwined.

I graduated from college after the tumultuous years of the late-60s, early '70s, and returned to my dad's farm because it grounded me, and it was the only thing in the world that made sense to me at the time. Soil, crops, and animals are as basic as life gets. It was mental survival and it breathed life back into me. The farm had saved me.

There I could retreat within myself. I could be alone out in the field. No one to bother me. I didn't need to go anywhere. This seemed to confuse my dad at times because he would occasionally ask during the summer if I was ever going out. I said I was fine and he left it at that, often walking away shaking his head at not being able to comprehend his son, the UW-Madison graduate.

I didn't need anyone or anything. I was completely comfortable with myself as my only companion. Perhaps that became embedded within me and would resurface in later years. Oh,

I could go out and socialize with the best of them, but I would choose it on my own terms. I was not unhappy and I didn't feel myself superior to anyone else for my seeming reticence. But I found I was the best company I could find at that time. Or, as one of my buddies once said when we talked about my infrequent dating agenda, "Well, at least then you wouldn't make someone else unhappy." Point taken.

My first published article appeared the summer after I graduated. It was an interview with an internationally known dairy magazine editor at Fort Atkinson, Wisconsin, and appeared in the quarterly magazine published by the national agriculture fraternity whose Madison chapter I had joined my first freshman semester.

During my college years, I had met Mary for the first time. We didn't have any classes together but I would run into her at college parties. When I took two semesters off mid-way through my four years, she graduated a year ahead and we went separate ways. We lost touch. She got married. I returned home. Life went on.

Mary and her husband eventually settled in my home town as a convenient access to both their jobs. I would stop in occasionally. She tried numerous times to fix me up with her single friends but none of them worked out. I really wasn't interested.

Eventually she and her husband separated but Mary continued to live in their house and continued her attempt at match-making for me with no success.

By that time I was getting an article published in a monthly national dairy breed magazine whenever I pitched an idea. Ironically, it was Mary who first introduced me to the owner and publisher.

I knew Mary was an excellent editor. Our interest in purebred dairy cattle, especially black and white Holsteins, was mutual.

She grew up on a dairy farm near Eau Claire where her parents raised purebred Holsteins like my parents did. Before sending in my manuscript, I would ask Mary to proof-read and edit it. And so it went.

Until.

I could pinpoint the moment when the scales that covered my eyes fell and I saw Mary for the first time outside our friendship. In that instant, I thought there might be a future for us together. It was a moment quite like the one I had thirty years later when I awoke in the hospital after being dead and saw everything in a completely new light.

After our marriage, Mary continued to support my writing while she focused on her business career, later starting her own. She sent me off to writing classes, encouraged me to submit pieces to magazines, even *The New Yorker*. She thought I needed to reach for the big leagues.

That was echoes of Mrs. Perry.

Then came Marcus. Two years later we moved back to my family farm from Minneapolis, where I had moved six years earlier for Mary's job after our marriage. Our move back to the farm was intentional so that we could raise Marcus in an open theatre. We both instinctively knew that he needed more space and the small lawn we had in a big city would never hold him. We didn't want to stifle his enormous energy even if we couldn't keep up with him. Neither of us wanted to stuff his life into the small box of a backyard we had, nor did we want him running in the streets. We'd have more room in our farmyard than he could ever have dreamed of having out the back door of our rented ranch-style house.

Writing took a backseat to milking cows, plowing fields,

making hay, fixing farm equipment, all while I worked with my brother again. We had semi-separated after I moved to Minneapolis but I returned to help with field work or clean out calf pens when I could.

Julia came along a year after we returned and with two extremely active children, farm work, and milking cows, my writing life was put on hold for several years. I had no regrets because I was able to watch them grow up and I got to do the normal things parents of young children did as it went along. Doctor visits. Dental visits and braces that almost broke the bank. Parent-Teacher conferences. School band concerts. Piano and ice skating lessons. 4-H meetings and Future Farmers of America (FFA) functions for both. Exhibiting their dairy heifers at the county and state fairs. Dance recitals. Being a comforting lap during crying sessions and disappointments. Celebrating and shouting during the accomplishments. Those were things I remembered and cherished the most. Not editor deadlines.

The flames crackled as I kept tossing papers onto the pile. The fire flared as I watched the printed words that no one would ever read disintegrate within the flames, bidding me farewell. I had no regrets watching that inferno consume it all.

I may not have written much on paper during those years. But our kids wrote a lot on my heart that I could effortlessly tote with me every day.

And that means much, much more to me.

# Chapter Twenty

It turned a New Year. In more than one sense. The calendar flipped and what had been was now only a reflection. I was still alive but I was much different inside from what I had been two months before.

My experience in another dimension wasn't stuck in the past as a static memory, somehow fixed to a particular moment. It walked with me every day, right *beside* me, right *inside* me, it *interblended* with me. I couldn't escape it if I had wanted to. Nor did I because it became like walking with a pleasant friend as a constant companion.

My body parts were slowly waking up to what they used to do, although some seemed to lag behind others in a disjointed effort to move forward. My legs would work but the rest of me wanted to lie down.

It was analogous to training two new work horses to pull together in a synchronized rhythm. Their stomping impatience at getting started. Their sudden shifts sideways. Then their stubborn reluctance to move at all. Then their out-of-step jerks forward as if they had lost count of the beat with their feet as each tried either to take the lead or let the other do the heavy pulling.

One of my body parts seemed to try to get ahead of the others, only to decide it wasn't worth the effort and let the rest of my body steam on ahead without it. When my body was ready to go, my head spun around and I'd get dizzy. I'd drop things that my mind wanted to use but my hands wouldn't obey. I'd forget where I set stuff. I couldn't remember names but wanted to talk with people. My eyes could see but making sense of the sentences on a page or doing a crossword puzzle often eluded my ability to think of any words or their meanings. It was a rare morning when most everything seemed to be working in a synchronic effort. It was then I felt one of the most vivid sensations and found I had escaped from the cocoon of my former inner consciousness a changed person.

Whatever my movements had been in the hours, the days, the weeks, the months, and even the years before October fifth, I finally knew for certain that all of my actions over that time had been deftly aligning to converge at that precise location, at that precise time, surrounded by people who could help me. I could label it as luck, if I chose, but I don't. Because I now *knew* deep inside that those threads of disparate activities had been interweaving through time and were being slowly brought together until they all melded together in that one precise moment at the fitness center when I collapsed.

In that microscopic instant of convergence I flowed into the prism of Time and Space, and after passing through, I exploded out the other side and emerged into a new field of consciousness about myself.

Perhaps the physical world—the objects, the forms, the ways we navigate and engage with others, the stars in the sky—hadn't changed for anyone else in that moment, but my view of it and my relationship to everything around me did.

What I saw after that was a world colored much differently. It was painted with a brush that had been immersed in and saturated with a vision from beyond this dimension of reality that I could never have sketched upon my mind's canvas without having seen or experienced it. It simply would have been impossible for me to conjure or invent such a composition on my own.

I had help.

With the new year—my new life—the colors before me became different when I walked across the grass of our pastures, or saw the trees in our backyard, stood amongst others, or observed our cattle. They were all the same physical forms as two months before but inherently different in how I now experienced them. Shooting through that metaphysical prism was a demarcation point of *before* and *after* for me.

During the following months, I experienced numerous mental flashes that replayed what I had witnessed in another dimension. They continually validated my experience to me. It was like watching the daily action around me with subliminal images flicking before me when I looked at anything.

I knew I wasn't being delusional because I was fully awake when they happened. If I saw a boat on the Wisconsin River as I drove across the bridge to Madison, I could get a flash of the raft I had been in. If I looked at the bright sun, before me appeared the energetic waves coming from Source. If I stared up into the dark sky at night from our farm lawn to watch the stars sparkle, a flash of Eternity came to me again as I looked into its great distance. I wasn't hallucinating. Those were real images because I could touch myself and I knew I was still alive in that moment.

Any apprehension I had about how long I have here on this earth was no longer of great concern to me. Did I want to check out again tomorrow? The larger part of me most often said no, I'd like to experience another day with Mary and my family. I'd like to stay because of the pleasure they gave me. I didn't feel the need to stay because I had ownership of anything, although those things may be useful to me while I continued to exist here for some time yet.

But, the other part of me said that if I go, it's really pretty magnificent.

So I found myself in a dilemma at the beginning of the new year. To go. To stay. It really didn't matter in the long range of time because, eventually, at some finite point in my future, I will leave my body again. For good.

I'm not being cavalier about life. It's wonderful. It's precious. It's a gift from Source. It's all we have while we exist in this dense form. To simply want to chuck it all away would be rather silly of me. And wholly unnecessary.

The new year brought with it a much deeper understanding and acceptance that this body I inhabit is only a fragile, temporary location for the inner me that is truly wondrous in its own way.

I now understand that my whole body is greater than the sum of its parts. It is more than four limbs, some two hundred bones, three pounds of brain matter, one hundred billion brain neurons or nerve cells, a gallon and a half of blood, fluids, and lots of other bits.

There is also *something else*. Take away that *something else*—my spirit, my soul, my consciousness, my life force, call it what you like—and I'd still be left with all the parts I started with but not the *essence* that provided the spark, the flame, the ignition of my life.

That life essence is what makes me—makes all of us—greater than the sum of my parts. All the body parts after one's death could be added up and still come up short because that essence not included in the total sum is that part that returned to Source like mine did. While I was lying dead on the fitness floor, I had all the same body pieces I started with that morning but the life essence that had kept me alive was missing because it had left. When I returned to being alive that essence had reentered my lifeless body.

Since the body form I have is a product of creation from the physical dynamics that exist in this plane—parts from two human parent bodies that made a third—where then does this *life essence* originate since it's clearly a part of me?

From what I experienced, I saw it is created from what we may perceive as the ethers of the spirit world, or the spirit consciousness that exists. I have existed for as long as the Source because I carry that infinite DNA within me, just as everyone else, whether I experience it as human or an energetic consciousness. It is the materialization of my eternal spirit into a human form that allows me to be in union with the Source and also an extension of it in this dimension. I now know that this component of the soul is in vibrational accord with its echo that exists in other dimensions and listens for its reverberation with anticipation. I know I will have an eternity to explore other dimensions and other worlds, and to reframe myself an infinite number of times. And I have been doing this forever already.

Even if my human mind might not comprehend it or doesn't wish to accept it as so, it still exists there, and will, when it is experienced again after leaving my human form here entirely.

If I dismissed my claim that I am part of this dynamic, then I would be listening to and agreeing with those who doubt it can exist, or those who try to convince me or others that one cannot possess it here, in this existence.

I'm an eternal visitor in an interim human body suit that is the vehicle which allows my spirit to experience this dense level of vibration just as others condense into their physical forms that surround and engage with us—like the person standing next to me at the bus stop, or the grocery store, or movie theatre ticket line, or soup kitchen, or lying on the street, homeless—each who are experiencing it in their own way.

When I leave again, I will still exist as the full essence of my truest self. My body is simply the framework that allows the inner me—the spirit me, the essence me, the eternal me—to maneuver within and participate with this physical world. At the center of this innermost part of my being is the core of who *I am* and what I *will always be*. The self-identification I have taken as a body called Philip is only part of my total essence. And the same is true for everyone else.

This part of me never changes. While the body packaging it's enclosed within may age, may feel pain, may love, may help, or may lift others, it will eventually die. That part of me which exists from beyond this plane cannot be destroyed by anyone or by myself. It will reconfigure itself in infinite ways as I journey through Eternity.

How can I *not* think this after seeing the infinite dimensions that exist? What exists within those dimensions was there long before I arrived in this human form and will exist long after I leave here again.

The significant realization for me at that moment was that I was still *alive*. Not in the sense that we understand it here on this breathing level, but I could feel I existed in another dimension and really had not *died*. I did not dissolve into nothingness. I hadn't disintegrated. I was not erased from existence.

It was an experience beyond an intellectual encounter. My intellect on a human level could not comprehend it until I experienced it in a vibrational or spiritual state first. Once experienced at that level, I can now recall it and understand it intellectually in ways I couldn't before.

I now can understand how I could experience this many times over in many other dimensions in my infinite past as I stand before my infinite future. And not be unafraid of either. It was a dynamic prism shift.

That is what felt so different from what I thought before the new year arrived.

So I'm on a journey, just like everyone else here. A finite journey that I now know will eventually lead me to those infinite dimensions that exist beyond my earth-bound comprehension but which I saw when in my spirit essence.

But for now, I wait. And I want to understand the meaning of what I've encountered so far. It was a need that kept prodding me as if it was an answer that wanted me to find it so that it could reveal itself.

I realized that what I remembered from my encounter with Source was only a small fraction of my full experience there. I understand that it was so vast that I couldn't possibly retain it all because my human brain isn't equipped with that kind of capacity. But my energetic consciousness understood everything it saw and was capable to access. It could comprehend the unlimited knowledge of Infinity because it was a part of it.

If I liken my brain's capacity to a computer's, I can explain this easier. Let's say I have a four gigabyte storage capacity in my brain and suddenly I experience something that required a thousand gigabytes of data to be *instantly* crammed into it. What would happen? I suspect my brain would crash. Frying my brain's internal circuitry beyond recovery wouldn't be of use to me. What human brain can possibly hold all the knowledge of the universes that exist in Infinity? That's why I believe I was given only the amount of memory from that experience that I could safely handle here without damaging my mental storage capacity when I returned.

And that meant *there was* a reason I had returned.

I had been told by the doctors that my memory would get better as my brain healed. I'm not convinced that's the full story. I believe the reason why it took my memory so long to reorganize over the two days following my collapse was more intricate: *I had been exposed to knowledge far beyond my human capacity to hold it.* And it was trying to readjust itself to that dynamic.

That was why I couldn't remember people's names when I met them again. That was why I couldn't remember conversations I had or plans I had made without writing them down. My short term recall was purposely abbreviated, and when I was told something one minute, I couldn't recall it the next. That was probably why I was frustrated with my inability to think clearly and logically at times.

It seemed to me that some portions of my brain's circuitry were intentionally turned off or amped down so I could more fully realize specific parts of my experience. It was re-forming and re-wiring the retention of my experience and allowing those new energies to emerge within my memory without them being inhibited or filtered by my past experiences here. They had been stripped clean of any interference or distortion.

If I remembered *everything* I had witnessed, I likely would never have agreed to come back, or I would find myself completely frustrated with this life.

That explained to me why my whole experience seemed surreal on a human level. Like it happened but never really happened, as my mind tried to comprehend and make sense of it in a logical way. My human logic had been supplanted by a higher energy beyond its awareness here, and I then understood that logic couldn't explain what I had experienced because the Spirit Consciousness that I witnessed inhabited a dimension beyond any logic devised by human thought.

In simple terms, I now understood why it seemed so weird in the hospital. My *human logic* was trying to mesh with my energetic self after having been in two different dimensions at the same time, and wasn't making sense of either. And since human logic doesn't exist in that dimension, my brain then couldn't make sense of the energetic panorama that my spirit self had inspected there and brought back with it because there was no way for my brain to understand what it saw. That explained why I was so confused about everything in the hospital—the place, the people, and especially time—after I finally regained my senses.

My memory retained enough bits and pieces to understand that what I experienced on another plane was real, as well as true, and allowed me to "see" the deep experience within me, even if I couldn't explain it.

I may have appeared physically unresponsive lying on the fitness room floor, but I believe my brain was still experiencing a continual flow of energy being released by those working on and around me but was storing that in a separate file, and all while I was simultaneously witnessing an out-of-body dynamic in another dimension while absorbing the energy emanating from a higher plane.

That's a lot to ask of any human memory storage system.

I now understood why my experience seemed acutely vivid and real in an energetic sense and, then later, when it seemed unreal or surreal after I was fully awake again. This was the reason that for eight hours I could talk with doctors and my family on this level but not remember any of it, and still be present in and experience a different level of existence while looking physically happy. I was oscillating between two dimensions and alternating between several energetic octaves, all at the same time.

*I had experienced a tangible link between spirit energy and human consciousness and now am fully aware of it.*

What then do I make of my journey? Of my temporary location and existence here? What of anyone else's journey who I come in contact with?

Forty, sixty or even eighty years of life may seem more than temporary. But in the full arc of the Eternity I saw, it's like a single grain of sand sitting on a vast endless beach. I now understood that and I became fascinated by it.

I used to think that I understood Time and what it meant. But now I realize that time is an illusion. It's only a marker developed along this lifeline to aid our navigation in this universe. There is nothing wrong with this but beyond our physical existence and our human-constructed dynamic to calculate it for our use, time doesn't exist. I can't create more of it. I can't delete any of it. I simply move through it from one moment to the next. Tomorrow never comes because I only exist in *this particular moment.* I can make plans for tomorrow or next week but there's no guarantee that that specific moment I plan for will arrive. I assume it will, and it often does, but I can't really be certain. So time itself as a structured equivalent is a limitation. But the infinite exceeds this limitation because it operates in a different vibration. So, if I can change my perception of time, then why couldn't I also change how I perceive myself within it?

I had no sense of time, as we use it, while I was gone from my body. None. But while I was "there" I could *feel* the *timelessness of each moment.* I distinctly sensed that I must have been there for "a long time" when, just as quickly, that became a feeling of already knowing I had been there for "centuries" in each specific moment. But the records show that I was "only" gone from my body for six minutes. Then after I was revived, I reentered my human form on the fitness room floor, and I returned to the shared agreement of the time-construct I use here, to be able to call it "a very long time."

The energetic emulsion which coated the image plate of my spirit's memory and imprinted my encounter with Eternity on it allowed my inner essence to transport it back into this dimension and see that plane of reality in my human mind. It was like bringing back a painted post card after traveling to a distant country.

*This transmutation of my energetic experience into my human memory is the alchemy through which I remember my encounter and can claim it.*

It is the echo of those tones that I still see. It is the color of the Source that I still hear. I see and hear that echo and that color which are brought back to me through the vibration of Eternity even now when I wish to reclaim my experience with it. I know the fabric of another dimension is permeable because of that alchemy.

I remembered all that. I can claim what I saw in my memory. When I claim it *as true* in my memory, I am once again standing before the Source, the Divine, because if it was a false memory, this could not happen. The energy vibration between what is true and what is not feels unmistakably different. It's like the sound of a bell that rings clear compared to an imperfect one that doesn't, and hearing and understanding that difference.

The tones I heard were the anchor to which my raft was tethered. It was the reason I didn't drift away. I had been melded with the mosaic of vibration from Source. And I felt uplifted by energetic guidance.

During the previous weeks I was home, I had been asking myself *why* this happened. Was there a deeper purpose or was this simply a random act involving me? Was I just plain lucky to be in the right place, at the right time when I collapsed like others said?

I now realized I was phrasing it the wrong way.

My question was not why it happened but rather, why didn't I stay? Why was I given that experience yet allowed to return?

*That was the answer I was really seeking*, I realized. The others were less important. And now I had been given the time to find my answers.

# Chapter Twenty-One

My questions of why I had returned challenged me at first until I realized they were only my doubts trying to assert themselves into the discussion.

Was it something I did? Something I didn't do? Was I not worthy of being there? Had I done bad things that barred me from staying? Didn't I do enough good things to warrant my acceptance? Asking those questions, however, was not a requirement for me to get an answer.

Those internal doubts served to interrogate me so they could question my memory, question my human logic, and they urged me to even question myself. They could feed on the suspicion born from any agreement I *might make* to listen to other opinions, with other agendas, rather than to trust and believe in my own experience. Those doubts were simply masks that disguised the voices of self-deceit, a cloak of shadows distorting the truth, all waiting to be released if I allowed them. But those doubts are lies, and the lies that speak the loudest have the most to hide. But it is the whispered lie that is the most dangerous—the lie with undertones that softly urges me—or us—to doubt ourselves.

I now understood that my doubts and fears could be agreed to by me *if I chose them*. If I internalized those doubts, they then would appear as if they were my creation—something deep within me that I'd made, when they were only something I had agreed to and opened the door and asked them to step inside to live within me. But I don't have to invite my doubts into my house.

I can brush them aside. I don't need them because I *know* what I had witnessed was true—is true—regardless of how other opinions may have tried to tell me it wasn't or that I was imagining it. Others may shake their heads from side to side saying no, it's not true. I will nod mine up and down and say that it is.

In the end, it is my certainty that matters to me.

I can't alter or change what exists in Eternity because that dimension has already been created and will not be affected one bit by me or my perception of it. It doesn't need me but it wants me, just as it longs to unite with each person here, and knows it eventually will regardless of my opinion while I'm here. I am a part of the whole of Infinity because I exist there already.

We generally accept the fact that there were people who lived here before us. That's our obvious history, our ancestry, our parentage. We can probably agree that there will be people who live after us—our children, grandchildren, nieces, nephews, cousins, friends, and neighbors.

Yet if we stop and think about it, we are living in Eternity right now, in this precise moment. Those who have died may have thought about some time in their future after they were gone and that they would never see it. That was their idea of Eternity. We are now living in, walking around in, driving in, what they thought was their Eternity. So in that sense we are already residing in it.

Our children, grandchildren and so on, will be living in our Eternity. One hundred years, a thousand years, a million years from now will exist in Eternal Time whether we are alive in this dimension or not. Our Eternity will be witnessed by others here while we experience it in another dimension. Even if this planet or our universe completely disappeared, Eternity would still exist.

So I understand that our concept of Eternity rests on how we place ourselves within that frame and the dynamic of Time.

I believe we compress ourselves into an experience with Time that becomes a shared agreement with others to help navigate our lives here. But we deny the truth that we can exist outside of this agreement, that we cannot experience a sense of timelessness while we inhabit a human form. Because I saw Infinity during those six minutes, I experienced that sense of timelessness. And I can claim my realization of being outside of linear time, as we understand it here, because of that.

I know the membrane of Time is permeable because I went back and forth between different dimensions. Even if I was talking, answering questions, and speaking with my family, whether in the ambulance or the emergency room, I could register no sense of my physical body or surroundings for eight hours when I passed through that membrane. It stripped away all the feelings I encountered here.

I was here but not here, fully. I was there, but no longer fully.

At that moment, as I was reintegrating with my body again, I felt myself release the amorphous state that I experienced myself as in a higher plane. During my transition back to a solid form, my energetic essence returned to re-enter my body which others recognized *as me* when I started breathing again. But they had not seen what I had been at the moment I left, nor where I had been before I came back.

Once I understood that the law of Time had been broken—which simply meant that time had no meaning there—and my place within it, I realized my entire existence here would be different. After having a true experience with the Source of All Creation *nothing* can ever be the same for me again.

It is simply not possible for me now to go back to what I was before October fifth. I cannot un-see what I saw. I cannot un-hear what I heard. I cannot un-experience what I experienced. I cannot deny the realizations and perceptions I have received that I know are true.

The sense of peace I then experienced was supported by remembering that while I was in a spirit consciousness state, I had no agenda other than to *be*. That was it. Nothing more. And that was enough. I didn't have a job to rush to, or bills to pay, or bosses to appease. I didn't have to create or develop any plans. I don't have to prove that something exists on the other side of the wall.

I can simply *BE*.

A significant realization for me was that I didn't need to "earn" my passage to another dimension. No amount of praying I could do would change that. No penance needed to be done. No money or personal sacrifice had to be offered in return. No genuflection. No prostration. Good deeds were not a requisite, although they are worthy of my time here. All was freely given to me even if I had not asked for it. There was nothing to bar me, or anyone, from returning or reuniting with Source where we are accepted as equals because we all are fashioned from the Source's love.

I finally understood that those eight hours passing into Monday evening were a time during which my spirit self was trying, *perhaps even resisting*, to reintegrate itself with my human form and then having difficulty readjusting to this reality once it did. My body had restarted and like the machine that it was programmed for—to breathe, to talk, to answer questions, to joke—it did all that without needing to be fully aware that it was actually performing its required functions.

I had one foot here in this plane and one foot still lodged in another, both at the same time. I was in co-residence with two dimensions, straddling them like an energetic tug-of-war. I understood that this was why nothing made sense to me for a long time later because I wasn't fully here either.

*Why wouldn't this be so?* I asked myself.

Having returned to the higher plane it once resided in and experiencing eternity again, why would my spirit self wish to come back here? It was returning to Source and then all of a sudden it was released and asked to return and re-enter my human form it had just left. During that abbreviated journey my spirit self passed back through that membrane which dissolves our understanding of Time and then had to realign itself with my body to become compatible again with, and conform to, our linear construct of it here.

No wonder I was confused about what time it was that Monday night.

Now I understood why it didn't make sense that I lost eight hours once I regained my awareness here. My previously agreed-to construct of time here was severed the instant I collapsed. My tether to it snapped. I was no longer tied to our time construct in any conscious way when I entered a higher dimension where there is no time, and that presence just *is*.

So, if I go back to consider that eternity already exists in this present moment and that it becomes a matter of how I relate to it and realize it, why then, couldn't I have been experiencing both dimensions of Time—our linear construct and Eternal Time—during those eight hours I couldn't remember?

Although I was beginning to understand this question better, I still didn't have my answer to why I was given the experience of another dimension in the first place. Especially now since I was aware that I wasn't going to stay there.

So I wondered, ok, if I'm allowed to encounter the Source—to stand before and see the Creator face-to-face—by passing through alternate dimensions, why then can't spirit guides in that dimension enter into our plane to abide amongst us in whatever form they choose? Or communicate with us in various platforms or through people we would not expect? Since I know the membrane of Time is permeable, why can't that be possible too? Why can't there be some back and forth transmission? Or are we so isolated in some backwater corner of the universe that they can't find us? I don't believe that to be the case.

I believe there are spirit "Guides" who surround me but don't interfere with my actions here. I believe they support me in ways I didn't fully understand at this level until I experienced them at a higher energetic plateau.

I believe the alchemy that allowed me the transmutation of my energetic experience into my human memory is available for everyone. It is not uniquely mine.

Even though I returned to my body, I had been given a pathway I can follow back. Because I have this avenue, I've found I can take this journey *any time I want* simply by thinking about it, and then I'm immediately transported back before Source. So *I know* we can slip through the portals of Time and Space and enter other dimensions or realities while still here, if we choose.

Because I have done it.

I was intrigued that I could access that dimension and relive my experience by simply closing my eyes wherever I happened to be and at anytime I chose. It was like receiving a lifetime ticket for the front row seat to view Eternity whenever I wanted.

It was at that point that I recalled what I heard, and I finally understood the humming sounds that permeated the background vastness of Eternity. It became crystal clear to me one morning while listening to a choral rendition of the Kyrie from René Clausen's *Memorial*.

I sat in a back row with Mary beside me and I closed my eyes and listened as the choir began. *Instantly* I was conveyed back to the presence I had witnessed when I first found myself before the Source of All Creation. The human chorus replicated the modulating octaves in my spirit hearing. I no longer felt present next to Mary. I simply followed my previous pathway, interlocked with the energy drawing me back. It was as if a trail of breadcrumbs had been left for me that I followed back.

*Finally! Now I understood.*

The octaves I heard while sitting in my raft were like the sound of a tuning fork. It wasn't a humming like I first thought, it was the rising and falling of an infinite range of octaves, all variations of one infinite tone. Each octave was in a perfect state of equilibrium with the others. I understood this as the voice of Source that speaks across the eternal dimensions in vibration. For me this was a moment of illumination to realize that this was the song of the universe that thoroughly permeates everything—people, trees, soil, cattle, bees, apartments, oceans, mountains.

*Everything.*

These modulating tones are vibrations that function as compasses or homing beacons that all energies can align to and follow back to the Source. Just as our bodies can perceive a physical vibration, our spirit selves recognize an energetic oscillation and can follow it. I can feel these vibrations as I write these words.

These tones permeate all dimensions and all energies and meet each of them at the level of vibration they inhabit in order to guide them home. If some have lost their way or can't navigate their own return through the vastness of Eternity, guides like I have encountered, assist as shepherds across Infinity.

I know these vibrations are calling to all that has passed through whatever existence it inhabited, in whatever form—human or not—as we understand them, and are calling *all* home to the Creator. I understand this to be the call that beckons us to our ultimate destiny. I know that no one will be left behind or discarded because our Divine self that inhabits each of us would never refuse to return to the *Nest of God*. We cannot destroy what has been created from a higher Source Energy.

I finally understood that the small jets I saw racing away from the sphere of Source were heading out to whatever destination they were meant to experience. There are no boundaries in Infinity and our planet is not their sole destination. If I think that we, on this planet, are the only energies ever created, or that we are favored over another, then I place the Source of All Creation in a tiny box of my own human design, and with an intention to be used for my own purposes. I witnessed that Divine Creation is of such greater magnitude than my, or any, human brain could possibly comprehend. I understood that all of this was revealed while I was in spirit presence and had brought it back with me. It took time for my human brain to process it, but it recognized it when my mind's ear heard it again and instantly took off to unite with it once more, leaving the human me back at my seat.

During the middle of the night, not long before that moment

of my and Mary's listening to the singing of the Kyrie, I had been awakened from a deep sleep and told why I was back here.

The next morning at our kitchen table Mary said she had taken some notes of what I had said during the night.

I said, "You're kidding."

"No," she said. I sat up in our bed and started talking to myself. She thought it might be important, so she grabbed her notepad on the small table next to her to write it down.

"I don't believe this," Mary wrote as I talked.

"Don't believe what?" she said she asked me.

"I didn't ask for any of this," I said.

"Any of what?" she asked.

"I've been sent back to be a conduit of hope for those who don't believe there is any," I said.

I reached across from my end of the table for the notepad she held out. I studied what she had written.

Mary looked at me. "You don't remember that?"

"No," I said. I didn't remember any of it.

"What happened then?" I asked.

"You laid back down and went to sleep. That was it."

I didn't remember saying anything in my sleep. I didn't remember asking for a job when I was lying flat on the fitness floor. I didn't remember even qualifying for it. And now I had been sent back to explain my experience to those who are afraid of what life holds. Or are afraid of what happens after life in our physical form ceases.

I was to be a means to deliver that message. Not a messiah, not a prophet, not an evangelist, and certainly not a saint. Just one human being given an extraordinary experience to relay to others to consider.

Sitting during the Kyrie, I had instantly slipped off again to the presence of the Energetic Source I first witnessed, but I knew I wasn't going to stay. I had been told I still had work here and *that was my answer to why I had returned and the answer to all my questions.*

Now *everything* made sense to me.

That was why I was "energetically guided" to go to town instead of staying home and working on our farm. That was why all those who helped me—all the staff, all the EMTs—were in the exact place, at the exact time I needed them. That was why all my vital signs returned to normal so quickly even with the trauma my body went through. That was why I appeared in a physical state as if nothing had happened to me. That was why I looked happy in the hospital. That was why I could leave the hospital in only three days after having had a sudden cardiac death.

That was why I heard my guides say to me: *"Since you're already in there, you have a problem with your heart that needs to be fixed. Then you can get on with your work."* Until then, I had no idea what they were talking about. I'd been given a task that wasn't finished. I had accepted it on some higher level and I had to be alive here to accomplish that.

And I was completely at peace with it.

The Kyrie finished its final phrases of the meditation. I hesitated to open my eyes because I didn't want to leave that experience again. I almost begged to stay. When I opened them, I realized tears were running down my cheeks.

Mary had turned to me. She'd been watching and thought something happened to me again, like I was in pain because I was dripping tears. There was an urgency in her voice.

"Are you ok?" she asked.

# CHAPTER TWENTY-ONE

I nodded my head and reached for my handkerchief to wipe my face.

"Yeah," I whispered. "I was just there again."

She understood because I had explained all this to her after it became fully formed a month before. And now she smiled because she knew what I meant.

The possession of that moment stays with me. Constantly. If I stop, anywhere, anytime, to listen, I can hear those octaves. At those moments I can go beyond this universe. I can go beyond the dimension I saw before me. I can be outside my body but still find my way back. In those moments I feel neither time lived, nor time lost, nor time present. I just am.

I'm not telling anyone what to believe, but I know those octaves are calling for each of us. They will be there when our experience here in this dimensional reality ends. We are not rushed to that end by some unseen hand, we each reach it at the time we agree to. There will be a tone to serve as a beacon to guide each of us back to the safety of our Source.

I need to share that I've seen no one will be left behind—no one, regardless of their circumstances here. Our energy, our soul if you will, will seek that beacon and those tones because it knows it already and will remember that's where it was born. We will be transformed from this dense body back to the energy form or vibration we were before we chose to enter this human experience.

I realize that it is the illusion of time that supports our fear of death. The framework we hold up through which we examine our understanding of death is shaped by our limited perception of it on a physical level. Once we understand that, yes, this human body ceases to function but the eternal self within us never dies, then we can confront our fear of death as something to be avoided at all costs.

If we experience only one end of life's spectrum—our birth—we would be stuck in this human form forever. And why would we want that, especially given how easily it breaks down? Just as we need to realize time to understand what timelessness is, I believe we need to realize death to fully understand the life we've lived here, even if we aren't around to recount it to others.

I don't know if everyone will have the exact experience I did when they leave here. That's not mine to determine. Our loved ones—family, friends, neighbors, and even those we don't like or can't tolerate—will all experience something similar because every person has the Source of All Creation energy embedded within them, even if we refuse to recognize it in others.

I have no doubts that those we knew and loved, and perhaps, greatly miss, are experiencing what I did when I left for those six minutes. I also believe they may not wish to leave the dimension where they now exist, and are content where their spirit energy finds itself. I need to accept that, and that is good enough for me.

My sudden cardiac death made me think about the story of Lazarus because I now had a better sense of what an actual resurrection feels like. The story recounts a man who died, was wrapped in burial linens, and was placed in a sealed tomb.

I wondered about that. Maybe he had two artery blockages like I did. The story says that he was called out from his tomb. I could just picture it: him walking and shuffling down a gravel pathway but without socks with gripper spots on the bottom. I doubted a nurse was nearby or that there was a wall railing to grab hold of to steady himself.

I wondered what those around him would have thought after

seeing a dead man get up and walk? Would their disbelief be different from what the EMTs may have felt when they saw me finally come back alive and open my eyes? And how did people treat him later? Would anyone rush up and unwrap him? Or did he have to do it himself? Would they hug him for being back? Or would they run because they thought they saw a ghost, or saw their greatest fear arise?

I tried to imagine myself standing there in that crowd and wondered what I would think. How significant would that moment be in my life? Would actually witnessing a dead person come back to life change what I thought, how I felt about mine, what I would want to do with it? Or would I simply shrug my shoulders in disbelief, turn, and then get on with the rest of my day? Would I not want to think about it because if I did I might find that being locked in a cold, dark tomb was too scary to my liking. Maybe I wouldn't want to confront my own mortality.

But metaphorically, I was in a tomb. My body was cooling down with each second that passed. And yet, I did walk out of it after hearing a voice no one else said they heard. There were enough people around who witnessed my return to life in that room to know it was all true.

I wondered what Lazarus thought when he saw he was wrapped in burial cloths. Did he realize that he had died? I certainly didn't. Not until several people told me later. What did he ask of others when he was finally returned home? Did he wonder what everyone was standing around for? What they were doing there? What all the fuss was about? I know that confusion.

Was that the purpose of the Lazarus story or of my collapse? To understand that it is all about the possibilities that exist beyond this life? To come back to explain to those who may be willing to listen about experiencing a Great Energy beyond what we can see?

When I stopped to think about Lazarus—that his story ended with walking out of the tomb—there were still a lot of unanswered questions. But, then, maybe that's the point.

If I couldn't believe what happened to him and the power of Divine Energy passing into this plane, then perhaps I wouldn't believe what he did with the rest of his life either. Maybe that's also the point—not to make history something sacred that has to be revered but, rather, to learn how we can relate to it and not be embalmed by it. I can examine it but I don't have to claim it as my history. I know how all that was possible then, because it still is now.

I know now that death, as we experience it here, cannot erect boundaries around us because it does not exist in that higher dimension. I saw no Eternal Death. I saw no hell, as we would prescribe human language to it. I felt only love, a love extended to everything that exists.

Each death is an individual experience. Others may mourn it, regret it, pray for it, or even wish it. But in the final analysis, it is still only that individual's experience with it. I understand that it is a fundamental human emotion to grieve the loss of those whom we have developed a love for or an affinity with in this life. And I'm not saying we shouldn't. Grieving is a normal human response and I would never say that one shouldn't express that in whatever way they feel appropriate without hurting someone else.

But a person's departure doesn't need to be with a sense of loss. A physical death is simply the transformation from this plane to a higher level of energy where they will reside in a different form, but still exist. I understood that that higher energy level cannot accommodate our human body tagging along, nor is this fragile body needed any more at that point. I know that we will all become energetic holograms of ourselves again.

I believe that much of our emotional attachment to someone who dies is the eruption of sadness about *our* own fears of loss more than it is an acknowledgement that what the person is experiencing may be for *their* highest good. We make their death our loss which, when you consider it, is a rather selfish emotion. *How dare they die when they didn't ask me? How dare they die and make me sad?*

I certainly didn't ask for anyone's permission to leave when I collapsed.

In other words, this person is not ours to hold onto in the first place. Yes, we existed alongside and we may have had shared experiences. But I believe our sadness and pain is as much about what we think *we've* lost as it is of actually losing that person.

We often have invested heavily in certain habits, certain family rituals, traditions or narratives, certain expectations of ourselves or of the deceased person. We may seek divine intervention. We may pray for outcomes to be different. But looked at closely, that is our selfish wish so that we don't have to experience the human pain or heartache that may accompany it. We can mourn them if we wish, but I believe that it is our loss we are most mourning.

But a period of intense externalized mourning may be able to lead one back to the land of the living. Repression festers. A checking in on one's signposts, guideposts or guidelines that one can draw from whether it involves a family, a community or some personal, religious or spiritual ties can be extremely useful. Everyone has a right to a personal meaning of their grief, sorrow or loss. But also, everyone has a right to a future happiness, joy and laughter once the time for sorrow has ended. We needn't mourn forever.

I don't need to be selfish or judgmental. I can let them have their life, even if I didn't agree with it or how they lived it, or what they believed, because *it is their life, not mine.* I can let them have their death, even if it is something I might want to delay, because it is *their experience with death, not mine.* I can let them go their own way because it is *their life experience to learn from.* Not mine. Not others to control. It's theirs.

Our companions who walk with us and beside us to share our journey here can be of great comfort and support. We can honor them after they're gone in a tribute. That alone can confirm our humanity towards others. But wouldn't it be even better for their memory—and ours—as we choose to remember them, if we took the time *now* to honor them while they are still here?

I know that this plane's physical death is only a step through a portal. I stepped through that portal and witnessed all that was before me and I returned back through it unharmed but dramatically changed.

# Chapter Twenty-Two

It arrived without notice in the middle of May.

The depression they spoke about in the hospital as a possible residual effect of my sudden cardiac death didn't slam into me like a tsunami to pitch me into the deep waters of melancholy and feelings of helplessness. It snuck up on me.

I didn't really believe them when they came into my hospital room three times to discuss it. It had been the same questions every time, only with slight variations: "Are you feeling depressed?"

Each time a clinician from St. Mary's staff came in for a chat, we ended up on opposite ends of that question—she asking it and me always responding with a "No, I don't think so." It felt like a standoff during the final visit.

I had difficulty understanding the point of the question because why would I be depressed if I was still alive and in fairly good shape, all things considered? But I was never convinced that she believed my answer when she wrote it down on a page in her file folder. Maybe she was writing something else, I had no idea.

We talked about other topics and she asked me how things were at home, my marriage, my children, our finances, my job. Did I sleep well before? Did I worry much? Did I enjoy myself? Did I have any hobbies? What did I do in my spare time? The questions went on and on.

There was some comment during one of those sessions I couldn't fully recite later about a heart attack being the cause of depression. But I didn't pay enough attention at that time to comprehend the statistics involved. I had to research them later when I felt I could understand them.

The second visit was shorter than the others as it was sandwiched in between the first and last. She only asked about my room and visitors. Did I like it? Did I like the nurses? Did I like the food? Did I have anyone to come visit me? Did I want to see anyone? A chaplain maybe? A priest? A Buddhist? Was I interested in watching TV?

I realized the questions were different and I began to wonder. I was paying more attention at the third visit. Maybe they had noticed something about me that I was unaware of. Maybe a change in the way I reacted to the hospital staff. Maybe my attitude had changed while they observed me and I didn't notice the shift. I was only looking at me from the inside, they were watching me from the outside. I was probably biased, they were objective.

After she left the third time, I realized I had not been asked if I was happy. It seemed to me that searching for a negative condition might be a positive approach. Being alive was a positive outcome, I thought. So why would I be depressed?

That is what they call hubris.

For all I knew those were standard questions for every patient in fourth floor cardiac care. Maybe I was an atypical patient they needed to watch closely while I was there. But then, maybe every other patient there felt the way I did.

In return for my answers, I generally got a subtle facial response that bordered somewhere between mild suspicion that I might not be fully forthcoming, and anticipation that I might want to reconsider my answer before she wrote it down.

I wasn't sure she thought I was telling the truth of how I really felt or if I was saying what she wanted to hear. Or, maybe that was simply my inverted thinking, and it had become clouded by the drugs and all the weirdness of the past few days. Maybe I was looking for phantom excuses that didn't exist in order to be happy.

*Maybe I really was depressed.* Maybe I didn't see it while others did. I didn't have a measuring stick to compare it to anything else.

Those daily chats ended when I was released. During her last hospital visit, the clinician said that it might take six months before signs of depression finally surface.

"If at any time you have those feelings and they seem to persist please call for an appointment. We can work with you on it," she had said as she left my room for the final time.

Seven months after I left the hospital, the depression she spoke about finally arrived. It had been stalking me in the background from the beginning like I was a target of prey when it finally zeroed in on me.

For a week I began to feel differently by increments—downward increments—each day and for no apparent reason, and I tried to hide it from Mary.

That was probably the worst thing I could have done because while I was trying to deny it from myself, I was falling into the same rut as others who experience depression by hiding it from their family.

It wasn't that I felt sick, although at times I'd feel different things: helplessness, that I wasn't good for anything around the farm or for Mary; hopelessness, that nothing I was doing meant anything to me and probably to anyone else, bordering on self-pity; a feeling of gloom like a dark cloud enveloping me through which I couldn't see an exit, which was more sinister than feelings of sadness or pessimism; apathy, which made me feel empty and like I had nothing to offer to anyone.

It wasn't a single event that seemed to have triggered it but, rather, a dozen little things in the background that mixed together—the bills, the frustration caused by my inability to work much or at length, the uncertain future, the burden of dragging myself out of bed each morning to face the same things—became a potent brew of melancholy.

I began down a slippery slope by thinking that my family would be better off without me. Mary would be relieved of my being a constant concern. Marcus and Julia would be able to get along without me. Besides, Marcus was about the same age as I was when my dad died, and I survived it. Julia wasn't that far behind. Why would my friends miss me? I didn't see them that often anyway. And those I didn't know wouldn't care if they saw my obit in the newspaper or online anyway.

All that seemed very reasonable in my mind-set that week. I didn't know how to break free or even if I wanted to. I felt that my life was over, regardless of my experience in another dimension.

Maybe I had already laid the groundwork for my exit. I had burned a lot of stored papers. I had rid myself of my childhood collections. I had given away books I no longer needed. Did I then unconsciously realize that this feeling would be in my future and I was preempting it? That I was preparing myself for an easy exit? I had tied up a lot of loose ends already.

Most people who have been pulled back from the brink of self-harm or suicide are grateful later that they did not complete their mission. In that moment when a decision has been made one way or the other, there must often be a resignation or realization that can't be explained to someone else.

I know that because that's how I felt at the end of that week. I tried to avoid Mary as much as I could so I didn't have to face her and then, in turn, face myself.

I can't fully explain how I broke free but the information I had been given by the clinician at the hospital during her last visit helped me face my feelings. And that they were not unusual for anyone with my heart history.

I had shifted stacks of books and papers on my desk, considering how I would dispose of them before I left, and ran across the papers she gave to me to take home.

"Yeah," I had said with little intention of doing so because I was just fine.

Hubris.

But as I started to read, I recognized myself as one of the group classified as a heart attack survivor who had returned home. I read that forty percent of the survivors would experience mild or major depression afterwards.

*That's me,* I thought.

Ironically, it didn't help as I read on. It said that patients with major depression were three to four times as likely to die within six months of a heart attack and often returned to the hospital. During her last visit, the clinician said those same things and it might take six months before signs of depression finally surfaced.

I looked up and did the math. October. May. Seven months. I was overdue. But that bill had appeared to be presented to me that week. I felt on the edge again and I knew she had been right.

Hubris.

No wonder they kept asking me questions. Any heart event could unleash intense waves of emotion—feelings of fear and nervousness about the future—even though survivors were grateful to be alive. Or even if I had an extraordinary experience, I was not immune.

Depression was not like a broken bone that showed up on an X-ray. It's detected through behavior and attitude assessment, like the visits I had in the cardiac care unit while I was there.

Before the clinician left my room the last day of my hospital stay, she said that if I experienced *any level* of depression, it wasn't a *normal part* of my recovery, to please call her. Better yet, have my wife observe me closely and ask me questions. She handed me a card with her phone number on it before she left the room.

I found the clinician's card on my desk and toyed with it for a moment, turning it over in my fingers and tapping the edge on the glass surface as if giving a Morse code S-O-S. I reached for my phone and was about to type in her number.

Then I stopped.

Maybe this wasn't what I thought it was. Maybe it all was just a week-long panic attack. Maybe I was making a big deal out of nothing. Maybe it would pass. *I could always call her,* I convinced myself. What good would having an appointment in a couple days or maybe weeks do for me right at that moment anyway?

I put my phone down.

It felt like I had lost something in those few minutes. Then I realized that it felt like I had lost *me.* Perhaps the frustration had been building over the past seven months and it was only now surfacing. Like finding myself in a cage and not knowing where the key was to let myself out and then banging against the irons in futility.

It was confusing.

Or, could this be a side effect of understanding there were aspects of myself that I didn't want to confront? That I hadn't made complete peace with what happened even if I thought I had.

*Could I really be immune from things other people feel—like depression—just because I had an existential experience?* Did I think that gave me a pass from normal human things in this life?

Did that give me greater insight than others? Or was it from a sense of frustration of having to move around in the sludge of daily life here again?

Or was it all a slow-motion body and mind adjustment I was going through in reintegrating myself from one dimension that had no boundaries to one here where there were limits and I was feeling boxed in by it after experiencing total freedom?

The day slowly went on. I keep moving around outside just to stay busy, like I was trying to outrun something. Then a thought occurred to me.

*What if all this was an effect from the medications?*

Maybe what I was feeling came from their long-term side effects. The three meds had hit me hard. I was sluggish and tired every single day, all day long. Those little pills of solidified drugs that I ingested every morning must have changed my body's metabolism because I couldn't eat certain foods like I had before. My sleeping patterns changed because I woke up several times during the night. They had altered my marriage because I didn't have any interest in physical contact and I wasn't interested in talking. They had, indeed, changed my life. That seemed a lot of side effects for such tiny little pills.

I then recalled the odd physical sensations I had recently experienced.

It started two months after I returned home. One morning I noticed odors around the house that resembled burning rubber. I was the only one home when I first noticed it. I searched every room looking for an overheating appliance or electrical cord. I thought that maybe I had left the hot water pot on or that Mary forgot to turn off the clothes iron.

No. All the switches were turned off. The fridge was working. The computer cords seemed ok. I checked the electrical junction box in the cellar. That looked fine. I couldn't find *anything*.

Then the same odor happened when Mary was home and I asked her to check. She walked around sniffing at every possible appliance but came up empty.

"Sorry, but I don't smell anything like what you're describing," she said.

I finally resigned myself. The odors must have been a side effect of the meds and not something actually happening. I was stuck with smelling burnt rubber until it quit or my body assimilated the drugs differently, or maybe for the rest of my life. Or maybe it would end and morph into some other scent.

And then, just as quickly as it started, the burning rubber smell disappeared. Just like that. I was still on the medications but it never returned.

During the same time I smelled burning rubber, I developed an insatiable craving for yogurt. At least one bowl a day, sometimes two. I had never cared for yogurt before. But now *I had to have some*.

I supposed I had gotten off easy at taking only three medications. But that wasn't my decision. I knew others who had been on six. A friend of mine's father had been on ten. Each and every day. Some of his were given to counteract the effects of others he was taking. I was secretly thankful I wasn't on that many or I'd soon be a nutcase.

I became concerned that I was on a medication carrousel and might never get off. I began to suspect that for some people the reasons they'd been all prescribed was more from a fear that removing one drug or two might cause a person's condition to change in an unexpected way. That the medical personnel were hedging their bets or backsides. But I thought that it could just as well be the case that by removing one it actually might make the person healthier. I'd been to nursing homes enough to recognize this. I had seen the pill cart being ushered around the table at meals. I shuddered to think how drug addicted those people were, and not necessarily of their own choosing.

I do understand that drugs may be needed to control a person's physical system that's gone haywire. Ok, I get that. However, I wondered about the cumulative effects of ingesting multiple drugs every day over an extended period.

In my case, the doctors couldn't predict my future progress. Although they said the long-term prognosis looked good there were no guarantees, even with my implanted stents, that my heart might not stop unexpectedly sometime in the future. I was aware that it could be in the next minute. But that was the same hypothetical situation for everyone.

I understood that assessment and accepted the fact that I would be taking a beta blocker to reduce my blood pressure, a blood thinner to keep the prospects of a stroke or another heart attack at bay, and one for cholesterol to help keep the stents open. All those plus keeping a vial of nitroglycerin tablets in my pocket in case of an emergency.

*Would it kill me if I went off them?* That was the unknown I couldn't answer. And, apparently no one else could either.

But I also felt I had become an integral cog in the pharmaceutical industry without any options. And that was frustrating. However, I never had the feeling that if my three little drugs were removed I might be the cause of their financial collapse. I was a tiny drop in a very large ocean of drug prescriptions.

The only certainty I had was that I would be taken off the blood thinner after one year because I was told that studies showed there were no long term additional benefits for taking it beyond that point. That wasn't much consolation but I'd take it. At that point it would be one down, two to go. Something I looked forward to.

But there was something else nagging at me.

I considered myself a relatively healthy person at sixty-four years of age, even given what had happened. So if my somewhat healthy body had difficulty synthesizing only three daily medications, plus aspirin, then what must it be like for an elderly person who is on say, four, six or ten medications each day, every week of every month? How did their bodies synthesize all those drugs? Would it then surprise anyone that they may suffer from depression as their body rebels against the toxins infused into it?

Every case is different. But if my relatively healthy body had difficulty with only three drugs it seemed likely to me that older people who weighed less than my two hundred pounds might have more difficulty metabolizing their dosages. At what point do those drugs affect the chemical reactions in their brain and affect their mood? Or their quality of life?

Upon reflection, I should have taken the advice of the clinician and made the call I hesitated making. It would have been the prudent, as well as the smartest, decision. Were anyone to ask me now, I wouldn't dither, if for no other reason than to accept the help generously offered and protect myself and my family.

That was a week I had to confront my sudden and unexpected dive into depression. I had no idea where it would lead or when it might present itself again.

Because I had deferred their help, I would simply have to wait to see.

# Chapter Twenty-Three

I was smiling. They had dressed me in my best dark suit. My tie was knotted to perfection after Marcus' keen adjustment as he reached over me to straighten it. My slacks shimmered in the afternoon sun that streamed through the polished glass windows into the small private room set aside for family members. Everything smelled fresh and clean, not quite medicinal but not sterile. Not like the hospital I knew so well. My black shoes glistened, polished to within an inch of their lives. I was lying flat in a coverless wooden box with three shiny gold-colored handles on each side. I was about ready to be carried in by six men and presented to those assembled for a final farewell. And I was smiling.

That was the dream I had the night before Julia and Victor's wedding in early June but I kept it to myself. As I dressed in the morning for their special day, I pushed it from my mind. Yes, I was that close to being in a coffin but I wasn't. Not yet. I had more to do. I had a daughter who was getting married. I would be escorting her down the aisle later that afternoon. I was ready to live.

I stood in the wedding barn and looked at the pre-wedding decorations being assembled. The front area where they would stand to pledge themselves to a lifetime with each other. It had been set up the night before with a bare arch that was in the process of being garnished with an array of flowers and trimmings as I watched.

It was mid-morning. The overcast sky would clear to afternoon sunshine the weather forecaster promised. *Oh please let it shine,* I thought as I turned to look out the double door through which Julia and I would make our entrance and then I would pass my now-grown daughter to Victor.

I thought how fortunate I was to stand there in that moment. I knew I could be missing her special day if it hadn't been for those who helped me survive. I said a silent thank you and turned to help where I could.

The reception hall was full of decorations. Jubilant banners suspended along the walls. Colored lights were strung across the room in three rows to light the guests who would sit below. The round tables whose full settings were laid out the night before only lacked the guests that would come. Marcus and his soon-to-be fiancé Paige had spent the last hour gently placing peonies amongst the baby's-breath floral accents in the bridal arch. These were the same peonies that had grown around the perimeter of our front lawn for over a hundred years. They were a legacy of a former owner.

I was merely a by-stander to the controlled excitement and anticipation that fluttered around me. I thought back to mid-May and chuckled to myself. For two weeks I heard a voice beside the peony rows and found Mary standing and talking to them. She was coaxing them to get with the program if they wanted to be part of Julia's wedding. One-third encouragement, one-third enticement, one-third drill sergeant.

She told them they needed to be ready by the beginning of June. No earlier! No later! Your choice! They had one chance that year to do something really, really special, aside from just standing there and looking pretty in our yard. It was a pep talk unlike any I'd ever heard her give. Anyone who had worked with peonies knew how fickle they could be, blooming anywhere from mid-May to mid-June. But they needed "toughening up," as Marcus would say.

The peonies slowly developed at first as if hesitant they might get scolded if they did more as Mary walked beside them every morning to check their progress. With cool nights and warm days, they took stutter-steps to grow. Until finally the last week they were off and running to the finish line. Then Mary started to snip the early ones to put into cool storage.

On Wednesday night I thought I was on a movie set when I heard Director Mary ask them, "Who wants to go to Julia's wedding?" It was like asking a classroom of excitable school children if they wanted to go on a field trip or stay home.

I had never seen anything like it.

By Friday morning there was an explosion of opened flowers. It was like all those kids shot their hands into the air at once as if to say, *I'll go. I'll go for Julia!* They'd be the center of everyone's attention. Over three hundred peonies were gathered as decorations for the arch, the reception tables, and made into the bridesmaid's bouquets.

I stood motionless, leaning against the inside boards of the wedding barn, thinking I could have missed all this. I walked to the changing room. I put on my dark suit. I knotted my tie which Marcus adjusted. I rubbed the tips of each dark shoe on the back of my pants legs. My dress pants shimmered as I stepped into the afternoon sun.

I wasn't being carried in a wooden box. I was walking towards my daughter who was standing dressed in her stunning white wedding dress, holding a peony bouquet with both hands, patiently waiting to be married to the man she loved.

I gave her a hug. A father's kiss on her cheek. I told her she looked beautiful . How proud I was of her and her choice in a life partner. How thankful I was to be there for her special day. I reminded her that I kept my promise from the hospital to be at her wedding. She squeezed me close with her arm wrapped around mine without having to say a word.

We stepped arm-in-arm to the double door. I saw the guests as they turned to look at Julia and watched as we walked towards Victor and a new life for them.

And I was smiling.

# Chapter Twenty-Four

My life had experienced a significant physical change during the previous eight months. There was no doubt about that. I could feel it and perhaps others had noticed it in me as well. But it was the underlining level—the substrata of an emotional shift—that had taken place and that I hadn't fully realized, especially as it affected others.

I felt I could manage my own emotional landscape but I couldn't manage anyone else's whose lives I had impacted and affected by such a seemingly – to me anyway - simple act as collapsing.

How could my single action of dropping to the floor, of which I had no control, spill over to create such havoc in other's lives, especially those who meant the most to me?

It was a slice of the same question I had been asking for months about why I was still here. But I had yet to fully understand or recognize it as I concentrated on myself and getting healthier. My focus largely was directly inward, mostly out of necessity. If I didn't take care of myself, I might end up back in the hospital, or worse.

*Was that a selfish motive?* I wondered many times during those months. I barely had time for myself in my thoughts and actions. I found it difficult to sit at my desk, a place that was second-nature to me. I couldn't sit and read for more than ten minutes before falling asleep. Oddly, I could still write. Or write what I considered as coherent sentences, even if those I read in books or magazines didn't often make much sense. I could work with the cattle a bit more each day.

I shifted between thinking, or trying to think of different topics, and writing as a way to jolt my brain and its wobbly synapses back into action. Sometimes my brain just shut down and I could think of nothing. It was an odd feeling because I thought I had a good memory about those things I had easily worked with such as writing a topic on my family's history. That came easily before but didn't eight months later.

Before I collapsed, I was working on two non-fiction books of different topics. One was a branch of my family history and the other an agricultural-related book that I had been contracted for.

The final edits for a book to be published during the summer had landed on my desk two months before my collapse and had been completed and sent off. Another requested manuscript had been written on homesteading and submitted to them shortly after that.

I used my family history, a topic of which I had much knowledge, as a way to engage my memory and thought process. It was a subject matter that I was intimately familiar with and I felt that if I could use that as a spring board to get my brain to start clicking again that would be good.

I still had no recollection of the eight hours from that Monday. I was less concerned about that than my inability to retain thoughts I just had. I kept a note pad and pen or pencil with me most times, especially if I was driving because there seemed to be uncanny occurrences while driving when something would pop into my head that I thought I needed to remember.

So during the summer after my collapse, I toyed with my writing skills trying at least to make complete sentences—subject, verb, sometimes with a predicate, other times not. I was glad the heavy lifting for my publisher's two manuscripts had been completed as it allowed me the breathing space to make only simple changes if they were needed and not a complete rewrite of the text.

One morning Mary walked into the kitchen with a stack of papers and gently set them down in front of me at my end of the table, as if she were delivering a fragile dinner plate. We had been discussing the challenges I was having in processing my thoughts and she had gotten up and walked out of the room for about thirty seconds, and returned holding two hands full of papers.

After she set them down, she asked me to, please, take the time and read them. She said she had stashed them away but felt the time had come for me to read them.

*Jeeeezzz,* I thought. What's this about?

I braced myself because maybe they contained some deep, dark secret from her past, or worse, from mine, that had snaked its way through the Internet and finally flashed on our computer screen.

I stared at the inch-thick pile as she turned and left the room. I lifted a near corner of the stack and thumbed through the edges like I was shuffling a deck of cards, letting each page fall on top of the one before it.

*Phew,* I whistled. *Man, that's a lot of emails.*

I took the top sheet and looked at the date. October 5, 2015. 5:41 p.m. Replies from my brother and sisters about what happened to me at the fitness center.

I looked for what Mary had written to them but didn't find it. No matter, I thought I could get the drift of them from their replies.

Next pages. A series of texts from Marcus, Julia, Victor, and then a host of emails from Mary's friends who were responding to the news as it flashed from one person to another, and who then sent Mary a note of concern and support. And questions about how I was doing.

Mary must have spent a lot of time getting the information out in order to get this cache of notices back.

More pages. Emails and texts about making arrangements with multiple friends to cover the care of our cattle, chickens and cats while Mary was away. Times not able to be determined yet. Texts about final handoff of her church duties to other staff and volunteers.

Then dozens of pages that were much like the first ones. However, that really doesn't do justice to the heightened concern flowing in for Mary and our family as the time stamp got later into that day and evening. Some were aware that I seemed to be out of danger for the moment while others were only starting to find out and were "shocked" at what happened; often recalling the last time they saw me.

I was reading a diary of the circumstances surrounding my collapse as viewed by others not involved with it, and those who had heard it second-hand or third-hand as the messages continued to flood in.

The more I read through the stack, the more stunned I became. It was a digest of all the components Mary became engulfed in as the whirlwind events of that October morning unfolded and shattered her world.

Those pages screamed out the impact my collapse had on Mary, her friends, acquaintances, and even people she had never met but were a friend of a friend of Mary's friend. Messages from our Belgian friends. English friends. Holland friends. California. North Carolina. Arizona. Hawaii. Maryland. We were not so far removed from others as I might think.

Throughout the exchanges between Mary and those sending the emails or text messages, I read an outpouring of concern, support, offers of help, meals, and reminders of self-care for Mary.

All of this was happening while I was either in the ER or the ICU, and oblivious to it all.

*When did she have the time to send all these messages?* I wondered as I laid a page down halfway through the stack.

Not only when, but where did she find the time? She said she was involved with me in the ER and later in the ICU. Was she on her phone all that time?

I realized there was an unseen arena I had never known about in which there were active participants while I was lying on a table or bed. It was silent chatter in the background to me and it seemed like I was the only one left out of the loop.

The time stamp on many of the pages indicated they were written in the early morning or quite late at night. She was burning candles at three ends.

Then I got to the pages starting with the date of October sixth as I laid down the last page time-stamped on the fifth. I realized I had only just reached the end of a long, long, first day for Mary. I wondered if she had any fingertips left from all that typing.

What about the phone calls? I didn't see any of them as I shuffled back through the pages I had read. She said she had made a number of calls. But then—in a duh-moment—I realized that they wouldn't appear on those pages because they weren't written on a computer. Duh. I would have to ask.

I don't recall how much time I sat reading when I finally reached the last page. After I laid it back down and straightened the pile of disheveled pages, squaring all four corners, and turning the stack over to the beginning, I called to Mary to say I had finished.

I could hear her get up from her recliner in the living room and walk across the dining room floor, across the pine boards of the pantry floor, and looked up at her when she reentered the kitchen.

I let out a low, soft whistle, and then said I had no idea.

"I know," she said as she placed her hand on my shoulder and gave it a little shake. That was why she wanted me to read those pages. She said she wasn't trying to make me feel bad but now that I seemed able to comprehend most of it, she thought I needed to know the other side of what the reality was for her. At least some sense of it. Even if I thought I was ok somewhere else, she was dealing with real-life issues here in the present.

She walked over to her chair and sat down.

"But that's not the half of it," she said as she settled into it.

I looked over at her not sure what she was getting at.

"What you see on paper is only a portion of what happened in those days. I could go on if you want."

I said, sure.

"Well," she continued. "There were a lot of things that happened that didn't end up in emails or texts."

She said that she first had to get herself in a frame of mind to call anyone. She was still struggling with the shock of what happened let alone try to explain it to someone else. And she had been in the dark about a lot of what was going on because even though she was in the ER, they really didn't have any information to give her until tests came back.

"But you looked like nothing happened," she said. "That was so unexpected that I thought I might be dreaming the whole thing. It didn't appear outwardly to be a crisis situation, but it was. You had died and now you were talking to everyone."

She said in a way it was almost surreal. Like she was talking to me but really was talking to someone else who wasn't in the present.

"You saw one of the emails I wrote to a friend where the doctors were kind of scratching their heads about the 'why' since your EKGs, blood tests, blood pressure, and everything were all perfectly normal by Monday afternoon."

But then came the flood.

"It was like a dam breaking and this wall of responsibilities coming at me from all directions."

It became more than concern for my health. The magnitude of all she had to arrange for and cover seemed overwhelming, and that also came blindingly quick.

"First I had to let your family know what happened. That was after I called Marcus and Julia," she explained.

Then she wrote to my brothers and sisters, who contacted their families. She had arranged for Heidi to tell my mom because she didn't want Mom to hear it from someone else if she happened to go into town. Word had quickly spread to certain quarters of the town's population and she had many friends who lived in Sauk City and Prairie du Sac, who might call her to ask about me.

"I needed to cover for the care of the cattle, the chickens and the cats because I didn't know how long I was going to be away from home," she said.

She had to arrange to pick up the vehicle that I had left behind at the fitness center. Then she had to finish arranging her work with the church staff.

Mary hadn't taken much time off from work during the past year, so, before that Monday morning, she had scheduled to take two weeks off from her position so that we could go to the wedding up north and also have some time after we got home to do a few things on her own. She had spent significant time lining up extra staff, and had volunteer help in place to cover her absence. On Monday morning she was wrapping things up when the call came in from Lieutenant Travis. On Tuesday and Wednesday she continued her wrap-up while attending to me at the hospital.

"So my vacation pre-planning started out as visits to you in the hospital," she said matter-of-factly and without any hint of malice.

My collapse had disrupted her whole schedule and had snatched that time from her. For the two weeks she would have been on vacation, she had me as a patient in the house instead of being able to relax like she had planned.

Then came the insurance issues. It had started while she was in the ER and it continued to the next hospital with my transfer. She had to check the insurance again. And again after she got home.

During that time, she was sending and answering text messages and emails from friends, co-workers, my family, and mutual friends from across the country and the world as they became aware of my situation.

While it was heart-warming and greatly appreciated, Mary said it took a lot of time and effort to get that information out, and sometimes she felt she was repeating herself in remote control. Then with each new piece of information, that went out as well across her network, and then with more replies and questions to answer.

"I could have used a personal secretary by then but I only had me," she said. "And through all that messaging, I still was concerned about you and found I had your stuff to manage too."

She needed to cancel the appointments I had made for that week with farm clients I worked with in the dairy industry. But first she had to find their phone numbers on my desk. Then she had to explain in general terms what happened and said I would reschedule when I could.

Mary said she wasn't sure how she made it through all that. But she did.

"No, that's not quite right," she said correcting herself.

She said there had been several prayer chains that she knew of.

"That helped because I actually felt it uplift me," she said.

She said those requests weren't for divine intervention because the worst had passed for me.

"It was a sense of being comforted by others, being held in their thoughts and hands," she added. "Most of the people I knew but others I didn't. I know prayer can mean many different things to people. But for me, I could feel being uplifted the whole time. Like I wasn't in it myself. That was comforting when I had deep doubts about what might happen next."

She said having others simply offering support and concern was emotionally helpful. Most times she thought she could handle what was coming. But knowing there were friends and family, and even others she didn't know, but felt she could trust if needed—even from those who had no idea what farm work entailed—helped ease the stress greatly.

"I had offers from some to help at the farm if it was needed," Mary said. "Or if I needed a ride when I felt I couldn't drive. Or a place to stay in Madison if I didn't want to drive home. Or simply a place to go to rest and lie down for a bit to get away from everything."

Mary said that, in an odd way, my collapse had helped her understand how broad her own support network reached. She knew it was there but didn't know the full extent.

"And maybe I'll never know," she said. "But, I guess, that's what a support network is about. You never know when someone is thinking about you and wishing you the best."

Mary fell silent after that thought. And then she got up and came over to give me a hug and left the room.

Until that morning I had little recognition of the magnitude of how that day or the weeks after had impacted her.

I was grateful that she shared it with me. I was grateful she was willing to sacrifice all she did and was willing to endure it for me and not simply walk away.

I remembered all those others who had been with me at the time of my greatest physical need and unselfishly gave of themselves.

Now I had Mary to thank for being there at the time of my greatest emotional need, and for her network that was there for hers.

I think I still owe her that two-week vacation.

# Chapter Twenty-Five

The cure became the cause. It was August. I was ten month's post-fitness center collapse and another tipping point was imminent.

Each day that arrived during the spring and summer passed with perpetual fatigue. Mary began to suspect that the medications were the cause for the way I felt. I couldn't simply ditch them and go cold-turkey because I couldn't pinpoint it precisely. We had suspicions, yes, but no evidence to challenge the medical directives. If I, or Mary, was going to challenge any doctor's assessment, we'd have to have some evidence to support it.

I had long-since completed my cardio rehab program. I was on a light, self-imposed, but unsupervised fitness program, although the Wellspring staff members became extra alert the first few weeks after I stepped through the door and said hello again each time I entered the room.

Every morning I fought two frustrations: the feeling that I had to lie down three hours after I got out of bed, and the feeling I might as well have stayed in bed in the first place. I made only short drives to be sure I could get back home without any trouble or falling asleep at the wheel.

The days I felt normal, or what passed for a new normal, I functioned at half speed. On days I was exhausted, I put it down to overextending myself from my light exercise routine. *How could the cure cause this?* I wondered.

Until Tuesday morning, August thirtieth.

That morning found me at the apex of my daily up-and-down swells, and I fell over the side of the boat to the bottom of the river trough.

After I woke up that morning, I went downstairs as usual. Again, I didn't sleep well. And I didn't feel any better after I had been up. I wasn't hungry. I was numb. Numb, as in I couldn't feel my feet. Numb, as in looking through a gauzy curtain and not seeing clearly behind it. My legs were two pieces of wobbly rubber searching for the edge of each step so not to tumble down the stairs.

That morning was much different from others. But I was still too stubborn to admit it.

Mary had dressed and was finished eating and about to leave for Madison when I slowly swayed into the kitchen trying not to show my awkwardness. I tried to maintain an image that nothing was wrong until I couldn't help myself and plunked down on my chair. Mary had gotten up to place her dishes in the sink.

I slurred a few words and she gave me a questioning look.

"Are you ok?" she asked. Although I probably didn't sound ok to her, I nodded so as not to give myself away to fast.

"Just another bad night," I mumbled as I looked away.

She said she could stay home.

I figured she was probably tired of hearing about my routinely bad nights. Because it was repeated every morning. I knew that if she stayed she'd have to spend extra time changing her full schedule. I decided not to make a fuss.

"Nah, go ahead. I'll be ok," I said as she gave me her skeptical *I've heard this song before* look.

No, really, I told her. Just a little off center this morning. Didn't sleep well that's all. I'd be fine.

But half an hour after she had left, I wasn't.

My first mistake was not calling an ambulance.

I began breaking out in a sweat and wondered if I could even call if I had wanted to. My fingers and arms were getting numb like my legs had before. I was lightly dizzy. I hesitated to call because it will mean an added expense to our already backlogged hospital bills.

Which would be worse? I thought. Adding to our expenses or having to admit to Mary she was right. I went to sit down in my recliner.

Another thirty minutes passed before I decided I better do something or she might come home and find me on the floor. My body started to shake as I got up but I didn't have any pain.

*So how bad can this be?* I thought.

If it was a heart attack, surely I'd feel some pain. If I had been clear-headed, I would have recognized that as wishful thinking because I had collapsed once before without feeling it.

Then I made my second mistake.

I figured I'd get to the clinic faster for help if I drove rather than if I called for an ambulance and waited here for them to drive out to our farm.

*I can drive there in fifteen minutes*, I convinced myself. So I put on my shoes, grabbed the keys and promptly dropped them on the floor. I bent down to pick them up, almost toppling over from dizziness before I headed out our back door, stumbling with a purpose.

I was rather pleased with myself after I backed out the garage without ripping off the mirrors. After the first few miles I felt certain I'd made the right decision.

But halfway into town, my head started spinning and I got

really dizzy. I gripped the steering wheel to keep from passing out and falling over into the passenger seat. I could feel my hands gripping tightly, turning my knuckles white. I still talked myself into believing I could make it. But then, for a brief second, I sensed that my poor judgment just might catch up with me as my head dropped to the wheel. One moment I thought I was fine, but the next I felt I wasn't. At that point, my best choice, had I been able to consider all the options, would have been to pull off to the side of the road and call for the ambulance. I reached into my pocket for my phone and couldn't find it. I looked over at the seat beside me. It wasn't there.

*I forgot my cell phone!*

Now what? I kept going that's what, and hoped I didn't cause an accident by crossing over the center line. Maybe if I swerved a little, a police car would pull me over. *Then they'd see I was in trouble.* I thought it ironic that the one time I wanted to get stopped by a sheriff's car there wasn't one around.

I opened my window to let the cool air hit my face. I steered the car on the far right edge of the road. I even sang to myself!

When I was two miles out from the clinic, I began to relax as the buzzing in my head thankfully lessened.

*I'm going to make it after all,* I thought. Or was I fooling myself again?

Two stop signs and two sets of stoplights later, I drove into the clinic parking lot aside the building and found an open stall. I got out and staggered towards the front door like I'd been in a bar all morning. Patients were checking in. The first three reception stations were already occupied so I wasn't noticed until I reached the last one at the far end.

I stepped up to the counter and leaned forward on it with both forearms and my head dipped into my chest. Seconds passed before the woman who sat in her small cubicle finished reading her computer screen and glanced up as if I was another routine check-in.

I tried to speak but nothing came out. I pointed to my chest. Half words finally spilled out …. *breath … here … can't … breathe.* I felt a sharp pain in my back.

*Maybe I am having a full-blown heart attack.* I thought. I had all the symptoms I had read about.

She rocketed out of her chair and pressed her necklace button to call for help. She rushed around the counter as I began to fall and lost my balance and grip on the counter.

Time morphed as things went a bit crazy after that.

I was eased into a chair against the wall across the entryway. Doctors appeared from nowhere and surrounded me. The room was spinning. Someone was unbuttoning my shirt. I felt a cold disc press against my chest and smelled the shampooed hair of another person pressing their head near it—listening.

Someone yelled for a cart. More people in white coats materialized from behind closed doors. Then a call for an ambulance. My vision went blurry.

Electrodes were attached to my chest. *No, not that again! They'll rip the hair off* was the only thought I had to help keep me awake.

But it wasn't good. I left this world again.

When I opened my eyes, I wasn't in the ambulance. I blinked to clear them. I smelled hospital. I smelled sterile. I knew that smell well enough to know it wasn't from another dimension.

I saw lights on the ceiling. Bright white lights. Not golden light. I was on a bed that had me half-propped up. My jeans were still on. My shoes were gone but my feet still had socks on. My shirt was open. I saw the patches on my chest with wires hooked to them.

*This can't be happening,* I thought. *Not again.*

Maybe this was just a flashback from the past ten months. Maybe I was still sitting in my recliner having a bad dream at home, falling asleep again after Mary had left. But the beeping of a monitor next to my right arm sounded like an orchestra kettle drum. Each beat thundered into my ears.

*This isn't a dream. I'm in a hospital,* I realized.

I was sick because it felt like I had regressed and was starting all over again. I didn't want to go through that whole process again. *Maybe I should just die and be done with it,* I thought. I wanted to cry because of the welling futility but didn't have the energy.

Moments passed before I tried to lift either leg. Nothing. They felt like logs. I tried to raise my left arm. It felt like lead. *Maybe I'd had that stroke.* My left hand had an IV needle stuck in on the backside again. My right hand had a finger monitor attached and I had another familiar wrist bracelet. I had been banded by another hospital.

An ER nurse with a Kathy name tag was talking to me. Asking questions. Always questions. What day was it? Did I know where I was? Did I remember anything? Was I in pain anywhere?

She was tall and leaning over me to check my eyes. Her gentle voice helped soothe out the drum beat from the monitor.

I had no idea how I got there or how long I'd been out.

Mary was called, again. I was alone for the time being. I wondered if she would want to come and see me in a hospital again. I wouldn't blame her if she didn't. I'd caused her enough trouble over the past year. I'd caused enough expense to last several.

Nurse Kathy was talking with me and seemed satisfied that I was stable before she left the room. It was quiet except for some beeping. The head ER nurse later walked in, her shoes squeaking on the polished floor with each quick step. She made sure I could understand what she was saying before she explained they were consulting with St. Mary's staff. Their preliminary tests didn't indicate any signs of a heart attack. Or a stroke.

I exhaled, relieved that it wasn't either.

"We can't be sure what's happened to you," she said. They had reviewed my file and needed to be extremely cautious because my previous history concerned her.

"At this point we can't say what's caused this. It could be minor. But we aren't set up to perform the tests you need."

There was a long stretch without any activity or conversation in the room. I nodded off and then woke up when Nurse Kathy came in to check my IV. I could only lie there and look at the blinking blue numbers on the monitor. *Those numbers seem awfully low*, I thought. Much lower and they might stop. But then I nodded off again.

The head nurse came back in after I woke up and said they were waiting for a bed to open and when it was available I'd be transferred to Madison.

More waiting. I noticed Mary still wasn't there. Maybe she had decided *not* to come out. Maybe she would meet me in Madison. Maybe … Maybe … Maybe …

Nurse Kathy came back in and said she'd read my history as part of monitoring me.

"How have things been going? Other than today?" she asked.

I was groggy but said that I was mostly tired all day long.

"I can't do things I did before. But I have kept up an exercise program and my diet," I explained as if to justify my being in her care and trying to deflect any blame for my presence in the room.

She glanced up at the monitor without giving away any

expression. She glided her fingers down my IV line to make sure it was flowing. The beeping didn't seem as loud. I was starting to feel my arms again. I lifted my right leg slightly. Then my left because I wanted to check to confirm their statement that I didn't have a stroke.

I told her that the morning was different from others when I woke up and didn't feel well.

"Hmm," was her only response. She was making mental notes, I just knew it. She pulled her stethoscope out from her side pocket and was steadying it to place on my chest. She listened.

"It's my second time in an ER since last October," I blurted out as a confession. But I realized she already knew that.

"So what happened?" she asked. "If you want to tell me."

I gave her the Cliff Notes version of my sudden cardiac death and my other dimensional experience.

"Do you ever talk about it?" she asked, now seeming curious enough to disregard any hesitation she may have had about asking a patient a personal question.

"Only if people ask and they seem interested," I replied. I wouldn't push it on anyone.

She said she'd be interested because she was close to her sister who passed away the year before. She had heard of people who had near-death experiences but never met anyone who did. Even in the hospital.

Then, as if conjured by a magician, Mary appeared in the doorway.

She stepped into the room and Nurse Kathy explained what she knew about what happened. She went through my present condition, my vital signs, and said there were no indications that my heart was in danger.

"Everything seems to be fine but he'll need further tests," she said.

Mary came over to where I was lying and asked how I was doing and smiled, as if she couldn't think of anything else to say.

"How did you get in here?" she asked after surveying the entire scene.

I shrugged my shoulders. Some things could wait. I'd never make a reliable criminal accomplice because when questioned under pressure by the authorities, I'd promptly spill my guts about the whole caper. I did that with Mary.

She sat down in a room chair after I finished, as if trying to distance herself from someone who clearly was crazy and had callously put himself in harm's way. And perhaps others as well.

*Now* I felt foolish. I had pulled her away from work again but this time she had to drive twenty-five miles to reach me.

The periodic comments went back and forth for the next hour until the head ER nurse came in again.

"They have a bed for you and you'll be taken to St. Mary's as soon as the Baraboo Ambulance can get here to do your transport," she said and then left the room. Mary said she would come down later after they got me settled. She had to call a friend to help ferry the vehicle I drove to the clinic in order to get it home. Again.

She said she'd pick up some clothes for both of us because we didn't know how long I would be staying in the hospital. Again. She seemed more exhausted from the stress of dropping everything and rushing to get to my side again than upset for what I did.

*The calm before the storm?* I wondered.

The ambulance team arrived and two EMTs transferred me to their gurney and rolled me out the door and into the back of their ambulance. I was locked in place and was on my way to

Madison again for the second time in ten months. I was fully conscious during my ride. I thought it might be something spectacular—riding in an ambulance while fully awake. But it wasn't. It was simply a ride while fully awake.

There was no small talk because the soft-spoken young man with an armful of tattoos was focused on checking the monitor every ten seconds as if concerned that the numbers might change if he turned away. He made notes on the sheet attached to his clipboard each time he checked the monitor. The second EMT drove at what appeared to be the speed limit because cars zipped by us when I raised my head off the gurney to look out the back window at the receding roadway. Mostly I laid there looking up at a white interior roof and listening to the wheels grinding on the highway.

We arrived at the hospital and I was pulled out and then wheeled to the elevator. I was delivered to the same cardiac care floor as the previous October but not to the same room. I never thought I'd see that hallway again. Or ever wanted to.

They brought me a white sleeveless hospital gown with two tie strands to loop around my neck and asked me to change out of my street clothes. *Where'd my shoes go?* I wondered. I was observed by a nurse to make sure I didn't fall over while changing. I looked at the white board and saw my name printed at the top. It looked like I had made a reservation. I resigned myself to not being in my bed at home that night.

I was tucked into my bed and shortly Dr. Peter came in to introduce himself. He shifted his glasses on his nose as he reached out his hand to shake mine. His grip was firm but his hand was slight like I imagined a surgeon's to be, if I were to knowingly shake a surgeon's hand.

I notice hands. I was brought up to shake someone's hand when they offered it because it was the polite thing to do. Most of the hands I shook when I was young were older farmers' hands. These were invariably calloused, thickly-muscled, and with an iron grip at the finish. Some squeezed like a vice wrench as if they derived a dark pleasure from seeing a young boy yelp out from the pain.

I was most impressed with the hands of my great-uncle that were bear-like paws to me. They were *huge*. But then he was a big body. My hand was engulfed in his so that I thought I'd never find it again. Until he opened it, and there was mine submerged in the center of his. I released Dr. Peter's surgeon-like hand.

"I'll be supervising your stay," he said.

And just as quickly as he came in, he left.

Then shortly, I was giving blood again left and right.

Almost four hours later an Assistant Cardiologist came in and explained what they had found. Or, rather, didn't find. She said it without sounding disappointed that they couldn't pinpoint my problem right away.

"We can't detect any proteins that would indicate a heart attack," she continued. However, they were concerned with my low blood pressure and low heart rate. That was something they wanted to monitor closely. Both had lowered to dangerous levels.

Dr. Peter returned later and said I needed a stress test so they could do an EKG and take pictures of my heart. They needed to eliminate the possibility that other blockages had developed since last October.

*That didn't sound too bad*, I thought.

Then they'd proceed from there. But he didn't elaborate on what exactly *there* would be. This wasn't the plan I had for my afternoon when I got up that morning. Again.

To do that stress test the next morning I wouldn't be allowed to eat until after it was completed. He apologized and said he was sorry but if they let me eat it would affect the chemical balance and then I'd be in here much longer.

Water was the only thing on my menu for the next twenty-four hours. I wasn't allowed to walk the hallway or to get out of my bed without help. I was left to myself except for someone drawing blood every two hours as they continued their tests for my panel profile. Not even the room cleaner came in. Mary called and said she'd be there soon. She needed to take care of stuff around the house and check the animals.

Again, I felt awful. *It's not fair that I cause all these problems for her,* I thought.

After Mary arrived, she hung the clothes she brought for me on the hangers in the closet. She was quiet most of the time she was in my room. I explained the vague plans they had explained to me and that I was back on a water diet until further notice. She seemed distracted as I watched her shut the closet door. She went to the chair next to my bed and settled back into it. I could tell something was bothering her but she wouldn't open up when I asked to tell me. So I let it go.

She said that on her drive to Madison she had booked herself into the B & B again because she didn't want to drive home again from Madison because it would be twice in one day.

"Once is enough," she said softly as she looked away. I wanted to hug her but I wasn't allowed out of my bed without a nurse present. She said the cattle looked fine in the pasture and the chickens and the cats had enough to eat so everything was fine.

"Besides, that's the best I can do," she added and then fell silent. She sat there quietly for an hour, sometimes nodding off before snapping to attention as if she was startled by an unseen hand shaking her awake. Finally she decided there wasn't much point in her keeping me awake since I would have tests the next day. She was going to leave and try to get some sleep.

"I'll see you tomorrow," she said. "Sometime." Then she left the room after leaning over my bed to give me a quick kiss.

I wondered if there was something else really bothering her.

The night passed with no food, a lot of blood tests, but thankfully no one asked me to pee into a jug. The next morning a nurse quick-stepped into the room to explain the plans for my heart pictures and stress test.

"Dr. Peter decided not to put you through the treadmill stress test," she said. He saw my chart and how unstable I had been yesterday. He was concerned I might fall during a walking test so they'd use a medical stress test on me.

She said I'd be collected in twenty minutes.

*What in the world is a medical stress test?* I wondered.

She didn't stay to explain.

That test would later rank as one of the strangest physical experiences I'd ever had. It topped my first airplane ride in a single-engine, two-seater when I was twelve. My dad's friend had built that plane out of material that could have come from a hobby store. It had only a cloth exterior that flapped in the wind over its wood frame, and an engine that may have been ordered from a Sears catalog. The only barrier between me and the ground six hundred feet below, when he tilted my side of the plane to give me a better view, was the notched, heavy leather strap that belted me to the seat. I was thankful he didn't do a plane roll.

That stress test was even stranger than when I noticed my dislocated pinky finger at a ninety degree angle on my right hand during a high school baseball game after I was tripped up making a double play at second base and landed on it.

Those two experiences were strange but that medical stress test was spectacularly strange.

I was helped off my bed and eased into the wheel chair brought into my room for my ride. The wheels were unlocked, I was turned and then whisked out the door, down the hall, and into the same machine room where my heart pictures had been taken the last time I was there. Yogi Berra's famous comment, *It's* déjà vu all over again, topped my thoughts.

Two people were present when I arrived. One was the technician who said he would operate the camera in the adjoining room and a nurse who would administer the injections. That nurse seemed vaguely familiar as if we had met somewhere before but I couldn't place her in the commotion of getting out of the wheelchair and onto a cot against a wall.

"We inject drugs that will cause a simulated workout without you actually doing a workout," she emphasized as if I had somehow lucked out. She said that may sound strange but it would increase my heart rate. I'll get short of breath. And then I'll start sweating. I will exhibit all the signs of working out but not have to do any actual exercise.

Getting the benefits of a workout without having to actually do it. *There must be a good fitness marketing plan in there somewhere,* I thought.

"Are you sure?" I asked in a doubting tone. I burrowed my eyebrows and shook my head slightly. I was skeptical. I wanted her to prove it.

"Oh, yes. That will happen. It never fails," she replied, certain that she wasn't mistaken.

*Ok, then, this could be interesting.* But I still didn't believe her.

She said the drugs used for creating these effects will quickly disperse from my body except for the heart muscle.

*Maybe not a good marketing plan after all.*

"Because your heart muscle is denser than other muscles, it will retain the drug longer. Enough of it stays behind to outline what's going on inside your vessels." There wouldn't be any lasting effects after it's over.

While she was explaining that, she laid out different color-coded, liquid-filled bottles on a small rolling table next to my cot. She asked me to lie still while they took final measurements of my chest and arms.

She made one final check of the IV line and then asked how I felt.

"Ok. I think." I was still suspicious.

"Good. Then we can begin," she said as if the curtain was about to rise before the show.

The blood pressure cuff was placed on my upper arm. She removed the stethoscope curled around her neck and spread the earpieces apart and clamped them to her ears to listen.

*Pre-game routine,* I thought.

I watched as she broke the seal of one bottle and drew its liquid into a syringe. Then flicked it with her middle finger as a small excess drop flew off the tip of the needle. She pushed the needle into the drip chamber of the IV line and eased the fluid in.

"It will take a couple minutes before you really notice it start to work," she said. I wasn't to feel alarmed. They would be there the whole time.

We wait. The only sounds came from a machine in the

adjoining room. Throats were cleared. Feet shuffled between one table and another. Time moved microscopically slow.

The nurse continued to listen to my heart. My breathing was still normal. The technician watched the IV line. I laid there waiting for something to happen. Anything.

Then it did. Like the joker who jumped out from behind a closed curtain to scare the crap out of everyone.

My heart jumped and started beating faster. In seconds, I became short of breath. I gasped for air.

My heart began pounding. I could feel it. I started to think *this must be what a heart attack really feels like. And it's intentional!*

The nurse listened closely with her scope on my heaving chest.

I began sweating. Breathing faster. Then faster. In seconds my heart was throbbing as if I was halfway through a marathon. I thought it might pound out of my chest. Sweat began running down my face. It dripped into my eyes. My hair matted. I was thirsty. My gown became soaked.

*What if they're wrong? What if I'm an exception to their rule and this test does the opposite of what they say? What if my heart explodes?*

I couldn't clear the sweat away from my eyes because my arms had tubes sticking out from them. They started to sting. I blew water off my mustache and the drops landed on my belly. Maybe in the nurse's hair. I couldn't tell.

I tried to catch my breath. I couldn't so I gasped. Suddenly it felt like I was suffocating. I must have run two miles by how much I had sweated.

*Finally!* I screamed inside my head. My heart beat started to slow down at least. It stopped pounding like it wanted to escape as much as I did.

Seven minutes had gone by before my breathing eased. That was only a minute longer than when I was on the fitness room floor almost a year ago.

She still listened closely and had cranked up the pressure cuff several times to check it. Finally, she eased her stance over me and relaxed as she released the air for the last time. She said it was over.

She said my breathing would be back to normal shortly. I was doing fine.

"This has gone well," she added, smiling that the test had been successful.

*Well for whom?* I thought. *I'm drenched.*

The sounds from my heavy breathing were broken by the technician's movements in the other room where he had moved to set up a machine.

He came back and said they could take me in now.

They rolled my table before the huge EKG machine that sat in the center of the room.

"Was this here last October?" I asked as I wondered if this was the same machine. I said that it looked familiar.

"We haven't moved it," he said from behind the monitor stand.

I assumed that meant yes.

I was helped as I slid from my cot to the long, narrow table that would again be inserted through the machine. Adjustments were made to the two metal plates positioned above me. A few more alterations as the panels were shifted into position.

While I waited, I stared at the white ceiling. Some dentist offices put pictures on the ceiling to look at while you're reclining in the chair, I said trying to make a joke. *A video screen might be useful.*

No response.

"Ok. I'm ready," he said. He told me to lie very still and not make any movement.

With arms at my sides, the table inched forward and then stopped. More adjustments.

Then slowly I moved until my chest was in line with the overhead plates. The table stopped again. My feet stuck out the other end. More adjustments were made. Then I was moved into a final launch position.

The stillness in the room was broken by a sudden click from the machine. It began moving. Slowly. Then a bit faster. Then faster like it is warming up to throw a pitch. Then faster still until it was whirring at full speed. *Man, that thing really spins!* I thought.

Lights on the tubes flashed and blinked. The camera plates taking 3-D pictures spun around with the tube. For a moment I felt like I was on the starship *Enterprise* and wondered when Captain Kirk would step in to ask the medical officer how things were going. It all felt so futuristic with the sounds, the lights, the whirring, and the strange spinning donut.

The first set of pictures was completed after what seemed like ages. I had to close my eyes during part of it as I got dizzy watching it spin. It finally slowed until coming to a complete stop. The lights keep blinking as if waiting for the next command. The plates were reset.

The whole process restarted and the whirring began again as the machine powered up until it reached full speed. I laid there another five minutes before the procedure was finished and the machine powered down before it slowly came to a final stop.

"Ok. You're finished," the tech said from behind his dashboard. "We'll take you back to your room now."

I was slowly retracted by the moving table and helped to sit up. I wanted my head to stop spinning and said that I needed to sit for a moment. The nurse firmly gripped one shoulder, making sure I didn't drop off the table. After a few breaths, I was helped off it but stood swaying unsteadily before I was eased into the wheel chair again. I was pulled away from the machine and returned to my room. Finally, I was told I could eat. I was handed the menu card while I sat in the chair in my room. I had asked if I could sit there for a few minutes because I didn't want to go right back into my bed.

I looked over the menu for a long time and found what I wanted. I called down to the cafeteria and fifteen minutes later I was looking down at a plate of food. Carrots and green beans. Rice with a low fat gravy spread over it. A thick slice of ham. A raspberry jell-o container. A small carton of one percent milk. And a hot tea. I hadn't eaten like this in days. *Maybe it's too much to eat*, I thought but I pushed my hesitation aside and dug in like it might be my last meal.

It was mid-afternoon before Dr. Peter stepped in with some good news. All the tests were normal and the pictures didn't show any new abnormalities.

"We can't see any further damage," he said as his colleague cardiologist entered the room and stood beside him.

I was relieved.

My stents looked good. There were no new blockages. They were aware of my extremely low blood pressure and pulse rate that I had come in with. They still weren't sure why I had the episode at the clinic. They reviewed my incident report from the Prairie Clinic, analyzed all my lab results, studied the pictures of my heart, and they couldn't find anything physically wrong. They looked over my medication list and knew that I'd been through a cardio rehab program and that I routinely exercise. Through the process of elimination they felt confident they had found the cause.

"We think it's the medications," he said.

*Mary was right.* I thought. The cure had been causing my problems.

"We've concluded that the likely cause is the medicine. The beta blocker. It seems to be causing too much suppression of your heart rate and blood pressure given that your exercise seems to be helping both."

*With its side effects of dizziness, lightheadedness, tiredness, depression, dry mouth—no wonder I was always thirsty—and depression, why would this be a problem?* I thought somewhat sarcastically.

At last they understood what Mary had sensed all along. She sat in the chair next to my bed with an expression that said she knew that was the problem all along but no one would take her questions seriously when she asked.

Dr. Peter said he and his colleague had discussed my condition at length and both were now confident they could remove the drug without causing me any problems. I'd be released later that afternoon.

I would still need to check in with my primary doctor the next week to make sure things were still the same and that I wasn't experiencing any problems.

"We'll let your doctor know what we've found. And we'll schedule you for a visit with your cardiologist in three weeks." Then he and his assistant turned and left.

I was speechless but I had my evidence to support what Mary had thought to be the problem. But I had to collapse again, and end up in the hospital, again, before anyone would believe us.

*How many more will there be?* I wondered.

But that thought quickly became the least of my worries because the signals I got from Mary were more alarming.

# Chapter Twenty-Six

I was released late Wednesday afternoon and Mary drove me home. She was quiet most of the way and I couldn't pry out of her what she was thinking. More than once during the drive, she would shake her head and wonder how they missed that in the first place.

At 5:30 p.m. I was back in our house. The first thing I did was to go outside and start a fire in the pit near our grass pasture. After it burst into flames I tossed in all the remaining blood pressure pills I had left over and made ashes of it all. I had endured another tipping point and had survived two quite strange days. I didn't want any of it stuck to me but that all paled in comparison to what Mary had been through in the background.

The Monday following my return home from my second hospital stay in less than a year, I received a call from Lisa, our local hospital's director of the emergency services. She said she had heard about what I experienced the previous October and wondered if she could come and talk with me.

That was fine, I said. We set a time for her to stop on her way home after work the next day.

She settled into the chair at the end of our kitchen table.

"I hope I'm not intruding. But I'm very curious," she said before she paused. Although she lived about five miles from our farm, our paths never crossed. She sat with her hands folded in front of her on the oak table and toyed with the ring on her left hand. She wasn't uncomfortable being in our house but the subject matter she was about to ask me didn't seem like something she had encountered before.

"I've read about and heard of people who had near-death experiences but I've never met anyone in person," she explained. "Would you be willing to tell me about it?"

For the next twenty minutes I told my story.

After I finished, she sat quietly.

She hesitated as if unsure she had any right to ask her question.

"Would you be willing to talk about your experience with the ER nurses?" She said she thought it might be good for them to hear it.

"Sure I can do that," I replied.

She said she would call to arrange a time about a month from then in October.

I went to my doctor's office the next week for the two-week checkup set up for me by Dr. Peter, and found that nothing had changed. But he wanted to see me again in six weeks.

Two weeks after that I met with my cardiologist who, again, said I'd made a remarkable recovery. And that I had a heart that has healed very well. He was lucky Mary wasn't with me to hear what she thought about the whole thing, especially after what happened in August.

It took three weeks before the effects from the blood pressure medication finally seemed to leave me alone. Dr. John said it takes three weeks to change or break any habit. I told him there were still days when it seemed like a hidden pocket of medication burst into my system. Like it had been tucked under a rock in the water and suddenly shifted and then got released into the flowing stream.

On those days I'd be thrown back into the sluggish state I

knew before. I could feel it and each time it occurred I anticipated a trip to the hospital. Most times nothing happened except that I needed to lie down for a short time to let it pass. Flushing that drug completely from my body was more difficult than I expected even though I wasn't pouring any more of it into my system.

But after three weeks there was a noticeable change. I slept better. I wasn't nearly as tired when I woke in the morning. I didn't need to lie down two hours after I got out of bed. I could stay awake during the afternoon. I could greet Mary at the door or even have a meal ready when she got home. It had been a long time since I could do that. The first time was a real surprise for her and she checked what I made before committing herself to eat it. I could even stay up until nine at night!

Mary had noticed that change in me. But there'd been a change in her as well. One Saturday morning we're talking about how differently I felt when *her* frustration exploded before she could catch herself.

"It was when we talked with our insurance agent about our farm this fall that I realized how much this all had affected me," she said. "And that was almost a year later."

She explained that it was just the stress of the whole situation and her emotional reaction to it. She had bottled it in because she thought it might affect my recovery. That I would be worried about her worrying. It had turned into a vicious cycle.

Mary recalled that our agent asked that I make a list of things I couldn't physically do on the farm that I had done before my collapse as it might qualify under different coverage.

"When I looked at your list, I wondered who was doing all that stuff?" she said. "And then I realized it was me, along with my fulltime job."

That, she said, was when she realized she was on remote control.

"No, it was somewhere between remote control and high alert," she corrected herself. "Every time something shifted in our lives or the days you didn't feel very well, it tripped some signal for me to be on guard to what might happen next."

There were other things.

"Mostly I was really, really upset because the pharmaceuticals were screwing you up. That made me mad. You couldn't function. Your pulse was low. Your blood pressure was really low. I could see it all before me and then we were told at your doctor's appointment that this is what they did for everyone."

I wasn't surprised at her anger but it had been a long time since I had witnessed such an outburst. Maybe I was secretly cheering her on. We both had been affected. Although those medications had an immediate and expected impact on me as primary recipient, she silently endured the effects as a form of collateral damage, which no one took into account. She was the silent partner that was largely ignored.

"Well, excuse me, this isn't working," she had wanted to point out to anyone who would listen. "I wasn't mad at you. I was mad at the whole medical protocol that there was no one I could call. You could get on new medications easily enough but you couldn't get off any of them when it was affecting you so badly."

She said it seemed the spouse was always the last one to be asked how they felt. She certainly never was asked during the whole time I was in the hospital last October and now, again, the previous month. I was the sole focus. Mary said she didn't resent that but felt her opinions were completely neglected and she had to suffer in silence for the good of her husband.

That explosion of anger came out a year after my collapse. That was now history. The blood thinner medication was history as well after I was informed not to renew my prescription. I could have kissed my doctor! I no longer had to bleed like a stuck hog when I cut myself.

I was now off two of the three medications I had started with. It had been a long road and I'd reached a milestone. Unfortunately, so had Mary. While I felt I was getting better, she wasn't.

In mid-September the full story of what happened to her during my second stay came out. It was like picking at a scab until it started to bleed again. The rawness of her emotions simmered just below the water line so they weren't seen by anyone else until they erupted like they had a few weeks earlier. But these emotions were different. These weren't about me, they were about Mary.

In an awkward moment when there didn't seem any topics of conversation left to go over, I mentioned that I had started to write down some of the things I could remember about the events following my first hospital stay. I said I was trying to piece together things that didn't make any sense.

By that time I had a stack of medical reports that I had requisitioned from the two hospitals involved, the EMTs and the ambulance reports, and the local clinic. As I studied them, I found there were gaps in what I recalled which, no surprise to me, were quite frequent.

Mary was patient in answering my questions until I got to my second hospital stay, only a few weeks before. It didn't come out as an explosion of anger. It came out as silence. Deep silence as she sat there with a look that seemed to take her back to that afternoon when she brought my clothes and hung them up in the closet of my hospital room.

# CHAPTER TWENTY-SIX

"I don't know how I got there," she said after what seemed like minutes.

Her shoulders sagged as she sat at the other end of our kitchen table, in a posture that said she was almost resigned to a never-ending round of hospital visits that could happen again at any moment.

She pulled her chair up to the table and rested her elbows on the edge as she leaned forward.

"I really don't know how I got there," she repeated as if trying to make herself believe she actually did it and it wasn't some dream.

I looked up from the reports I was reading to watch her slowly shake her head from side to side. I hadn't seen this type of resignation in her face for a long time. Not since her mom had died.

She rubbed her face with both hands as if that might wipe away her doubt.

"I wasn't even sure I would get there," she continued, following her previous statement.

"How so?" I asked.

"I turned into the wrong hospital," she said. "What was I thinking?"

I wasn't sure what she was admonishing herself for.

She said the second hospital trip for her the few weeks before had been the hardest. It really affected her but she didn't realize its extent until she backed into the landscaping stone at the B & B. But it was more than that.

"What stone?" I asked. That was all new to me.

She then recalled the morning she got the call at work from the local clinic where I had collapsed in August.

Mary said that after she explained what happened, her pastor walked her out to her car and asked if she was ok to drive. She thought she was but he offered to drive her instead. She said she'd be ok but the drive from Madison to our local hospital was a blur that morning. She realized that she shouldn't have been driving and that she should never have refused his offer to drive her out.

I realized that that was what took so long for her to arrive at the hospital while I was being observed and waiting for transfer.

"Before that morning, I felt I had started to recover from your first collapse," she said matter-of-factly. "Then all of a sudden I found myself back where I had started last October."

I had landed in another ER, and faced another transfer to Madison.

"I had to scramble again," she said. "I called a friend on my way out of Madison to see if she could drive your vehicle home from the clinic parking lot. But I had to find a time when she had a break long enough so she could get away to help."

Mary said after they put me in the ambulance for Madison, she and her friend ferried the cars home, checked the cattle, then fed the chickens and cats, and put together some clothes for me because she had no idea how long I'd be in the hospital. She packed some clothes for herself. And she had to arrange for another friend to do the farm chores.

"My friend stayed with me until I headed back to Madison and dropped her off back in town as I went through," she explained.

On her drive back to Madison, Mary booked herself into the same B & B where she had stayed before.

"I called and got a room because I didn't want to drive back home a second time the same day," she said. "Then when I got to Madison, I turned into the wrong hospital. I got myself turned around and finally got to St. Mary's. But then I couldn't find the parking lot."

It was after this that I saw her walk into my room and hang up my clothes as if nothing had happened.

"So I get into your room, and I see the same thing I saw last October. You're in a hospital. You're back in the cardiac care unit. You're lying in bed. What was I supposed to think?"

The doctors hadn't fully decided on a plan by the time she came in but it was explained before she had left for the night.

"Since you seemed stable, I left for the night," she said. "Then that next morning before I came back to the hospital, I backed into a landscaping rock at the B & B. I was trying to navigate a tight area and hit it. I could have screamed. No, not screamed. I was about to give up. With everything. You name it. I didn't hurt the bumper. And the rock survived intact. But I've never done anything like that. Or felt that way."

She said she had seemingly held everything together, even herself, for the best part of ten months.

"I now think I was kidding myself the whole time. That morning everything went off-center," she said. "I wasn't ok. I felt like I had lost my compass. Then when they concluded that it was probably the medications that had caused your collapse, I wanted to scream. I was mad because no one listened to me. I was frustrated because of how those meds had affected you. Us. I was empty from all of that. But I couldn't say any of that in front of you or even admit it to you because I was afraid it might affect you in some bad way. So I kept all that inside me."

Mary relaxed in her chair and took a deep breath.

"I guess the lesson I'd want others to learn from this is, if someone offers to help by driving even when you think you're ok, let them. Accept the offer. Accept the gift of their concern."

Lisa called the morning of October fifth to confirm my visit to the hospital ER nurses the next week. The irony of her call on that particular day wasn't lost on me as it marked one full year to the day. After the arrangements had been made, I took time to think about what I had experienced over the previous twelve months and appreciated what I had put everyone through, especially Mary.

I arrived at our local hospital shortly after noon and Lisa came from her office when I announced myself at the reception desk.

She escorted me to a room where nine ER nurses had gathered. Several were aware of what happened to me but Lisa explained that I was willing to share my experience and answer any questions. She began with an overview of the events the previous October and that I had given permission to let everyone read my EMT report. I had agreed because I felt they would read it differently than I would and I could ask questions about their interpretation of it.

I paused as they read through the report that each held in their hands. When most had placed their papers back on the table, I began.

I explained my blood pressure anomalies the previous summer and why I had started at the Wellspring Center fitness program. I told them that things had been going well. I didn't have any problems during my workouts or after I had stopped. I explained the things that I didn't understand about the whole episode, and what the EMTs did, and tried to unravel all the contradictions by studying my medical reports. Then I described my experience in another dimension.

It was *very* quiet after I finished. There was a l-o-o-o-o-o-o-o-n-g silence.

Finally, one nurse spoke up.

"Did you feel any pain from the chest compressions? While it was happening?"

I said I couldn't remember any pain because I wasn't there while it was happening. I only became aware that they did compressions to me after I was told about it much later. While I was in the hospital I had realized something must have happened because the muscles across my chest became sore, like I had been repeatedly punched. And I couldn't recall my chest feeling like that while I worked out. So something must have happened but I didn't know what until I began asking questions later.

"That's helpful," she said. Just to know that because sometimes they had broken ribs on fragile people while doing CPR. To know the person doesn't feel it seemed comforting.

I said I understood that emergency personnel needed to perform certain mechanics to save a person. So if it was me applying the compressions, with what I knew later, I wouldn't worry about it. It needed to be done.

"Is that helpful?" I asked.

She nodded that it was.

"I'm also impressed and thankful that you are willing to work that hard to save someone you probably never met," I went on. I said that at first I was most interested in learning what happened in the fitness room during those six minutes before I was finally brought back. I was awfully curious about what actions were being taken by those surrounding me.

"That was the period when I was experiencing another dimension, another plane of existence," I said. "You can believe that or not. It was as real as me sitting here now."

I looked at each of their faces but couldn't read what they might be thinking.

Another nurse shook her head slightly.

"I'll admit. I'm surprised," she said. "You were very fortunate.

It depends on the person, but five or six minutes is the outer edge for those electrical impulses to function. Six is exceptional. After that they likely will cease if the heart hasn't restarted by then."

A silence settled across the room. That thought seemed to float from one nurse to the next. Perhaps they each recalled a specific case they had worked on.

I said that was interesting but it didn't disturb me. "You probably have seen both end results in your work, where one person lived while another did not."

Several nurses slightly nodded.

"And yet, I'm sitting here with you."

But I didn't want them to misunderstand me. I was glad to be back. But I wouldn't have minded staying where I was.

Several eyes widened. They seemed surprised I would say that in such an unconcerned manner.

One spoke up.

"I've read about people like you who came back but I've never met one in person. I'm not sure what to think."

Others agreed.

I said I couldn't tell them what to think about what I'd explained. They would have to decide for themselves. And I certainly couldn't tell them how to react if someone they worked on didn't survive. I could only give them *my* perspective of having been on the receiving end and then to be brought back and realize later what happened.

I said I didn't think they needed to feel guilty if, after performing all the procedures, the person didn't survive. But that was their personal issue.

"That's easy for me to say, I suppose," I confessed to them. "Look, I'm not making a judgment on your skills. But now I realize that the place I went to is far better than what's available here. This plane may be pleasant at times but it's not forever anyway."

I said I wasn't implying they shouldn't care or try to help someone. But if they're not successful in keeping that person alive than I believed it simply wasn't their fault.

"And from my experience, I don't believe anyone who has left here while in your care holds anything against you for not doing better."

I said that was my perspective after having seen the other side of death. I was here one minute. Then I was gone, and finally I came back.

"I don't have any religious motive for telling you my story. I'm not an evangelist. You can believe it or not. You can take from it what you want. That's not my concern."

I only asked that they keep an open mind even with all the medical and scientific training they've had.

Then the next question came.

"Could you have imagined all this?"

"That's possible, sure," I replied. "I've thought about that a lot. But I'm confident I couldn't have imagined it because there were things I experienced that I had no other way of knowing. They weren't part of my physical experience here so how could I know of them unless I was there."

I added that from time to time over the past six months there had been small confirmations along the way that what I experienced was true. I had no reason to make anything up. I could only explain what my experience was, as I believed it to be. But sure, in the end, we believe what we want to believe.

"Do you look at life differently now?" another asked.

"Yes. The pressure is gone. The pressure to perform to a certain expectation. I drop things to take more time with my family and friends. I've jettisoned a lot of the stuff I no longer need in my life. It's been freeing. There is nothing for me to be afraid of anymore."

I said it wasn't that I was expecting to check out anytime soon, but now I could distinguish between what is important in my life and what really doesn't make much difference in the end. So, yes, things had changed in my life.

I said I was more content with myself. If the end came tomorrow, I wouldn't consider leaving here a great loss.

"That probably sounds selfish," I explained. "Because it likely will have some effect on others. But the biggest thing I've learned is that leaving this life is not the end. It's the start to a whole new experience in a different dimension of existence and in a different form of consciousness."

So what's to lose by leaving? If I could talk about my experience then perhaps others would be able to handle any fear of death they had much differently.

"Maybe that will help make your jobs easier."

The time ran out and several had to return to their duties, and their lunchtime was over. Lisa walked me to the front door and thanked me for coming. As I stepped out the front door, I didn't know on what footing I would be tomorrow. But I had faith that, regardless of the steps I take, I need not fall into the depthless chasm of being afraid. That faith, which is probably unproveable from any scientific perspective, is supported by the extraordinary fact that on two separate occasions, ten months apart in which my life was on the brink of ending, I had collapsed each time within an arm's reach of professional assistance.

Is that extraordinary luck? Is that simply a matter of being extremely fortunate? The cynic might say it is but I prefer to believe it was more than that. It was more than I can understand at present but eventually will fully at some point in my future.

I returned home and changed to go out to check the cattle. I grabbed my walking stick and opened the gates so I could slip through. They were out in the center of the field again as I walked up towards them. I thought about my discussion at the hospital.

*Have I deceived myself into believing I experienced something that seems so preposterous to human logic?*

I got my answer as I walked across the grass.

*No. I'm not deceived.* I *did* experience it. I heard it as clearly as I heard the birds chattering in the field.

The grass beneath my feet grew from the soil that was as old as the earth itself. I am a human infant in an adult world across time. The universe and earth were formed by the Source of All Creation. As I walk on it, I touch another dimension, I touch the beginning of Eternity. I am kissed by the soil. I am kissed by the billions of years of life from which it was molded. Whether I walk on this soil in my human form or in the energetic hologram after my physical presence ceases, matters less to me now as I stand before our cattle. Because I *know* what I had experienced. It's a *confirmation* that I had not been deceived and that I, in turn, have not deceived myself.

Before I turned and headed back for the house, I stopped and slowly did a three-sixty. In that moment I had no need for the flashing lights of any city. No need for the glitter of financial accumulation. No need for the popularity of social media whose fads change quickly. No need for the flash of celebrity. These are all temporary and illusions. Smoke and mirrors to enchant me, to distract me. Fog that dissipates in the breeze. A hall of curved mirrors that distort how I see myself. All born out of a fear of never seeming to be enough or have enough. These are things fashioned from a template held out to me that are the dreams of someone else. But they do not need to be mine.

If I considered that what I had was abundant, regardless of how I measure it in quantity or quality, then I had enough. It wasn't that I couldn't have "more" or "better," it was a question of why I would want it in the first place, and what benefit it would be to me after I left.

But, yet, I still need more. Much more. I need my family—Marcus and Paige, Julia and Victor. My mother, brothers and sisters. My friends.

I need the solid timeless soil beneath my feet. It supports me. It makes me whole. It speaks to me of yesterday, of today, of Eternity. I need only that.

And Mary.

# Chapter Twenty-Seven

November First. It was the day Mary and I celebrated our thirtieth wedding anniversary. A lifetime for some, perhaps, but I came to realize it was not nearly enough time for me.

It began as a pleasant late fall day. The air was cool in the morning but with the promise of sunshine during the afternoon. There wasn't yet any hint of winter that was to come soon enough.

The past thirteen months had included two hospital stays, nervous expectations, the sale of most of our cattle, a significant diminishment in my work abilities and the emotional stress that spread throughout my family from the effects caused by multiple medications. Mary and I agreed we needed a break. It was time to regroup. Time to celebrate still being together. Time to celebrate life as it stood before us, patiently waiting for us to embrace it.

To my surprise, even with the distance from our wedding and my recent mental lapses, I could recall that day clearly. So we took the day just for ourselves. We unplugged from the demands of the farm, of Mary's job, of the bills piled on the table, as we simply decided to walk away from it all for a few hours.

More than a year had gone by from my first hospital stay and our feelings about it still loomed large. It was a touchy subject even at this late date and our emotions were still raw from two hospital experiences, and the rough edges accompanying all of that hadn't yet worn down.

I knew Mary had been affected but until we really talked, I had no idea as to the degree or depths. She'd pushed her feelings into the background. She'd buried them mostly.

She was probably not unlike many women today, or even in generations past, who set aside their own concerns to care for a spouse/partner/friend/parent/child and took a backseat as the focus was directed to the person in care. They became invisible, blended into the background, or were often seen as white noise to those who interacted with the patient. Seldom listened to and likely dismissed when they offered their opinion. Mary's feelings and emotional strain had never been addressed unless she engaged with close friends about her concerns and thoughts. But never with me. I was oblivious to it because it was always about me. How I felt. How I was doing. How I could be above it all and disassociate myself from it all because I'd had an extraordinary experience. I didn't make more demands or complaints than necessary. Often I sat in silence, turning within myself instead of asking for help. We were two fragile eggs dancing around the room with each other afraid that touching and reaching out, either physically or emotionally, would crack our shells beyond repair. Humpty Dumpty might fall.

But on that November day, Mary was different. She was more relaxed then I'd seen her in weeks, no months. Maybe something had shifted within her and I'd find out what it was. Maybe something had shifted in me.

On our drive to Madison we bounced proposals back and forth like ping pong from her passenger seat to mine about what we each would like to do.

"Why not Picnic Point?" Mary asked. And that settled it. There wasn't a need for further discussion about our destination.

We'd take a walk out on Picnic Point, around the corner from the university's campus.

During my four years of college I had never once set foot there. We both had attended UW-Madison where we first met. So it would also be a homecoming of sorts and, hopefully, a second chance again for us.

Picnic Point is the local reference given by a contemporary society. In earlier days the Ho-Chunk Nation considered it a spiritual and sacred site. If they had their own name for that particular area it had been lost in time. It must have been significant because they built scattered mounds across this slim peninsula that was now a popular walking area. And more.

It had developed a reputation as a romantic getaway. Many marriage proposals were inspired by a walk out to the Point. It had been named by one publication as perhaps the 'kissingest spot' in North America. I secretly considered conducting my own scientific study while we were there. But I'd need a willing partner.

Although a foggy morning had greeted us when we hit the road, it began to clear as we arrived, and almost replicated the morning of our wedding after it lifted. The crispness of the air. The low sun of the season filtered through bare-leafed trees. The fallen leaves were still wet from the evening dew, matted to the dry grass on the sides of the path or lying slick where we walked. Their pungent odor smelled of resignation to their fate because their seasonal job was completed.

*Did they gracefully leave the tree behind?* I wondered. Did leaves harbor angry thoughts at the tree that had once created them after they were released to their fate? Or did they go peacefully without regret? In return for their birth from the limbs, they soaked in the sun's energy and transformed it into nourishment for the tree. Did they understand that when they died they would become compost to feed the same tree again next spring, a part of themselves reborn within the cycle of continuity?

*Are we so unlike them?* I thought as I kicked at a pile with the toe of my boot. *Is our position in this cosmos so different?* I wondered. It's all transformation. It's all change regardless of whether we want it or not, regardless of how we try to deny or ignore it, no matter how we try to hide from it because the enormity of it might scare us. Change sought me out no matter how invisible I tried to make myself or pushed back against its tides. For me to surrender to and accept the idea of change was simply to embrace my inevitable future.

We were joined on the trail by couples walking hand-in-hand like we did. *Perhaps on their own scientific mission.* I smiled inwardly as I squeezed Mary's hand. Runners puffed hard as they darted past and shifted to avoid those slowly ambling ahead of us. They pinged from side to side like a billiard ball bouncing from one rail to another while trying to avoid any contact with those on the narrow path.

Some hikers took pictures of their partner or friend against the backdrop of tall trees. I wondered if it would be a photo they kept, or deleted if they thought it unworthy of their phone's storage space, realizing they were caught up in a moment of inspiration or emotion that no longer seemed significant when reviewed later.

*Do we have memories like that?* I asked myself. Snapshots of a moment in our lives that we keep to show ourselves later what we were once, what we did with our time. Or do we effectively delete them because we don't want to be reminded. I'd spent a year trying to reclaim the snapshots of my memory. Some days I did well, others I didn't. But my time in another dimension was still my most vivid impression. After a year, nothing from my experience had changed of what I remembered. Neither had my mind altered any of it. It stayed as pristine as when it happened.

It was like my memory was exposed as negative film to my experience and captured every nuance, every microsecond of my six minutes in eternity and brought it all back with me to develop in my human memory dark room. If a picture was worth a thousand words, then each second I recorded contained a book of its own.

Mary walked on ahead while I stopped to catch my breath. As I watched her walk away, I remembered why I was grateful she didn't do that last year during the many rough days we had. Sure, I probably could have taken care of myself. I probably could have lived on my own. But it was much better with her being there.

She reached the Point ahead of me and sat down on a stone bench built into the shoreline at the water's edge where I joined her. We looked out to the blue water. At the Point, the lake seemed much larger than when looking back in our direction as seen from the opposite shore. The lake was the *same size* regardless from which vantage point one looked. I realized it was an illusion. From where we sat it looked like any other round shoreline in the distance. But viewed from the campus across the way the Point looked like you've stuck your pinky finger out into the water from the shore. Like so much in life, its reality was the perspective one brought to it.

Sailboats were tacking towards the wind as they slowly arced across the center of the lake. Boats sidled next to the shore as anglers silently trolled back and forth looking for the pockets of fish in the deepest holes. The breeze rustled the remaining leaves above us as Mary and I silently looked out. We saw the traffic on the distant streets but heard nothing as the sounds of their motors and horns were smothered by the heavy air and the distance.

I turned to Mary and leaned over. I began my own scientific study and could later confirm its validity. It was, indeed, a good place to kiss.

We sat. We talked. We silently observed. We listened to the seagulls plaintive calls. We watched as eagles swooped, lowered their talons, and snatched their dinner from the water, plucking a fish that ventured too close to the surface.

I sat thinking that if I drew two columns down a sheet of blank paper, one marked *Before* and the other *After*, about how I'd changed or been changed, the *After* list would have far more items penciled in because of the last year. Maybe I was less observant of my actions or aware of my behavior before but all those events certainly provided a focus for what had happened since my collapse.

"I have something to say." Maybe Mary was about to break her silence.

I picked up a small pebble at my feet and tossed it underhand into the shallow water. We watched as its small expanding ripples were quickly consumed by larger waves bobbing into shore. Here for a moment, then gone, engulfed by a larger universe the stone didn't know existed.

I waited.

"After your collapse you came back to the person I had married," Mary confided. She reached for my hand to hold it close as if making a physical connection would allow the words to flow more easily.

"Somewhere along the way before, you had drifted off to almost someone I didn't know."

There was a pause before she said that at one point several years ago, she felt I was ready to die.

"You seemed to want to go at that time. You didn't seem to want to stay here. Not that you didn't love your family but that you already seemed somewhere else, unsettled."

She thought that if I did check myself out, she'd probably leave the farm.

"I remember talking with a good friend about it. You were in your own world. Not in a bad way, it wasn't your habits or anything, you just seemed to be drifting away from me on your own. So the real plus from all this is that you're back to the person I knew. Your persona is different. You've returned to me."

*Wow*, I never realized that.

The door had opened and Mary continued.

"We left the hospital and the next day we took off for the wedding. I wasn't in favor of that at all but you wanted to go. So I said, ok. But I was hoping nothing would happen to you. I really thought you were being careless but you didn't seem to think so."

Mary said I couldn't even grasp what happened. That it was completely beyond me to understand what had happened to my body. My heart had stopped! I had no comprehension of how serious that was.

"But I did," she said. "And that was so frustrating. You didn't seem to care. Maybe you did but you never showed it. You were off in some other world most of the time. You were happy while the rest of us were aching inside. I could have screamed at you so many times but I couldn't. I could have screamed about our lives falling apart but not in front of you because you would never have understood."

She reminded me that while driving up north, she checked each exit we passed looking for hospital signs. She was constantly on high alert. All the time, every day, and that was tiring. It wore her down.

"You were still vulnerable. And you still wanted to go! I didn't have any down time that whole week. I was doing all the running back and forth to see you at the hospital while still doing my job and taking care of things on the farm. *Everything* centered on you."

She paused but I caught myself from jumping in and just shut up. She had the floor. That was the most we had talked about her feelings all year.

"Sorry," she said. That sounded callous and she didn't mean it the way it came out. She said that of course she was concerned for me and how I felt in the morning. But it didn't leave any time for her to relax or let down her guard.

Then there was that wedding up north. She came back to it again.

She realized that might have been the last thing we did together. We had just gotten home from four days in the hospital. *After you'd been dead for six minutes.* She said my heart wasn't in the best of shape as far as she was concerned even if the doctors thought it was ok for me to be released. On top of that I wanted to take off the next day for a long weekend! As if I thought I had just been in some hotel room on vacation for a few days and now was going to go on a picnic.

She shook her head as she recalled the absurdity of it. Like she really couldn't believe what I had wanted to do.

"You wanted to go. You wanted to feel alive. You really, really had a need to feel alive. I could sense that. I suppose on some level I could understand it. But after that week I didn't think I had the energy to drive that far. Then at the reception you even snuck away with Sarbs for a drink. You thought I didn't notice but I did when I was standing with Kathy. I was half expecting to see you being wheeled out to an ambulance again."

I watched the lapping water near our feet slowly shaking my head with a little smile that I didn't show Mary. *And all this time I thought I had gotten away with it.* I thought. I could never fool her!

"Then after that you were tired each and every day. Every. Single. Day. I'm sure part of that was from what happened to you physically. But I was convinced it was also from the medications."

Mary said one thing she finds herself doing even after a year, is listening to my breathing at night.

"After you got out of the hospital the first time," she said. "Every time I woke up during the night I listened for your breathing. To see if you were still alive. I'd have to hold my breath so I could hear yours because it was so light. Your pulse had dropped to the high 30s when it was checked. Those signs should have alerted them that something was wrong. Your blood pressure was consistently low, something like ninety over forty. Sometimes I thought you weren't breathing until I could finally hear it. Then I'd be able to go back to sleep and hope you would still be with me when I got up in the morning."

Mary said that was draining because it became another constant presence. She ended up exhausted from not getting enough sleep at night and then having to drive an hour to go to work the next morning almost half-asleep.

"And the next night it would happen again," she said. "It became a cycle I couldn't break."

And it masked other feelings.

"I was angry, yes," she conceded. "I was angry that it happened to you in the first place. I was angry that I had to deal with everything at home on the farm and at my job. I was angry because I wasn't sure if I could go anywhere and leave you alone because I never knew what I'd find when I got home. I had nowhere to direct my anger. Not at you. Not at Marcus or Julia. So I buried it. But it all cascaded and hit me again after your second trip to the hospital."

I stood up to stretch because the stone seat was hard on my butt and needed to get some feeling back into my legs. I made a slight turn to leave thinking that session was over but Mary didn't move an inch. She wasn't finished with me yet.

I sat back down and shifted closer to Mary on the cold stone bench trying to absorb some of the warmth radiating off her as she talked.

She said there were some early signs that something was different last October.

"I've had time to think and look back on that morning. I didn't see the signs when they were there. I missed them."

Or maybe she did see them but just brushed them off. She wasn't sure. It was easier later for her to see them more closely.

"That Monday morning you gave me a much longer hug than usual before I left for work. I noticed it right away but didn't say anything at the time. But maybe it wouldn't have made any difference if I had said something. Now I think I understand it. Maybe at some level you were saying goodbye to me. But then maybe you changed your mind while it happened."

The other difficult thing was the financial pressure we experienced.

"You couldn't work so I had to make the income. All the medical bills came cascading in. That reminded me so much of what happened with my parents. Every time I turned around there was another bill for them and now there was another one for you. It was like I was caught in some vortex and couldn't escape. It seemed to follow me. I was trying to break that pattern of anticipating the worst from insurance companies but it was hard. Fortunately our insurance covered the vast majority of the expenses you had. I can't imagine what it's like for those who don't have any, or those who have it taken away from them because politicians think it's a good thing to spend that money somewhere else."

Mary exhaled as if the load of the world had lifted off her shoulders. Atlas couldn't have done better.

She stood up and reached for me as we hugged like that Monday morning in October or that November day thirty years ago. I sensed it was some sort of wedding renewal. I said thank you. We kissed and then decided it was time to go.

I now appreciate the gift of walking with Mary and sharing this life with her.

We hiked a different route back to our car. Our path took us past downed trees decaying in the undergrowth, signs advising us not to leave the trail, a spring which Native Americans used for fresh water thousands of years ago and was still bubbling.

We walked by a former shelter, now disused and standing derelict. Then up a small rise until we reached the top of the crest and saw the remains of a farmstead that belonged to an early settler who was long since gone.

We reached our car and found we had unintentionally committed a parking *faux pas* by not getting a pre-pay window stub to place on our dash. I was glad we didn't get towed but I had no guilt after sliding into the seat and driving away with Mary.

In five days I would celebrate my sixty-fifth birthday. It was now just a number to me. Nothing more. *Every* day was now a *birth* day from my perspective, even if it might be my last. I couldn't be sure but I wasn't afraid. That alone was more than a good enough reason to join with my family for a few laughs.

That November cooled by Thanksgiving and December brought rain and snow and, finally, the year's end. We passed through the longest day of darkness but that didn't last either. And as surely as the sun came up, each day's light got longer that would be a herald for spring.

Just before Christmas, and for a week after, I caught the first cold I'd had in over eight years. I surprised myself by almost welcoming it because I then knew for sure I was human again.

# Chapter Twenty-Eight

Three years after experiencing my sudden cardiac death, I was able to take a deeper breath in reflection about the consequences of what happened than I had in the immediate aftermath, or even weeks and months later. While the events I witnessed and the sensations I experienced hasn't changed one bit, my realization of what it all meant has evolved.

If someone told me that I would have a significant life-changing experience that October day, I likely wouldn't have believed them. It would have seemed preposterous. Why would the next day be different from the rest? That I did, is a testament alone to the folly of making any predictions of how tomorrow will turn out. And that understanding has been an unexpected gift.

The immediate result of my collapse was an intimate introduction to the life-saving efforts of several acquaintances and by many people I had never met; a four-day hospital stay; two stent implants; a reassessment of my diet; a step into the pharmaceutical maze; a re-evaluation of our beef grazing program; and an examination of our long-term farm plan.

I would never wish a sudden cardiac death on anyone. But, oddly, I'm very thankful for the whole experience. In that sense I've learned that what first presents itself as a tragic situation may be something wondrous and immensely beneficial to me later. Without it, I would have been the same old me, bumping up against life as I had done every other day, and not having the vision to see or experience what exists beyond or outside the edges of the canvas that I had painted for myself. I would have continued to brush strokes across it to represent what I had wanted to see, what I had wanted it to represent, and not what really is or could be.

It has given me the latitude to yes, make plans, but not fret if they don't go according to the way I felt they should proceed. Because *should* contains within it a directive of expectation, and I now know that expectation diminishes my present. I have been given the gift of patience which has allowed me to take an extended, long view of what I encounter here to realize that nothing is permanent except that which is within me or each of us.

While I can choose to change my actions, my habits, my intentions, or any other thing that physically motivates my day, I realize that everything around me is also in change, regardless of how I might wish to hold it in place, or want to push back against its evolution. The tide of change cannot be stopped by anyone, and certainly not by me, no matter how much I, or anyone, wish things to remain the same, or to go back to a time in the past that may seem or appear to have been better. I now realize that wanting that is all an illusion, and a deceit we may perpetrate on ourselves.

I have learned that I cannot hold forever a moment that has passed. I can have the memory of it, but not that moment itself. If I concentrate on that past moment too much wanting it to return, then I've just missed the present one that slipped by while I was longing to return to a time gone by. I don't get a do-over of that moment, but I can engage with the next one that presents itself to me.

But really, why would I want to stop change even if I could?

If I had the same experience every day, repeated daily over

the course of decades, how boring would that be? I'd be a robot. If that becomes my routine, my life, how can I expect to explore things outside my static orbit? Why not a new experience, a new encounter, a new path to take, a new engagement, or a new lesson to learn?

My sudden cardiac death has opened my eyes to things beyond what I saw before. I realize that for me to have this experience, others had to endure their own emotional challenges. My family was foremost affected by my collapse. But there may be lessons in that for each one of them as well. Just as it is for anyone else who's experienced an event to which we might conveniently attach a label as being traumatic.

My change came in two forms: the physical change of how my body reacted to a lack of blood flow and included a restructured lifestyle, and my emotional change which followed after I understood what I had experienced while away from my body.

Both worked in an odd conjunction. It has opened my ears to octaves beyond my human hearing. It has opened my mind to understand that what I learn here does not exclusively bind me to the systems created by humans that would have me doubt the existence of knowledge beyond humanity's logic and comprehension. It has allowed me to examine language and find it can transcend verbal and written comprehension to exist in vibratory potential and opportunity. It has confirmed to me that my spirit consciousness is real, that I can commune with it without anyone's help, and that it exists in whatever form of infinity I could imagine. It's not some dream. It's not some deception. It simply *is*.

Dying was so easy, so effortless, so uncomplicated. It was so simple. But, I've had a second chance because of people who cared, probably more than I did at that moment. They pushed the reset button of my life, and now I get to begin again. I was given a clean canvas on which to paint something new—intellectually, emotionally, and spiritually.

It is not simply that those who helped—Diane, Josh, Sandy, Kevin, Chris, Josh, Sarah, Rikky, Dean, and a dozen other people— had worked to bring me back to this life. They pulled me back with an incandescent experience that I can now describe and explain as best I can. I can remember the hologram image of myself in energetic form. I can remember seeing the depths of Eternity—what it looks and feels like in a human vocabulary. I certainly didn't take any of that with me when I left. I experienced and witnessed it there—beyond this plane—and then carried it back with me as I re-entered my body. So I'm extremely grateful for that.

If they had not been successful in their efforts, I would still be *there*, beyond this life. And I would be merged with the Eternity I saw. I would be a part of that dimension, exploring the Eternal in ways I couldn't here all while existing only as a memory to others still here. Had I stayed there, however, I would not be able to tell my story of what I witnessed, at least not in this way.

Since that October fifth, I've been asked many times if my experience of death has changed me. I find that question has many facets to consider: physically, emotionally, psychologically, and spiritually being the top ones.

Except for the medications I was prescribed, and finally was able to eliminate from my daily intake, I don't feel physically different from before. Although I'm now in better cardio-vascular shape because of my continued fitness regime.

I'm more emotionally and psychologically attuned to my reactions to things around me. I can still get angry if I want. But it's far less often. Besides, what good does that anger do for me? Will it make me feel better? Today? Tomorrow? I don't need it, especially when I consider that my anger is of no interest to anyone else. I do not have to accept or even acknowledge any desperation energy that may want to surface to entice me to do something that is unnecessary.

Yes, I was given an extraordinary experience, but I still need to navigate the same environment here that others do. Maybe I can change it now in how I engage with it and others around me.

My past included the accumulation of stuff, for lack of a better inclusive term. The possessiveness of my things has dissolved and I could relinquish them without any sense of losing something. They may have been useful to me while I'm here but I won't be taking any of it with me after I leave. Those things are of temporary ownership anyway and will change as well. Perhaps be taken up by someone else, or perhaps transformed into something other. Everything changes. Eventually. That's the one constant in life's experience here.

And what of my spiritual evolution? This is not a religious tract nor is it intended as one. But my inner essence, my spirit consciousness, that kernel of inner presence—what I described earlier—is as real to me as my fingers are before me typing these words. I need only to close my eyes to find myself back to the dimension where I witnessed so much. If I feel anything now when I let myself drift back, it is the billowing warmth that immediately wells up within my chest every time I voluntarily place myself back in that dimension.

This awareness has given me a sense of peace with which to confront deep-seated segments from my past and deal with them unafraid. I am more forgiving than before. I've forgiven the guys who stole my girlfriends in high school and in college. I've forgiven the slights I've received, the comments that I wasn't good enough for the team, wasn't smart enough to accomplish what I wanted, wasn't talented enough to succeed. These matter little now and I can release them and let them recede forever into the river that flows into my past. I forgive by allowing the other person to be who they are regardless of what *I* think they should be.

This idea of forgiveness is not so much for the others as it is for myself. When I forgive and bless another, I bypass the narrative of history I may have previously assigned to them by their actions. When *I* stop agreeing to the narrative I've created, I dissolve my conflict.

It doesn't matter to me anymore what others may think of me, and what I think of others is more gracious now than I may have been before. Forgiveness is the release of the discord which was of my own creation anyway. The other person may never know I held something against them in the first place. It is my issue but also my opportunity to change. I've found that forgiveness, as hard as it may seem at the moment for me, finally lets love enter where I might not have let it in before. I've found that if I close my mind or my fists in anger, then I push love away.

I've also found that prayer is whatever I want to make it. There is no prescription about how I practice it, what I need to wear when I decide the moment is right, what form of words I need to recite for it to be acceptable, or what attitude I need to participate in it. And it need not be for the asking of divine intervention. We pray for miracles while we fail to see the miracle in front of us—ourselves. We are the miracle as we step outside of our expectations and see how we can learn acceptance for what we cannot control.

However, I've also learned that the manifestation of prayer resides in equivalency—I must be willing to become that for which I ask.

I've found that gratitude is a form of prayer. That kindness is a form of prayer. Singing is a form, and so is weeping. Prayer, in whatever form I observe it, makes me stop for a moment to lift myself and others to the potential of a higher octave of experience that I might otherwise not imagine to be possible.

I have a physical past that doesn't need to define, to entrap, or regulate my future. I have a vivid spiritual memory that has given me a window to view what exists beyond this dimension, one which we largely perceive as the only reality we can ever experience. I can hear the vibrations of my eternal presence whispering back to me that there is more to be encountered, more to be experienced, more to be enjoyed as we understand that in human terms.

That is the sense of Hope that I wish to impart to those reading these pages.

In recounting my experience, I have attempted to demagnetize the stigma and, hopefully, the anxiety which have clung to the word *death* that have layered our experience with it. I have tried to peel away those layers that have enveloped themselves around the word itself.

This does not diminish anyone's ideas or attitudes they hold but if I can neutralize that word, if I can release the lineage and morality it has become encased within, then I can re-examine it and separate it from its previous symbolism and decoration and re-shape it into something with a different meaning which then can be dissolved. I'd like to offer a way to level the playing field from my experience.

The body I inhabit is only temporary. I knew that before October fifth, but my understanding then was less solid and almost hypothetical. Now I have an intimate sense of knowing its reality after the experience I had. I stood toe-to-toe with death. It was not a specter, not a hooded black cloak with a scythe. It was a transition to which we've assigned a word, a name—nothing more. I was embraced by it. I walked with it. But it didn't hold me. My sudden cardiac death was the key that released me from this body I inhabit, and that allowed me to return to where I had first come from. Without that key, I'd be locked in this body forever. If I die tomorrow, I know what lies ahead. I now understand that behind the veneer of human or other physical forms, everything is made of spirit energy and has embarked on its own infinite journey. I will liken it to being on an energetic superhighway as I journey through Eternity. In 1951, I took an exit along the way, and the off-ramp led me into this plane—onto this planet—and I was born into the family I am a part of—at this moment in infinite history—for whatever time I have here. This is the same for everyone else—those beside me at a restaurant, driving a car in the next lane, those I see on TV in other countries, speaking other languages.

I stepped onto planet Earth so that I can experience all that is before me—my family, my farm, my cattle, my collapse—in ways I never could if I stayed only in a spirit state. When my body has used up its fuel supply and ceases to function —as it will—my spirit self will depart and will once again take the on-ramp to rejoin that energetic superhighway and continue until I decide to get off at another universe or dimension for another experience. I will have an infinite amount of time to explore an infinite number of experiences. And I will keep re-doing this forever because I will have an Eternity to accomplish and learn much more from each stopover. Just as my father, my grandparents, some of my friends, my nephew David, Marcus's dog Lucky, and Julia's cat Baby—all are doing this in their own way, in their own future, as a gift from the same Source, but simply in a different expression than mine.

Our points of departure from here may be different – some early, some later – perhaps from opposite sides of a shared life, yet we will arrive at the same end point in different dimension from here. Maybe I'll return here reconfigured, maybe somewhere else in the infinite dimensions that I've seen are available.

I've realized that what I may think is my singularity here— where I am separate from others or that I am here by myself—is a total misconception.

We are the jets that have raced out from the Source of Creation. We are all like drops of rain that fall from the clouds. Each one is born in its singularity—its distinctiveness—although they originate from the same cloud.

As each singular drop embeds the earth with itself in different lands, at different times, for different purposes, and while it may claim itself to be different from other raindrops, it is born out of the same Source. But eventually each singular drop of rain remembers to return to the vast ocean from which it came, to re-merge with its Source.

This topic surfaced during a discussion I had with a friend whose sister had died. I knew her and that she meant much to others before her death, not unlike how many others feel about their loved ones who have left.

He asked if I could recall my friends, my family, my jobs, my hobbies, my cattle, or even my pets while in the other dimension?

His question was about remembrance.

My answer was that while it may be important as humans to want to be remembered or to remember others—and there is nothing wrong with this—it became less important once I sensed myself merging again with the vast ocean of infinite energy that was radiating before me from Source.

I learned that we will remember everything we experience here. We will remember everyone we knew here in this lifetime we have—our family, our friends, our activities. But these remembrances will be transformed through a higher octave of energetic vibration that we will agree to inhabit and that will re-form them through an eternal lens of love and acceptance. What we refer to as our memories here will pass through a membrane of re-articulation that will align them to a spirit consciousness in which we existed long before our entry into this plane of existence. We will take those re-articulated memories as part of our eternal journey as we move to our next infinite expression. And it will freely come at no expense to us. These will be the gifts we receive simply because we *are*. What could be better than this?

I thought much about this later and realized that for many people the fear they have of death is not necessarily the act of their physical form ceasing to function but, rather, that the finality of it here might render their life anonymous.

The fear of anonymity—of becoming nameless or forgotten—at the end of our lives, I think often serves as a motivation for recognition. We can see it all around us. We erect gravestones and monuments with our names carved into them, perhaps as pushback against mortality and trying to propel our memory into the distant future, hoping time will not erase them. Names get emblazoned across buildings, parks, inventions, awards and much more, as a way to be memorialized. That this can be found all over the world attests to our collective anxiety of anonymity.

In my absence for six minutes from this life, I learned that all will be remembered and loved by a greater love than these words could ever convey. I understand with greater clarity than ever before that the love we have for another will always align with them and go where they will go into the eternal planes of their future. And a part of what they offer to us will always travel with us into ours. That love is never lost in Time. It will go with us when we leave here.

When I have once again returned to that nest of Creation and become reformed and reconfigured *within* the DNA of Source, then what I will remember will be on a higher plateau of energetic memorial than I could possibly understand here.

So, yes, I do believe we will remember those we know here on this plane of existence, but in a greater and more profound way than we can comprehend now. Because we will interweave and braid together with them within the Creation DNA, we will all commune together in experiencing the totality of Eternity. We will all become part of that vast energetic ocean from which we were born. We will all be remembered. We will then have no need for our singular identity even if it is allowed us.

Perhaps for me, the most surprising reaction I've had to my entire experience is my inability to feel sad at someone's death. This doesn't mean that I don't care about that person or their families, or that I don't have any human emotions left. But it's because of what I've experienced that I can't conjure up any sorrow because I know where they have gone and what they are experiencing. Why would I want to deprive them of that? So, I say thank you for sharing some of their life with me and let them go. They've gotten back onto the on-ramp of the eternal superhighway and are heading for their next experience, that's all.

Today. Tomorrow. Before. After. These are demarcation lines we use here in understanding our human constructs of time that will simply blend together in Eternity with no real consequence.

The physical outline of my human form contains within it the emotions I've built upon that were instilled into me by my parents, my family, my ancestors, my friends, my teachers—everyone I've been in contact with while here. It's my data of personal history. While these things I've absorbed may be useful for me to express myself to another human, they will be background lessons I've experienced to be part of me when I leave. But I can appreciate them now for what they are.

So I can walk across the same fields that my father did. I can place my steps onto the same soil that my grandfather did, and his father, and his father, reaching me back into my past. But it is only my past in the sense that I am now in a human form to know it as that. My past is my idea of existing at a certain point before. My present is where I can only experience something new. My future is yet to be. And though I may wish to recall my past, I can never bring it back. Nor do I need to. It belongs there in its own time and space of before.

When the weather is good I go outside to where I do my best thinking. Out in the open I can look around and be immersed with the sights and sounds of our farm. It's fundamental to life. Now it's fundamental to my life. And it's the foundation of humanity. It's what allows us to exist here. Without the sun, the rain and six inches of topsoil we all would cease to physically be. Beyond these basic elements everything else in life is window dressing and pageantry. No amount of money that one can accumulate, no position of authority held can change that dynamic. In the eyes of nature, we humans all are equal. There is a message in that.

I go outside to sit at our table and watch as the steam curls up into the air from my tea cup before the wisps blend and fade away in the cool morning. My thoughts focus on the idea of faith and what mine is defined as now. I realize it's not a faith in the religious sense of some church organization or structure, or theology or tenet. It's a faith that, regardless of the horrible things I may witness, life is still the best thing I have to experience while I'm here, and all that goes with it.

What does it mean? What is faith in oneself or the ones you love? Faith in your spouse or partner? Faith in your family? Faith in humanity? Or if you wish, faith in a Source of All Creation, a God, or whatever form of a higher energy or enlightenment you may wish to acknowledge or label it, or faith in nothing at all?

As I sit, I recall one scene from the movie *Indiana Jones and the Last Crusade* that resonates with me about the idea of faith, regardless of whether any religious meaning is attached to it or not.

Near the end of the movie. Jones reaches the edge of a cliff and looks down into the chasm below. He must cross it but there seems to be no foot bridge. Overhead we are shown the depths below him as he kicks a stone and it falls and falls and falls, careening off the sides as it drops.

Nothing appears to support him if he steps out into it. In this moment of crisis, he faces a choice. He can step out into the unknown, completely against his better judgment, and take his chances and assuming he will fall. Or, he can do nothing. His failure to act means his father will die. He has reached an intimate crossroads with himself which he may have never before confronted. Time is running out.

He realizes the only choice he can live with is to take that step regardless of what happens. He anticipates what the consequences will be if he steps off. But he knows deep within himself that he can't go back and live with the consequences if he does nothing. He straightens and resigns himself to his expectation that he will likely plunge to his death below. But by his action that can't be explained or logically justified, he takes a step out into the void anyway. So his response, in the end, is to an emotional stimulus. Not unlike what I, or you, may often face.

He's surprised when his foot lands solidly on something he cannot see. He's unsure but then gingerly plants the other foot next to the first. He slides one forward and then the other when he realizes there is something supporting him. He continues small steps until he reaches the other side. Once across, he turns and throws dirt back onto this seemingly invisible foot bridge. For the first time we see what was there all along.

Sure, it's a contrived plot piece. But the point this has for me is that what is first presented is an illusion that we buy into because it's what we expect from past experience. I wouldn't have believed the foot bridge was there because it was hidden from my normal sight. I assumed, from my own history, that nothing was there because past experience told me what I would expect to see.

Because of this, I dismissed the possibility that anything else could exist. Or that anyone could step out into an abyss and walk across a non-existent foot bridge.

*That's not possible,* I say.

Then, when the truth of what's there is shown to me, I have a new understanding of the same image because my own experience with it has changed. I see it in a completely new way because I now understand it through different eyes.

This is what I experienced when I found myself supported in my raft in another dimension. I view everything differently now because of my experience with it, when before, I may not have had any rational reason to believe it.

I step out onto that unseen bridge each morning. The choice is mine, and mine alone. As it is for everyone else. I can take that step. Or not. You can take that step or not. Before when I encountered something new, my first reaction may have been to see it through the filter of my past and maybe hesitate. Now I realize this is stepping out into the unknown without the certainty of the old.

The point, to me, is that what we label as faith—that unseen element of human emotional dynamics—is our embrace of stepping out into an unknown that leads us to where our true inner essence resides. It becomes a profound encounter with a vibration greater than we would otherwise acknowledge and for which human logic falls short. Faith is simply a potential that is already here but not yet operating in expression. It is the recognition of possibilities and saying *Yes* to what lies ahead regardless of the uncertainty.

I can choose to turn around and go back to what I knew was behind me and where it seems safer. I can keep reliving my past if I want. There I don't have to risk anything new because I've already experienced it. It's comfortable. But I'm also stuck with a history I may not like, may not want, or may not need. Then I've put myself on a drug I can't get off and I'm self-prescribing.

Every day when I take that step onto the unseen bridge, it reaffirms my experience in another dimension. I can take each step into the unknown with a faith I can't fully explain in human language.

My sudden death experience could be likened to a message-in-a-bottle tossed in some far end of Infinity that washed up upon the shore of Now for me to open. It was an experience that here, I, a modern man—a member of what is considered an advanced, but often cynical, world society—could accept the possibility that an impossible message was sent as a communication originating from a distant shore I had not thought existed. And yet now I stand before the in-rushing waves of the shore on which I now reside and hear the words written on the invisible paper inside that bottle and see that distant shore of Eternity.

Early in my recovery I asked myself often if I wanted to leave here and return to my raft where all was so good? I've finally learned that's the wrong way for me to phrase it. It's not whether I want to return it's that I'm not hurried to return there. I need to let my journey here take its own course to its destination whether it ends tomorrow or ten years from now.

The anticipation of discovery can be a wonderful thing. This means I can engage with this world while I am here, with open hands to accept what comes along, all with lessons for me to learn. And after I'm not here, I will engage with another realization, in another dimension, in another consciousness, to be re-known in another way. I will be changed again, just like everything will. I *feel* the energetic resonance that was encrypted within my spiritual essence and returned with me as I passed through the membrane of timelessness, and it allows me to be part of this dimension as well as others.

I also realize now that there is no finish line. That it's not a contest of who has more in quantity at the end, or lives days or years longer. My future is infinite and no one and nothing can or will take that away from me. I've seen it is my destiny. Our destiny. It is our right. It is our gift. It is the promise to us that we will traverse through the elasticity of this dimension unharmed into the next. We are to become a part of a greater ocean that pushes itself to a farther shore. The great gift to me, I now understand, is that I had realized and fully experienced my inner self—my true self—in those six minutes and it was beyond any harm anyone could do to me here. I was not shattered by my departure as I transitioned from my physical form back to an energetic essence I was before.

# CHAPTER TWENTY-EIGHT

That is what I have seen.

The real *ME*, who was given and known by the name Philip here, is the one who I described while I was in the other dimension. That is the eternal expression of *ME*, which was transposed at my birth into a human form but is the one who exists *ALWAYS* and is the energetic signature in vibration with the Source of All Creation. I had tasted the elixir of forever and it has extinguished my fears of what may come.

To embrace this idea is to embrace the innermost core of my essence and to commune once again with that kernel of light I was before I arrived here. I know I can take each step, every day towards that future. And it can be done without the need to be afraid about what happens to my body here.

My testament to all I experienced is the words I've written. I have presented my experience, as best I can describe it, as a pathway to help you if you wish. But it is not your experience. You will find your own, in your own way, by your own design, in your own time. You will have your answers when you seek them. The seeking we do is our effort for comprehension with no right or wrong way to embark upon our search.

Because you have agreed to read this far, I believe you have considered a possibility that may now have awakened something within you. I cannot tell you what that something is, but it is yours to examine. And you can do this fully without trepidation because I have seen that death is nothing but a portal to an unseen future.

This is what I learned from my collapse.

This is what I experienced.

This is what I now understand.

This is what I have returned to share with you.

# Acknowledgments

My life was saved by the selfless efforts of many people. Although it turned into a collaboration between three groups of professionals, certain people stand as my initial guardians. I owe my life to Diane, Josh, Sandy, Sarah, Kevin, Chris, Rikky, Dean, and a dozen others. To simply say thank you would hardly explain the full range of my gratitude for their skills, their tenacity in performing them, and their willingness to sit with me to recount their actions so that I could better understand what happened. Thank you to each of you.

While their initial lifesaving work was in progress, the Sauk Prairie Police Department and numerous members of the Sauk Prairie Emergency Medical Team quickly responded to assist. These included Keifpher, Ken, Shelly, Bob, Kelli, Janet, and Cassie. And later, two members the Middleton EMS paramedic team came on board during my transfer to Madison. My sincere thank you to each of them.

Others who preferred not to be named work at the Sauk Prairie Hospital's Wellspring Center, the University of Wisconsin's Hospital Emergency Room (Madison), and St. Mary's Hospital (Madison) Cardiac Care Unit. All had a hand in passing me along the chain of recovery. I wish to include my primary physician, Dr. John, who, besides being my friend for over thirty-five years, diligently monitored my recovery.

I've had tremendous support from my family, especially my wife, Mary, and our son and daughter, Marcus and Julia and their spouses, Paige and Victor.

For Mary, I owe a profound sense of gratitude and thankfulness because I've now put her through several traumatic health episodes but she's never wavered in her love and support. My mother, and my brothers and sisters, along with their families, stayed interested in my recovery with many words of support.

A sincere thank you to friends that include Beverly and Rick, Jim and Kathy, Kate and Gregg, Sonya and Michael, Phil, Mark, Myron, Jim, Patrice, Barbara, and many others too numerous to mention. All offered well wishes and tolerated my lapses in memory, and several who visited me in the hospital and/or accepted my request to read early drafts of this manuscript.

A thank you to Karl Jenkins for his composition *Benedictus* from *The Armed Man: A Mass For Peace*, which speaks to me in ways no other piece of music can.

Deep gratitude to Nadine Kenney Johnstone for her suggestions and critique of my manuscript which helped frame my story with greater clarity. Also, thank you to Amy Glaser for providing an avenue for this book to find a home.

A sincere thank you to Jerry and Ruth Apps, who besides being dear friends, have been valued mentors for most of my writing career. Jerry was the first to encourage me to write about my experience.

Thank you to Lisa Hagan for her belief in this book and my story and her willingness to present it to a larger audience.

I have referred to "Guides" who have helped me gain a new realization of myself and what I experienced. I first encountered them through the work of Paul Selig. I met them a second time, face-to-face in an unexpected way on a February day four months later, when they acknowledged and greeted me like an old friend.

**Channeled Literature by Paul Selig that
has helped me immensely:**

*I Am the Word*

*The Book of Love and Creation*

*The Book of Knowing and Worth*

*The Book of Mastery (The Mastery Trilogy: Book I)*

*The Book of Truth (The Mastery Trilogy: Book II)*

*The Book of Freedom (The Mastery Trilogy: Book III)*

*Beyond the Known: Realization*

## Books by Philip Hasheider

How to Raise Cattle

How to Raise Pigs

How to Raise Sheep

The Homestead Planner & Logbook

Family Cow Handbook, A Guide to Keeping a Milk Cow

The Complete Illustrated Guide to Farming

The Complete Book of Jerky

The Complete Book of Butchering, Smoking,
Curing, and Sausage Making

All Bottled Up, A History of the Sauk Prairie Area Milk
Delivery Routes

Creating Balance Between Form & Function; The Story of aAa©
Animal Analysis, Bill Weeks and Skyway Farm

Correction Lines

Building Early Wisconsin Community; The 150-Year Story of
Mills on the Honey Creek

Printed in Great Britain
by Amazon